T0375662

# RESURRECTION

# SHOCK

## Did the Disciples Get It Right?

### LANE SANFORD WEBSTER

# IF CHRIST HAS NOT BEEN RAISED, OUR PREACHING IS USELESS AND SO IS YOUR FAITH. MORE THAN THAT, WE ARE THEN FOUND TO BE FALSE WITNESSES ABOUT GOD, FOR WE HAVE TESTIFIED ABOUT GOD THAT HE RAISED CHRIST FROM THE DEAD ... IF THE DEAD ARE NOT RAISED, "LET US EAT AND DRINK, FOR TOMORROW WE DIE."

*— Paul of Tarsus, ex-persecutor turned tireless apostle, from his letter circa AD 55, 1 Corinthians 15:13–15, 32, quoting Isaiah 22:13 (NIV)*

# RESURRECTION

# SHOCK

## Did the Disciples Get It Right?

## LANE SANFORD WEBSTER

WESTBOW
PRESS®
A DIVISION OF THOMAS NELSON
& ZONDERVAN

Copyright © 2020 Lane Sanford Webster.

All rights reserved. No part of this book may be used or reproduced by any means, graphic, electronic, or mechanical, including photocopying, recording, taping or by any information storage retrieval system without the written permission of the author except in the case of brief quotations embodied in critical articles and reviews.

This book is a work of non-fiction. Unless otherwise noted, the author and the publisher make no explicit guarantees as to the accuracy of the information contained in this book and in some cases, names of people and places have been altered to protect their privacy.

WestBow Press books may be ordered through booksellers or by contacting:

WestBow Press
A Division of Thomas Nelson & Zondervan
1663 Liberty Drive
Bloomington, IN 47403
www.westbowpress.com
1 (866) 928-1240

Because of the dynamic nature of the Internet, any web addresses or links contained in this book may have changed since publication and may no longer be valid. The views expressed in this work are solely those of the author and do not necessarily reflect the views of the publisher, and the publisher hereby disclaims any responsibility for them.

Any people depicted in stock imagery provided by Getty Images are models, and such images are being used for illustrative purposes only. Certain stock imagery © Getty Images.

Scriptures taken from the Holy Bible, New International Version®, NIV®. Copyright © 1973, 1978, 1984, 2011 by Biblica, Inc.™ Used by permission of Zondervan. All rights reserved worldwide. www.zondervan.com The "NIV" and "New International Version" are trademarks registered in the United States Patent and Trademark Office by Biblica, Inc.™

ISBN: 978-1-9736-6710-0 (sc)
ISBN: 978-1-9736-6709-4 (hc)
ISBN: 978-1-9736-6711-7 (e)

Library of Congress Control Number: 2019908513

Print information available on the last page.

WestBow Press rev. date: 8/18/2020

*To Brooke,*

*who knows why*

# ACKNOWLEDGMENTS

Grateful am I for the friends, family members, colleagues, and teachers who reviewed one or more parts of this book, gave me their honest responses, and made more than a few worthy suggestions. Nevertheless, any errors, omissions, lapses in judgment, or other residual faults remain solely my own.

When barely embryonic, the book concept was incubated about three years ago when I presented it informally to notables of the Regent College community in Vancouver, B.C. Canada: Dr. Sven Soderlund, a New Testament professor who taught an epic seminar on the book of Hebrews; Dr. Donald Lewis, professor of Christian history, who originally befriended me in Oxford, England when I was an untutored lad on a year abroad; and a scholar in his own right, Bill Reimer, who for many years has guided with distinction what I still consider my happiest indoor place on earth, the Regent College Bookstore. Among the readers who generously and humanely critiqued specific chapters were Anthony Webster, Janet Weiner, Jeff Barneson, Joni Knapper, Josh Duff, Marie Kiekhaefer, Dr. Sven Soderlund and Tegan Webster.

Those who read a version of the entire manuscript displayed uncustomary valor: Berkely Webster, Dr. J. Carl Laney, Dr. Lambert Dolphin and Dr. Marvin D. Webster, my father, veteran pastor and valued leader on seminary and missions boards. At key intervals in the journey, further encouragement came from Dean Christensen, Merit Webster, Robert Bouzon, and my mother, Virginia L. Webster, compassionate teacher and classical, worshipful keyboardist. One other credit is due. Now gone to glory, Dr. Ray C. Stedman unknowingly influenced these pages when he took me aside for a season as a young man in Palo Alto, California and grounded me in a biblical strata of bedrock spiritual truths that continue to reverberate in my heart and mind. My gratitude goes out to all these exemplary people who have helped bring this extended endeavor to the light of day.

# RESURRECTION

# SHOCK

## *Did the Disciples Get It Right?*

## LANE SANFORD WEBSTER

# CONTENTS

# ABBREVIATIONS

## OLD TESTAMENT

| | |
|---|---|
| Gen. | Genesis |
| Ex. | Exodus |
| Lev. | Leviticus |
| Num. | Numbers |
| Deut. | Deuteronomy |
| Josh. | Joshua |
| Judg. | Judges |
| Ruth | Ruth |
| 1-2 Sam. | 1-2 Samuel |
| 1-2 Kings | 1-2 Kings |
| 1-2 Chron. | 1-2 Chronicles |
| Ezra | Ezra |
| Neh. | Nehemiah |
| Esther | Esther |
| Job | Job |
| Ps. | Psalms |
| Prov. | Proverbs |
| Eccles. | Ecclesiastes |
| Song | Song of Songs |
| Isa. | Isaiah |
| Jer. | Jeremiah |
| Lam. | Lamentations |
| Ezek. | Ezekiel |
| Dan. | Daniel |
| Hos. | Hosea |
| Joel | Joel |
| Amos | Amos |
| Obad. | Obadiah |
| Jon. | Jonah |
| Mic. | Micah |
| Nah. | Nahum |
| Hab. | Habakkuk |
| Zeph. | Zephaniah |
| Hag. | Haggai |
| Zech. | Zechariah |
| Mal. | Malachi |

# ABBREVIATIONS

## NEW TESTAMENT

| | |
|---|---|
| Mt | Matthew |
| Mk | Mark |
| Lk | Luke |
| Jn | John |
| Acts | Acts |
| Rom. | Romans |
| 1-2 Cor. | 1-2 Corinthians |
| Gal. | Galatians |
| Eph. | Ephesians |
| Phil. | Philippians |
| Col. | Colossians |
| 1-2 Thess. | 1-2 Thessalonians |
| 1-2 Tim. | 1-2 Timothy |
| Titus | Titus |
| Philemon | Philemon |
| Heb. | Hebrews |
| James | James |
| 1-2 Pet. | 1-2 Peter |
| 1-3 Jn | 1-3 John |
| Jude | Jude |
| Rev. | Revelation |

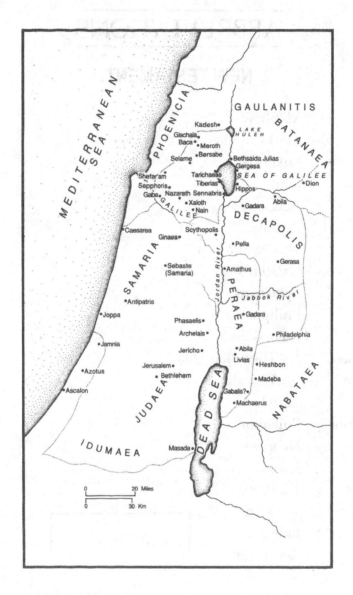

***Land of Israel in the Roman Era***. These are the towns and regions
during the time Jesus lives in the land of Israel. Note that the commercial
fishing center of Magdala on the Sea of Galilee is denoted by its Greek
name, Tarichaeae. Jesus bases his operation north of Magdala along the
northwestern lakeshore at the town of Capernaum (not shown). Excerpt
from *Baker's Concise Bible Atlas* by J. Carl Laney © 1988. Map originally
entitled "First-Century Palestine." Used by permission of Baker Books, a
division of Baker Publishing Group.

## PROLOGUE

---

# FOR THOSE WHO WONDER WHETHER JESUS EXISTED

---

ould we have heard of Jesus if we had none of the writings in the New Testament? Those writings describe him as a young man from a working-class family in a rustic, agricultural zone in a minor Mediterranean country. He lived during the reigns of the Roman emperors Augustus and Tiberius. He began a teaching and healing ministry. He gathered disciples. He held crowds spellbound in the country and later at the temple in the capital city. He threatened the priestly hierarchy enough for them to convince the Roman governor to execute him to keep the peace. Would we have known that he existed outside of the New Testament documents?

The answer is unmistakably yes, we would have heard of him. Start with the Roman historian Tacitus, writing in his *Annals* in AD 115. He reported how about fifty years earlier (AD 64) the Roman emperor Nero got nervous. He discovered citizens were blaming him for a devastating fire that mysteriously swirled through some sketchier parts of the city of Rome that most needed redevelopment. To dodge the charge, he blamed the arson on the followers of "Christus," as Tacitus at his acerbic best recounted.

*Consequently, to get rid of the report, Nero fastened the guilt and inflicted the most exquisite tortures on a class hated for their abominations, called Christians by the populace. Christus, from whom the name had its origin, suffered the extreme penalty during the reign of Tiberius at the hands of one of our procurators, Pontius Pilate, and a most mischievous superstition, thus checked for the moment, again broke out not only in Judaea, the first source of the evil, but even in Rome, where all things hideous and shameful from every part of the world find their center and become popular.*[1]

Even earlier, in about AD 94, the person of Jesus was noted by Josephus, a Jewish historian. He was an ex-military man from the northern region of Israel known as Galilee, where Jesus lived. As a Jewish general, he led forces against the Romans in Galilee but surrendered to them in AD 67. Early on, he saw that when it came to Rome, resistance was futile, so he joined their side. He translated for them during the siege of Jerusalem that ended in AD 70. He gained favor with Vespasian, the Roman military leader who later became emperor. He retired to Rome to write the history of the Jewish people for his Roman patrons. Scholars debate to what extent his texts have been altered by later Christian editors.[2] However, most accept that there is an original, authentic reference to *"Jesus, a wise man"* and *"a teacher"* in his writings.

*When Pilate, at the suggestion of the principal men amongst us, had condemned him to the cross, those that*

---

[1] Tacitus, *Annals* 15.44. From Cornelius Tacitus, *Annals*, Alfred John Church, William Jackson Brodribb, Sara Bryant, eds. (New York, NY: Random House, 1942), perseus.tufts.edu, retrieved 14 July 2017.

[2] For a lengthier but still manageable treatment of this evidence with comprehensive endnotes, see Lawrence Mykytiuk, "Did Jesus Exist? Searching for Evidence Beyond the Bible," *Biblical Archaeology Review*, Jan/Feb 2015, Biblical Archaeology Society. Available at biblicalarchaeology.org. The endnotes discuss textual and source issues regarding the references to the writings of Tacitus and Josephus.

*loved him at the first did not forsake him … and the
tribe of Christians, so named for him, are not extinct at
this day.*[3]

Other references in the same work by Josephus, *Antiquities
of the Jews*, cite the unjust stoning of James, "the brother of Jesus
who was called Christ" (20.9.1) and the imprisonment and death
of John the Baptist (18.5.2), a cousin of Jesus according to one
biblical report (Luke 1:36).

---

Textual Detail:
**Debate over Alterations of a Text from Josephus**

The spirited debate over to what extent later Christian scribes
cut and paste a section of original text by Josephus looks virtually
settled by the scholar Lawrence Mykytiuk. He points out the fact
that Josephus mentions Jesus not only regarding his condemnation
under Pilate but also later in his book. The ancient writer brings up
Jesus again in the course of identifying his brother James, whose
wrongful death in AD 62 brought down the regime of a high priest.
Further, the text refers to Christians as a "tribe," a Jewish term. In
addition, the text attributes the execution of Jesus to Pilate without
incriminating the Jewish leaders. These are two strong indications that
the author writes from a Jewish, not an early Christian perspective.

---

Early evidence for the existence of Jesus in history extends
beyond Roman sources.[4] In a section (c. AD 70-200) of the
Babylonian Talmud, the Jewish writer recorded how Jesus

---

[3] Josephus, *Antiquities of the Jews* 18.3.3. From Flavius Josephus, *The
Antiquities of the Jews*, in *Josephus, The Complete Works*, tr. William Whiston
(Nashville, TN: Thomas Nelson, 1998).
[4] For the following references to Jesus, see Robert E. Van Voorst, *Jesus
Outside the New Testament* (Grand Rapids, MI: Wm. B. Eerdmans, 2000).
He comprehensively discusses sources citing Jesus in classical Roman,
in Jewish, and in post-New Testament writings including Gnostic and
apocryphal documents. Also see the given references in simplified form

(denoted as Yeshu or Yeshua, with one manuscript adding "ha-Nosri" or "the Nazarene") was hung on a tree on the eve of the Passover feast, because he practiced magic as a miracle-worker and led Israel astray as a teacher (Sanhedrin 43a). This Talmudic mention views Jesus negatively, but nevertheless affirms Jesus as a real figure in history.

A Syrian stoic philosopher in a letter to his son also referred to a historical figure who is presumably Jesus. Imprisoned by the Romans, Mara bar Serapion (c. late first century or second century AD) listed heroic persons who suffered injustice, namely Socrates by murder, Pythagoras by burning, and what he termed "the wise king of the Jews" by execution. He counseled his son that the wise triumph over their foes in the way they live on through their teachings.

Other early writings indicate how Christians worship Jesus even in the face of social pressure. In a letter to his emperor Trajan, the Roman governor Pliny the Younger (AD 61-113) observed how Christian believers arose early in the morning "to sing a hymn to Christ, as to a god." After executing a few of them, Pliny doubted his procedure and wanted to know how much to punish them if they refuse to renounce their superstition. Later, in a biting satire, the sarcastic Syrian orator and author Lucian of Samosata (AD 125-180, from a city in southeastern Turkey) ridiculed Christians for the way they "worship the crucified sage."

As a result of such historical evidence outside the Bible, we know that Jesus existed. He died in Judea at the hands of the Romans. After his death, people worshiped him even at the cost of their own lives.

---

in Ralph O. Muncaster, *Evidence for Jesus* (Eugene, OR: Harvest House Publishers, 2004), 111-27.

# APPROACHING THE RESURRECTION HISTORICALLY

There is compelling evidence for the existence of Jesus in early sources outside the Bible (as demonstrated in the prologue). Yet the core Christian claim is not just that Jesus simply lived, taught, healed, got into trouble with the law, and died unfairly young and that his memory continues to inspire people to virtue and good deeds. No, the Christian claim is much more startling than that. The claim is that he died but did not stay dead. He was raised from the dead by divine power.

Is there any evidence for this claim of the resurrection of Jesus in history? Yes. We find it in letters written to communities around the Mediterranean region by a high-strung itinerant tentmaker, a Roman citizen to boot, from the southeast of today's Turkey. We find it in two separate biographies (one action packed, one reflective) sourced from the memoirs of two first-century Jewish commercial fishermen. We find it in another book that traditionally traces its origin to a Jewish man who served as a tax collector for the Romans. We find it in two superb sequential histories written by a medical doctor, probably a Greek native. All of these writings are undisputed first-century documents (though scholars differ on the exact decades in which they were composed). They are legitimate sources for historical inquiry.

The common names for some of these documents may be familiar: First Thessalonians, Galatians, First Corinthians, Mark, Matthew, Luke, Acts, John. At first, they circulated independently as letters or biographies and some for as long as two centuries. Then churches in the Mediterranean countries started to amalgamate the writings in varying collections (a famous example is a list known as the Muratorian canon).

A volume totaling twenty-seven writings became the canon of Christian scripture. The term *canon* derives from a Greek word meaning "measuring stick." It signified that any future assertions or beliefs were to be measured by these previously accepted writings. This canon of writings was established in history not by a specific church council but by an evolving consensus.[5]

---

Historical Portal:
**The Christian Canon Develops Organically**

The council of Nicaea in AD 325 is often cited as the point where the canon is authorized. No records of the council support this notion. The focus of the council was determining the relationship between the divine and human natures of Jesus. Smaller councils known by their locations (Laodicea, AD 363–364; Hippo, AD 393; Carthage, AD 397) reiterate the canon but do not decide it. In effect, the apparent absence of official council certification of the canon by debates and votes inoculates the NT canon from criticism that it was decided by "cultural elites" imposing their will on the masses. Instead, the canon bubbles up from believers using the writings and finding them speaking along the same lines. The publishing venture of Constantine in AD 331 does exert enormous influence on what is included and excluded from the consensus Christian canon. Eusebius, a scholar and church leader in Caesarea, advises Constantine on the contents.

---

[5] See Michael J. Kruger, "The NT Canon Was Not Decided at Nicaea—Nor Any Other Church Council," 4 June 2013, michaeljkruger.com. Also see Henry Y. Gamble, "Canon, New Testament" in David Noel Freedman, ed., *Anchor Bible Dictionary* (New York, NY: Doubleday, 1992), vol. 1, 852–61.

A major turning point came once the Roman Empire embraced the Christian faith. In AD 331, the Roman emperor Constantine ordered fifty Bibles in Greek for the growing church in Constantinople; they included the Hebrew scriptures in Greek translation (the Old Testament, in Greek known as the Septuagint) and most of the books of today's New Testament, all of them originally written in Greek.

Because these documents were canonized, there is a tendency among some scholars to discount them as historical documents. Supposedly, they are biased because they include faith claims. Not so fast, I respectfully object. Luke's Acts is just as relevant for historical inquiry as is Tacitus's *Annals*; a letter from Paul is just as eligible for historical assessment as is a letter from Pliny.

Ironically, a noted letter from the Roman governor Pliny (in what is today's northwestern Turkey writing c. AD 112) itself includes implicit faith claims—for the gods of the Romans. Pliny checked with his emperor, Trajan, to see if he was right to release

> ... *those who denied that they were or had been Christians, when they invoked the gods in words dictated by me, offered prayer with incense and wine to your image, which I had ordered to be brought for this purpose together with statues of the gods.*[6]

Clearly, the Romans had their own faith agenda. Having faith claims does not mean the document cannot be assessed for historical evidence.

---

[6] "Pliny the Younger Letters," *Harvard Classics*, XCVII. To the Emperor Trajan, bartleby.com. Also available at "Letters to Trajan," 10.96–97, faculty. georgetown.edu. Pliny is called Pliny the Younger to distinguish him from Pliny the Elder, his uncle, who is known as a Roman military commander, naturalist, encyclopedia author, and today mainly as the namesake of a purportedly excellent craft beer.

Historical Portal:
**Pliny, Pontus, Persecution, and Paul**

The Roman province that Pliny the Younger governs is Pontus/Bithynia, on the coast of the Black Sea in today's north-central Turkey. The Romans combined the two ancient kingdoms into one province but retained both names. Paul mentions how he senses the Spirit of Jesus preventing him from entering Bithynia on his second missionary journey. Instead, he is redirected first to Troas, where Luke joins him, then on to Greece, starting in Macedonia (Acts 16:6–10).

Later during this trip, Paul meets his friends and fellow tentmakers Priscilla and Aquila in Corinth, with Aquila noted as a native of Pontus (Acts 18:2). Pliny's letter to Trajan unfortunately concerns persecution, but it indicates a positive development. Despite Paul being prevented from entering Bithynia sixty years earlier, the message gets there eventually for there are enough Christians around to put the governor in a quandary over fitting punishments for those who refuse to worship Roman gods.

Treating these documents as having equal historical value initially does not necessarily mean they are completely accurate in everything they claim; it just means we take their claims seriously and use solid historical principles to determine whether those claims are more or less probable.

### More Like Law Courts Than Scientific Experiments

Establishing validity in a historical inquiry is much different from obtaining validity in scientific inquiry. The scientific method endeavors to establish cause and effect through controlled experiments that are replicated to prove that the effect is catalyzed by a particular cause or substance. The nature of history is that the exact series of events never can be repeated. The cause-and-effect relationship cannot be reduced to a controlled experiment that can be conducted time and again. Whether an event occurred and what caused it are subject to debate.

A better analogy to historical inquiry is the way a typical court case works in an adversarial judicial system. The parties seek to gather evidence for their respective sides. The judge or jury must decide if there is enough evidence to make a determination beyond a reasonable doubt. This determination by its nature involves probability rather than the type of certainty a replicated scientific experiment provides.[7]

In this inquiry, I bring evidence to bear on the resurrection of Jesus from first-century texts. In the Roman world just as in our day, people regularly did not see the dead raised. On the surface, a resurrection from the dead is an improbable historical claim. The categories of science also would consider it highly improbable. Experimentation has not been able to raise someone from the dead despite the high hopes of Dr. Frankenstein in literature and others today who in their wills order their corpses cryogenically frozen in anticipation of a scientific breakthrough.[8]

Yet that is exactly the point of the claim. The resurrection of Jesus is a shock. Because resurrection is not an everyday occurrence, because it is utterly improbable by natural means, if it happened, there must have been an uncommon power involved. This historical miracle is what these definitely first-century documents assert based on actual witnesses who saw evidence that this event occurred. To determine whether an event claimed

---

[7] Other books on the resurrection take this legal case approach including *The New Evidence that Demands a Verdict* by Josh McDowell (Nashville, TN: Thomas Nelson, 1999) and *Alive: A Cold Case Approach to the Resurrection* by J. Warner Wallace (Elgin, IL: David C. Cook, 2014). Interestingly, it is a former legal affairs newspaper editor who wrote the now classic book on the evidence for Jesus, based on interviews or "cross-examinations" with leading NT scholars. See Lee Strobel, *The Case for Christ* (Grand Rapids, MI: Zondervan, 1998).

[8] Currently, one of the people known to have his body cryogenically frozen is the famous Boston Red Sox baseball player Ted Williams. The literary figure of Dr. Victor Frankenstein appears in the book by Mary Shelley, *Frankenstein; or, The Modern Prometheus* (London: Lackington, Hughes, Harding, Mavor & Jones, 1818). This first edition was published anonymously.

to have happened in history did occur, we depend on witnesses and their testimony as we would in a court case.

### Four Biographies Agree on the Basic Resurrection Narrative

These witness reports primarily are contained in the four biographies of Jesus, commonly called gospels or books of "good news." Certain letters from Paul predate the gospels and contain brief witness reports as well (as described in the evidence in chapters 6 and 7).

In order of appearance in the New Testament, the gospels are Matthew, Mark, Luke and John. All four biographies are dated to the first century, all four circulated independently for several hundred years, and all four were written in Greek. Each qualifies as a biography but not as we today customarily define the genre. Just two of them include accounts of the birth of Jesus (Matthew and Luke, from which the famous Christmas story is derived). Mostly, they focus on the public career of Jesus as a teacher. He embarked on this career in his early thirties, and it ended with the gripping events of his last months on earth.

This approach is typical in the genre of Greek biography; it covered not the private lives but the public careers of important military and government figures. The presence of healing miracles and others in these accounts does not disqualify them as historical sources. Miracles were claimed in many Greek and Roman sources, and scholars chronicle reports of miracles in nearly every culture continuing to modern times.[9]

Each of the four authors has a particular emphasis as might be expected of people with different personalities. Matthew emphasizes how Jesus fulfills Jewish prophecies given centuries before his time. Mark, the shortest and fastest-moving account

---

[9] For a thorough treatment of miracles in these sources and in a larger global context across cultures, see Craig S. Keener, *Miracles: The Credibility of the New Testament Accounts* (Grand Rapids, MI: Baker Academic, Baker Publishing, 2011).

of the four, stresses the suffering Jesus endures. Luke accents the joy of Jesus and how he reaches out to Gentiles as well as to Jews, to women and children as well as to men. John focuses on the unique, intimate relationship Jesus expresses with God the Father.

Where they each begin their gospel is revealing. Matthew begins with a Jewish genealogy starting with Abraham. Mark begins with a prophecy from Isaiah about John the Baptist appearing out of the wilderness. Luke begins with a birth account of John the Baptist that connects his family with the mother of Jesus. John begins with Jesus in his preexistence with God the Father before the dawn of creation and his entry into humanity as the Light of the world. Though they begin their accounts of Jesus differently, they all end in a remarkably similar place.

Despite differences in emphasis and personality, the four gospel authors agree consistently on the basic facts of the resurrection narrative. By resurrection narrative, we mean the death, burial, resurrection, and appearances of Jesus.

- All four report that Jesus dies on a Roman cross after the Roman governor Pontius Pilate condemns him to death.
- All four record a group of women followers of Jesus mourning their loss at the execution site. His male disciples, scared to death, were nowhere to be found with one exception (John 19:26–27).
- All four present a man who suddenly emerges—Joseph of Arimathea. A member of the Jewish governing council, he receives permission to take possession of the corpse of Jesus. He brings the body to his family tomb nearby.
- All four report women rushing to the tomb in the early morning several days later led by Mary Magdalene.[10]
- All four report the women find the tomb empty.

---

[10] Mary Magdalene is the sole focus of John's account, but other women are implied in the plural noun she uses in telling the disciples, *"We do not know where they have put him!"* (Jn 20:2).

- According to all four, a messenger in dazzling white apparel speaks with them.
- All four indicate that the women are the ones who announce to the male disciples that Jesus is alive again.
- Three of the four gospels present appearances of Jesus after he rises (see chapter 2).
- Each of these three gospels includes at least one account where it is stated or implied that the body of the risen Jesus is physically touched by a follower.

We have four gospels, all by separate authors. Two gospels are independent works, Mark and John. They show virtually no signs of copying or depending on each other. The other two, Matthew and Luke, reveal they had access to Mark's gospel, and borrowed from it in many sections. They likely had at least one other source in common. Yet each of them also compiled unique material no other gospel covers. Especially valuable for our investigation are their unique accounts of the appearances of Jesus.

In *Resurrection Shock: Background Guide*, a companion book published separately, I go into more detail on these gospel authors and their relationships as sources. For these gospels and other documents that have demonstrated sufficient reliability to have made the cut for our sources, the guide examines their authorship, content, likely times of composition, and other historical issues that arise from this resurrection investigation. Other so-called gospels, acts or action narratives, and epistles in later centuries also purported to tell what happened to Jesus and his disciples. Some of these sources have been found relatively recently. In the *Background Guide*, I review these non-canonical and often comical documents.

I put these resources in the *Background Guide* to keep our focus in this book on the testimony and the lives of the resurrection witnesses. Given that focus, the issue of how the resurrection narrative (derived from our multiple sources) measures up to typical academic historical criteria is highly relevant, so I present that somewhat technical discussion in addition 3 at the back of this book.

## Discrepancies Can Occur Amid Overall Consistency

Along with major consistencies in the resurrection narratives, there are some discrepancies. This is common when there are multiple sources in historical events just as in court cases. Witnesses may get certain details different, but that does not change their agreement on the overall narrative. In case you have not noticed already, in this book I will not hesitate to discuss discrepancies when we run across them.

To gain proper perspective on these discrepancies within general agreement, an analogy is useful. Think of the gospel writers as if they were documentary filmmakers. They rummage through footage taken by other camerapersons to see which episodes are covered. They splice this older footage with newer footage that they take themselves (including their own eyewitness testimony if they were there or their interviews with eyewitnesses). They may tell a similar story, but the sequence of scenes may differ.

Also, they may edit the frame for a given scene. For instance, they take different angles on the women discovering the empty tomb (see chapter 1). John puts Mary Magdalene in a close-up shot. Matthew uses a two-shot with Mary Magdalene and Mary the mother of James. Mark includes three women in his shot— these first two women (in Matthew's two-shot) plus Salome. Luke features a group shot with at least five women; he mentions the same first two women, adds Joanna by name, and notes at least two other women were there if not more, but he leaves them unnamed.[11]

These decisions could have arisen from the writers' personalities, their views of their readers' interests or needs, from their differing access to sources, or from their emphasis

---

[11] For these contrasts, see Jn 20:1-2; Mt 28:1; Mk 16:1; Lk 24:1-10.

according to their own angles or themes. One can imagine all these documentary filmmakers working for the same studio executive (believers might assert that this executive would be the Holy Spirit), but they all are given poetic or artistic license to tell their stories in their own ways.

Nearly all discrepancies among the gospel accounts are *complementary*, meaning two or more reports could be true. The gospel of John says that Mary discovered the tomb empty, but this singular camera focus does not exclude the possibility that there were other women there, as Mark, Luke, and Matthew make clear. These accounts of the women at the empty tomb are complementary. In contrast, a *contradictory* discrepancy would be for example if one gospel reported that Jesus was crucified under the Roman governorship of Pilate while another reported that he was executed by a successor of Pilate, say Marcellus or Marullus. In reality, all four gospels report that Pilate was the governor who ordered the execution of Jesus.

Anytime there are multiple witnesses along with multiple writers composing accounts based on witness reports, some discrepancies are nearly unavoidable. Actually, discrepancies can add credibility when they involve minor details. Often, this can mean that the witnesses are relating independent viewpoints and not huddling together to perfectly align their accounts after the fact. This factor underscores the historical power of having four gospel accounts for the resurrection narrative. Even if they seem to show occasional areas of disagreement, they consistently agree on the major events and messages.

Of the four gospel authors, the only one to write a sequel is Luke. His sequel is commonly called Acts, or the Acts of the Apostles. It covers the next thirty years after the events of the epic Passover festival when the crucifixion and resurrection allegedly occur.

While Jesus's several years of ministry and his fateful week in particular are covered by the four gospel sources, Luke's Acts is our singular NT narrative source for the following decades of outreach by the disciples. Most scholars nevertheless consider

Luke's record to be reasonably accurate (see addition 3 and *Background Guide*, resource 1). The collected letters of Paul, Peter, John, and James add data and correlations to Luke's renderings in Acts. He claims to be a careful researcher who came into contact with eyewitnesses (Luke 1:1-4). Moreover, archaeological findings continually corroborate his Acts accounts as noted in succeeding chapters.

The first half of Acts focuses largely on the witness of Peter usually in tandem with John. The second half deals mostly with the missionary work of Paul in cities around the Mediterranean region. Luke himself met and traveled with Paul; he was present for many of the events he narrates. He also apparently had access to excellent sources for his accounts of Peter as we shall see in chapters 4 and 5. For our purposes of sifting historical evidence for the resurrection, I consider Luke to be a sufficiently reliable narrator.

### Message Is Designed to Get Out Through Witnesses

None of these first-century documents shy away from the fact that the entire case rests on the witnesses.[12] The risen Jesus himself as recorded by Luke in his gospel says that this straightforward approach is his plan. The way he intends his message to be spread is by means of the witnesses he appoints.

> *He told them, "This is what is written: The Messiah will suffer and rise from the dead on the third day, and repentance for the forgiveness of sins will be preached in his name to all nations, beginning at Jerusalem. You are witnesses of these things." (Luke 24:46–48)*

---

[12] For a breakthrough academic work on the neglected historical source category of witness testimony, see Richard Bauckham, *Jesus and the Eyewitnesses* (Grand Rapids, MI: Wm. B. Eerdmans, 2006), especially 4-8, 505-8. Bauckham deftly shows how understanding the notion of testimony goes a long way toward undoing the supposed conundrum of "the historical Jesus" versus "the Christ of faith."

This emphasis from Jesus on witnesses sunk deeply into the minds of the disciples. This explains the urgency they feel to replace the former disciple who betrayed Jesus and hanged himself (Acts 1:15–20). Any random follower of Jesus will not do. Peter, the leader among them, insists they must find a person who has been with them from the beginning who can testify to the entire span of events.

> *"Therefore it is necessary to choose one of the men who have been with us the whole time the Lord Jesus was living among us, beginning from John's baptism to the time when Jesus was taken up from us. For one of these must become a witness with us of his resurrection."* (Acts 1:21–22)

They end up nominating two qualified persons, praying, and then casting a lot that falls to a man named Matthias to round out the full slate of twelve disciples. Luke honors the runner-up in the account by including his name, Joseph, also known as Barsabbas or Justus (Acts 1:23). From then on, the reassembled twelve disciples are called apostles, those who are sent with a message and a purpose. (In this book, I use the terms *disciples* and *apostles* interchangeably, and in some contexts they may include other persons beyond Jesus's original eleven loyal recruits.)

These disciples turned apostles are the lead witnesses. They personally experience the events leading up to the resurrection of Jesus, to his ascension, and then to the initial giving of the Spirit in the streets of Jerusalem. Along with them are many other witnesses in the Jesus entourage that included women as well as men. They simply could not resist spreading the word of resurrection life to whomever would stand still long enough to hear their story. (For a full list of named and unnamed witnesses recorded in the NT, see addition 2.)

The simple question about the resurrection of Jesus that you and I engage with in this book is this: Did the disciples and the other witnesses get it right?

When we ask whether Jesus was raised from dead, we are asking whether he was raised in his own body and then in that body ascended to heaven as the witnesses reported. We are not asking whether he was raised in the sense that his memory was alive in the hearts of his followers, nor whether he was alive in spirit like any other human might be after death, nor whether he simply had obtained an exalted status beyond the normal human in heaven.

There are alternative theories of what happened to Jesus, which will be examined later (see chapter 10); but what we specifically are asking is whether the disciples got it right when they said that Jesus was raised back to embodied life, that he did not leave a corpse behind decomposing in an unmarked grave, a communal pit, or a tomb where his bones would be boxed up a year or so later.

In each of the first nine chapters, I present one line of evidence that increases the historical probability that the bodily resurrection of Jesus in reality occurred. No single line of evidence may seal the case, but taken together, the lines provide a cumulative weight. Despite all the evidence applied to our subject, I do not claim that the resurrection is proven beyond *any* doubt. Obviously, those who do not believe in God at all have difficulty believing he would raise someone from the dead. A case for divine interference in history can fall somewhat flat if one rules out from the get-go the existence of a Divinity to interfere.

What I do assert is that the wide array of evidence in the sources—looked at in historical context—raises the probability that things happened the way the witnesses reported. Put another way, the accumulated evidence makes it more difficult to disbelieve that the resurrection of Jesus actually happened. From that point, a person's individual decision toward or away from belief determines where he or she stands.

Our historical approach by no means eliminates the need for faith to believe in the resurrection, but it offers reasons to believe it. Faith is not blind to historical reality nor a giant leap into the complete unknown.[13] It is based on believing the witnesses and the writers who recorded their experiences. This book lets you look over the shoulders of these witnesses, many of whom Jesus appointed himself. From there, you are in a position to decide whether you find them credible—once you have had a chance to consider the historical evidence and their responses to what they persistently claimed to have seen, to have heard, and for a number of them, to have touched.

What the data compiled in this book firmly validate is this: to believe that the bodily resurrection of Jesus occurred in history is rational. This conclusion cannot be successfully dismissed as delusional because it has plenty of reasonable historical evidence to back it up.

### Embracing the Humanity in the Resurrection Narrative

I encourage readers to embrace the humanity of the resurrection witnesses and to an extent the humanity of the New Testament writers—some of whom were eyewitnesses themselves and all of whom reported eyewitness testimony. Yet this emphasis on their humanity in no way diminishes the perceived involvement of divine power. The faith perspective sees divine power supervising the sequencing and witnessing of the historical events and the reporting of the witnesses' experiences. Staking out the human dimension can enhance the sense of wonder at the power of divine working. It shows how despite our flaws and foibles and individual traits as human beings, God nevertheless works through imperfect people to bring the

---

[13] In matters of religious belief, there is always a need for personal decision or the so-called "leap of faith." This term was popularized in the mid-1800s by the Danish Lutheran philosopher Soren Kierkegaard. As the evidence for historical probability increases, the length of that leap is reduced to a more manageable "hop of faith."

message of salvation in Jesus to all nations so that everyone is given the chance to believe and *"that by believing you may have life in his name"* (John 20:31).

In short, my intent in writing this book is that whether or not you currently consider yourself a believer, you will get the opportunity to engage closely with the experiences of the resurrection witnesses. This way, you can make an informed decision about whether you agree with them. My hope is that you can feel in some way what they felt—their shock and awe, their recovery and joy, their confidence and peace, their irrepressible hope, and the overwhelming love pouring into their hearts all from the new life they found to be true and could not keep to themselves.

Lane Sanford Webster
Autumn 2019

## NOTE

---

# ON STRUCTURE AND USAGE

---

This book on the resurrection presents nine lines of evidence. At its heart, it is the story of the resurrection witnesses. Most chapters feature one or more lead witnesses up close and personal to the extent possible while remaining true to the historical sources.

Each chapter begins with a summary of one line of evidence. It is followed by a prelude, a short episode from an actual biblical account. Each prelude involves either a lesser-known person or a lesser-known moment in the life of well-known persons all documented in the Bible. Taking a certain degree of liberty, I have retold these episodes to focus on what these persons might have felt as they found themselves in a moment related to the resurrection narrative. The chapter prelude sets the stage for the chapter subject.

The main part of most chapters relates the experiences of resurrection witnesses largely in narrative form. These narratives produce witness profiles that will help readers evaluate the claims about what really happened. Near the back of the book, addition 2 gives a list of biblical witnesses to the resurrection to help you keep track of them all.

As you read the chapters, you will find boxes (or windows) popping out of the main text as already seen in the prologue and

21

introduction. These boxes give information that supports the main flow. They come in the following five categories.

### Found in the Ground

Archaeological discoveries often support or confirm the evidence in our textual sources. Each description includes an index number; the index is in the separately published *Resurrection Shock: Background Guide* described further below. The index features lengthier descriptions and source references for each of the archaeological discoveries, many of which are remarkable.

### Historical Portal

These portals are reports about figures or episodes in history known from nonbiblical sources. This background information often shows how persons figuring in accounts in secular historical sources intersect with the witnesses featured in the NT documents. Also, these portals provide context for the ancient Near Eastern culture in which the witnesses and the source writers lived.

### Interpretive Angle

These angles spell out how the biblical text is being interpreted in this book.

### Bible Sidelight

These sidelights are accounts from other parts of the Bible that bear on the subject in the chapter. Sometimes, they contain major truths in their own right but are labeled "sidelights" only with respect to our immediate context.

## Textual Detail

These details show up occasionally when there may be multiple manuscripts and some controversy over whether to include or how to translate certain phrases.

By its nature, a historical approach involves issues with sources, authors, document dating, alternative interpretations, archaeological discoveries, and other background questions. For readers wanting to inquire along these lines and go into more detail, I have written a shorter companion volume, *Resurrection Shock: Background Guide*, available in both downloadable and print versions. The main book refers to the background resources by their numbers (for instance, *Background Guide*, resource 1). To help you know which resource is which, the resources in the guide are listed with their numbers below. Note the exception is the archaeological index; it is referenced in the main book without a resource number but with numbers for specific index entries. Each entry has a number starting with the number of the chapter in which each is discussed and followed by the number for the order in which it appears in that chapter (such as Found in the Ground, 1.1). These are the resource subjects in the *Background Guide*.

Resource 1: Sorting Out the Sources
Resource 2: Estimating Document Dates
Resource 3: Calculating Timelines for Resurrection Week and Year
Resource 4: Reviewing Rabbinic Takes on the Servant in Isaiah
Resource 5: Surveying Jewish Expectations of Resurrection
Resource 6: Found in the Ground Archaeological Index

Should other key issues arise that deserve further treatment, there may be more resources added to the current ones in potential updated versions of the *Background Guide*.

In this main book, beyond the nine chapters each with its line of evidence, there is one more chapter that adds important information. Chapter 10 presents ten theories that deny the resurrection. These theories are evaluated, based on the evidence in the previous chapters.

After the ten chapters come four additions. Addition 1 provides discussion questions for each chapter. These are designed for individual study or for small groups that may wish to pursue a resurrection investigation perhaps by reading one chapter per week. Addition 2 lists the resurrection witnesses in the biblical records using several categories. Addition 3 shows how the resurrection narrative measures up to historical criteria customarily used by academic historians to determine the probability of events. This approach can get slightly technical, but it provides valuable perspectives on the resurrection sources and the enduring strength of the evidence. Addition 4 ends the book simply by quoting a section from Paul's first letter to the Corinthians. In it, the diehard apostle lets his language soar to rare heights as he renders resounding hope to the human heart in describing how the bodies of believers will be raised to new life through Jesus.

In the interest of clarity, allow me to briefly explain some of the particular terminology employed in this book.

### Counting the Years

We are taking a historical approach, but I do not use the terms for dating years now common in historical research. Most historians now use BCE to stand for years Before the Common Era instead of BC, Before Christ. Accordingly, they like to use CE to stand for "in the Common Era" instead of AD, the Latin abbreviation for *anno Domini*, "in the year of our Lord," counting from the estimated year of the birth of Jesus. We will stay with the traditional BC and AD. It is just easier, and this book is meant for the general reader. Be assured that in either notation scheme, the numbers for the years remain the same.

Most historians now agree Jesus was born several years before the commonly held year (AD 1) of his birth, but that does not change the accepted point from which the years in history continue to be counted. When years cannot be precisely determined to a single year or two, I use "c." for "circa," meaning the action occurred around the estimated year though not necessarily in that year exactly. A "d." means the estimated year a figure from history died.

## Measurement Systems

For measurements, I give distance measurements in terms of miles and kilometers and size measurements in feet or inches (ft or in) and in meters or centimeters (m or cm), usually spelling out the measurement indicator in full. Including both systems offloads the calculation readers otherwise might have to make.

## Source Abbreviations

To reduce repetition, I usually abbreviate references to gospel verses with two-letter indicators without periods (Mk for Mark, Mt for Matthew, Lk for Luke, Jn for John) with chapter and verse separated conventionally by a colon. Other biblical books are referred to either by their full names such as Acts or by common abbreviations with periods such as 1 Cor. for 1 Corinthians.

When I provide an exact quotation (from the Bible or from another original source) separate from the main text in block form, I spell out the full name of the book.

Usually, the New Testament is abbreviated as NT and the Old Testament as OT. For some readers, the term *old* may carry a negative connotation. It should be understood as the testament coming earlier, the first testament. The Jewish term for it is the Tanakh; the term is used increasingly in academia but is not yet common among general readers.

Two works outside the NT also are denoted in the main text with abbreviations. These two come from the Jewish-Roman author Josephus, also known as Flavius Josephus, a new first name he obtained once he started schmoozing with Roman royalty. I abbreviate his book *The Antiquities of the Jews* with the numbers following it for book, chapter, and paragraph, for example (*Antiquities* 18.9.2). His book *The Jewish War* (or *Wars*) is abbreviated similarly (*War* 17.6.3).

## Citations

Books and journal articles have long had clearly established practices for citation, and here we mainly use the Chicago style format. Regarding websites, we frequently run into missing pieces for citations when the practices for online resources are not as yet fully standardized. You may see the following terms: n.a. for no author, n.d. for no date, and n.p. for no publisher when any of these are unattainable.

*Wikipedia* offers no authors' names and rarely dates, so article titles are the primary identifier in these citations. I cite Wikipedia mainly as a source for well-known facts but rarely for interpretations.

I do not bother to provide complicated URL tracking codes because keyword searches on the internet almost always locate the source with the current advances in search technology.

## Italics

As is customary, italics are used in the text to emphasize a word or phrase. I also use italics in webpage citations for the *publisher*, and in books for the *title* of the book. Quotations from the Bible or from other sources are rendered in italics in block form, and also usually in italics when they appear in the main text, in order to highlight the material from original sources. In a few instances where I relate what is likely going on in the mind of biblical persons, their surmised thoughts also are shown in italics.

There you have it. Now you are all set to listen to the historical witnesses to the resurrection of Jesus, and to explore personally the multiple lines of historical evidence.

# CHAPTER

# LINE OF EVIDENCE

## SUMMARY

## 7:

Women, not men, are the first witnesses who observe that the tomb of Jesus is empty three days after he dies and is laid to rest in it. The women receive a divine message; they are commissioned to tell the men who will become apostles to the world that Jesus has been raised from the dead. No self-respecting Jewish writers who hope to be believed in the first-century Mediterranean world would pose women as their lead witnesses if they were making up the story. Women were considered less educated and more easily deceived and confused. Many courts of law did not admit them as witnesses. Nevertheless, the gospels report that as many as five or more women witness the empty tomb, and four of these women are identified specifically. Certain qualities about them as individuals, evident from the accounts, add to their credibility as witnesses of the resurrection events.

# PRELUDE

## CHAPTER 1

He was likely very angry. Angry at what had happened to Jesus, both the swift trial at night before the cunning high priest Caiaphas and the brutal whipping and crucifixion. He probably also was angry at himself for not having done more to speak up and try to stop the injustice. Now, he is angry enough to come out of his protective shell, go to the Roman governor, and ask if he can bury the expired body of Jesus. He is a rich, *"prominent member"* of the Jewish leadership council (Mk 15:43). He had not consented to putting Jesus to death. It is not even clear if he was present at the hastily organized night trial. In fact, he is a disciple of Jesus himself, *"but secretly, because he feared the Jewish leaders"* (Jn 19:38).

Fighting back guilt and sorrow, Joseph of Arimathea may have figured the least he could do is keep the body of Jesus from being tossed into a mass grave or thrown to the dogs. Only the Romans could carry out the death penalty in occupied Israel for civil laws, so they had custody of crucified bodies. He would have to go directly to Pontius Pilate, the governor, to make his appeal. In doing so, he would publicly self-identify as a Jesus sympathizer.

He finds the courage and is granted his request, but time is short. It is late afternoon, and bodies must be buried before sundown according to Jewish law especially when a Sabbath is about to begin that evening. Most of the crowd at the site is gone by now, but wailing and crying still fill the twilight air from those deeply distraught by the tragic death of Jesus.

As a wealthy man, he almost certainly has servants to assist him. (John reports another council member joins him, bringing a weighty load of burial spices, Jn 19:39.) Joseph has bought a linen shroud. He wraps it around the body, right after it has been detached from the wooden cross by the Roman soldiers, who will recycle the nails. His servants then transport the body, likely on a hand-carried pallet, to a tomb nearby. The tomb sits in a garden area not far from the barren, dusty crucifixion grounds. Just outside the city walls, the tomb is cut into the stone face of a hill, a former quarry. It is a new tomb probably meant for Joseph himself, and no one has ever been laid to rest in it.

Inside the tomb, his servants lay the body on a stone bench. In line with then-current Jewish practice, they wrap it in strips of cloth. Customarily, they tuck in chunks of spices to counteract the aroma of decomposing flesh. However, the men likely run out of time to apply the spices fully before sundown. Joseph assumes that in about one year, he will reopen the tomb. After the flesh has disintegrated, he will gather the bones of Jesus and place them in a small, carved stone box, an ossuary, to be returned to the family of the deceased.

As he observes his servants roll the massive, wheel-shaped stone along an earthen track to close up the entrance to the tomb, his eyes may have caught a glimpse of several tear-drenched women who were watching from a short distance. They must have followed him from the execution site. As the sun sets, he can hear the rustle of their robes as they hurry away.

# WOMEN ARE THE FIRST WITNESSES TO THE EMPTY TOMB

Jesus is arrested at night on the Mount of Olives by a mob armed with swords and clubs. As handheld torches flicker in the garden, the disciples flee for their lives (Mk 14:50). The more courageous among them, Peter (and one other disciple, most likely John) trail behind the armed guards as they bring Jesus down the mountain into the city and onto the grounds of the mansion where the high priest lives.

Peter makes it past the gate into the courtyard and finds a place by the fire on the cold night. Yet it does not take long for even Peter to be spooked after a servant girl recognizes him. She calls him out in front of others standing by and causes him to retreat in a discombobulated state (Mk 14:66–72). (For more on this interaction with the servant girl and how Peter recovers, see chapter 4.)

## *While the Disciples Hide, the Women Watch Burial*

Found in the Ground:
**Rock-Cut Tombs**

Jerusalem—Tombs are seen for centuries outside the walls in most directions. Some tombs trace back to the First Temple period, the ninth to the seventh centuries BC, showing Phoenician influence. The later wave of rock-cut tombs is dated to the period from when the Jewish Hasmonean regime began until the temple was destroyed (about 150 BC to AD 70). These findings confirm that the burial practice undergone by the body of Jesus as described in the gospels was indeed in fashion during his time. (Mk 15:45-46; Jn 19:38-40)

Index 1.1

At the site of the cross, in the hours of Jesus's most intensive suffering, the disciples have disappeared from most of the accounts (with one exception, Jn 19:26–27). They fear being killed alongside Jesus. They go into hiding. In contrast, a group of women who have come with him to Jerusalem from Galilee remains at the execution site weeping and mourning over Jesus as he suffers. Four of them are identified. Two of them stay on after Jesus expires. They follow discreetly as a prominent Jewish leader takes down the body from the cross and lays it in his nearby tomb. They get close enough to see how the body is prepared for burial (Mk 15:47; Mt 27:61; Lk 23:49, 55).

The custom at the time is to wrap the body in linen strips similar to an Egyptian mummy. The body would be left on a stone ledge in a cave-like tomb. About a year later, only bones would remain. The linen strips would be disposed of, and the bones would be stored in a stone box. The box would be shelved and the tomb readied for its next corpse.[14]

The two women position themselves to see how the men are

---

[14] Jodi Magness, "What Did Jesus' Tomb Look Like?" in Hershel Shanks and Ellen White, eds., *Jesus & Archaeology* (Wash., DC: Biblical Archaeology Society, 2016), 80–83.

wrapping the body of Jesus. They do not seem satisfied with the quality of the job. It is a rushed effort because it is dusk and the next day, a Sabbath, is about to begin. According to Jewish law, the body must be buried with the tomb closed before the sun has set (Jn 19:31).

Due to restrictions placed on commercial and physical activity during Sabbath days, the women are delayed in returning to the tomb. They wait until they can buy and prepare spices (Mk 16:1; Lk 23:56). (For more on their spice journey, see *Background Guide*, resource 3). They want to wrap the body of Jesus properly since it will be in the tomb for a year. Their first opportunity to return comes on the first day of the week (which in our modern calendars is Sunday).

Given the fear of the disciples and the courage of these women, it is not surprising what happens next. All four gospel accounts concur.

> *Very early on the first day of the week, just after sunrise, they were on their way to the tomb and they asked each other, "Who will roll the stone away from the entrance of the tomb?" But when they looked up, they saw that the stone, which was very large, had been rolled away. As they entered the tomb, they saw a young man dressed in a white robe sitting on the right side, and they were alarmed.*
>
> *"Don't be alarmed," he said. "You are looking for Jesus the Nazarene, who was crucified. He has risen! He is not here. See the place where they laid him." (Mark 16:2–6)*

It is not the men whom Jesus called to be his disciples who are up at dawn on the first day of the week to discover that his tomb is empty. The shocking discovery is made by women, the first human witnesses to the resurrection of Jesus. They encounter an angelic messenger who informs them Jesus has been raised from the dead. They are the ones divinely assigned to go to the disciples' hideout and tell them Jesus is alive.

### The Cultural Oddity of Women Witnesses Adds Credibility

Found in the Ground:
**Anklebone from Crucified Man**

Jerusalem—Found in 1968. Among the many bone boxes (ossuaries) found in tombs around Jerusalem was the box of an individual named Yehohanan, with an iron nail pounded through his anklebone indicating death by crucifixion. This artifact confirms that Jewish law permitted the burial of crucified persons with honor in regular family tombs if the violation was against secular Roman law, not Jewish law. This stunning find debunks the theory that Jesus had to have been buried in a trench or a mass grave, which is an attempt to discredit the gospel burial accounts. (Mk 15:45–46; Lk 23:53; Mt 27:59–60; Jn 19:40–42)

Index 1.2

Our culture today would not bat an eye at these gender role–bending accounts. Of course, women today might have more courage than the fear-ridden men did. Of course, they might be the first to know. However, in the patriarchal societies of the Mediterranean world, this would not be the case. Writers who made women their first witnesses to an event would be inviting people to question the validity of their accounts.

Women were not considered to be reliable witnesses in first-century Jewish society. Neither women nor slaves were permitted to testify in court according to the Jewish-Roman historian Josephus (*Antiquities* 4.8.15). Some sources trace the tradition to a proof text cited in the Talmud (Rosh Hashanah 1.8) while others trace it to Psalm 45:13–15. The psalm depicts a role model for women, a princess supposedly focused on the domain of the home, the private sphere, not the public sphere of the courts or government.

Maimonides, a highly influential rabbi, philosopher, legal

scholar, and leader of the Jewish community in Egypt in the late medieval age (AD 1135–1204), disallowed women as witnesses. He based the prohibition on the way the Torah used the masculine form when speaking of witnesses. His list of persons disqualified to be witnesses in court included those who were blind, deaf, minors, slaves, interested parties, wicked, contemptible, lunatics, and relatives, as well as women.[15] It is likely that the mind-set in first-century Israel unfortunately viewed women as less reliable or more gullible, possibly due to interpretations of the creation account in Genesis, when it came to matters of serious legal proceedings.[16]

Historical Portal:
On Women's Rights

This limitation on women as witnesses continues in Jewish traditions until 1951, when the nascent, three-year-old state of Israel ends this disqualification with the passage of the Equality of Women's Rights Law, which also brought protections against harassment and abuse. It is worth noting that it took nearly 150 years from the founding of the United States for women to get the right to vote in 1920.

Once the cultural context is understood, the assertion that women are the first witnesses to the empty tomb becomes an especially strong line of evidence for the veracity of the resurrection event. No first-century authors who intended to convince people of their era would invent out of thin air narratives that championed women as key witnesses. Yet the gospel writers in this instance remained unanimous and undeterred.

---

[15] "Witness," n.a., n.d., jewishvirtuallibrary.org, Encyclopedia Judaica, The Gale Group, 2008, *American–Israel Cooperative Enterprise*, retrieved 11 Aug 2017.

[16] For a more comprehensive look at the status of women in and around the first century era, see Tal Ilan, "Post-Biblical and Rabbinic Women," n.d., jwa.org, *Jewish Women's Archive*, Encyclopedia, retrieved 18 Aug 2017.

## The Four Accounts Agree the Sealed Stone Is Rolled Away

The four gospel accounts have major factors in common (with some minor differences we will consider below). All of them feature women (or one woman in John) heading out to the tomb (Mk 16:1-8; Mt 28:1-8; Lk 24:1-10; Jn 20:1-8). It is early morning on the first day of the week. Although in Mark 16:3, they worry how they can gain entrance with a stone blocking their path, all four accounts agree they arrive to find the stone rolled away. They look inside the tomb and see that the body of Jesus is not there. They encounter an angel (one in Mark and Matthew, two in Luke and John). The angel is intimidating, dressed *"in a white robe"* (Mk 16:5), *"in white"* (Jn 20:12), *"white as snow"* (Mt 28:3), or *"in clothes that gleamed like lightning"* (Lk 24:4). Initially, the emotional state of the women is one of fear and trembling. In Mark, they are *"trembling and bewildered"* (Mk 16:8). Luke adds, *"In their fright the women bowed down with their faces toward the ground"* (Lk 24:5), while John recounts weeping (Jn 20:11), and Matthew captures their feelings as *"afraid yet filled with joy"* (Mt 28:8). The women leave the tomb site and rush to tell the disciples.

Found in the Ground:
**Tomb Jesus Occupied**

Jerusalem—The tomb is rediscovered in AD 325 by Helena, mother of Roman emperor Constantine, and by Jerusalem Patriarch Marcarius. An elaborate Romanesque church called the Church of the Holy Sepulchre was built over the site. Formerly a rock quarry, the site stood outside the walls of Jerusalem at the time of Jesus. This supports with high probability the actual site of Joseph of Arimathea's fresh-cut tomb where he laid the body of Jesus. (Mk 15:45–46; Mt 27:57–60; Lk 23:50–53; Jn 19:38–42)

Index 1.3

## *Agreement on Essentials, Difference in Details*

In certain items, the accounts differ, but most differences are complementary, not contradictory. Let us look at the differences keeping in mind that some minor differences are normal when there are multiple independent witnesses to a major event. Multiple witnesses may experience the same event from slightly different points of view, and the gospel writers may be working from different witness accounts. This exercise will be brief, but some readers might consider it a bit tedious. Yet this way, we are sure to know what these women claim they experienced.

Discrepancies are duly noted in order to be true to the data, but they do not affect the overarching line of evidence. The fact that women are reported as the first witnesses to the news of the resurrection of Jesus significantly increases the historical credibility of the account.

> Found in the Ground:
> **Pilate Inscription**
>
> Caesarea Maritima, Israel—Found in 1961. The limestone plaque commemorates Pilate in his role with the title of prefect dedicating a building to the Roman emperor at the time, Tiberius. This confirms the gospel accounts of the existence and rule of Pilate during the time of Jesus, eliminating notions that he is a fictional figure. (Mk 15:1–15, Jn 18:28–19:22)
>
> Index 1.4

## *Number of Angels*

Mark and Matthew each indicate one angel is present. Their language does not eliminate the possibility that there could have been more. (Uniquely, the account in Matthew directly credits the angel with rolling back the stone; it also includes uniquely the occurrence of an earthquake.) Luke and John recount two angels; Luke has them standing while John has them sitting (Jn 20:12) right where Jesus's body had lain. Of course, they might have moved around a bit as they were not statues, so these variances are not contradictory.

### Words of the Angels

Three of the four gospel accounts have the core words of the angels in common: *"He has risen! He is not here"* (Mk 16:6; Mt 25:6; Lk 24:6). Angels ask a question in Luke, *"Why do you look for the living among the dead?"* and in John, *"Why are you crying?"* (Lk 24:5; Jn 20:13).

Matthew and Luke have the angel reminding the women that Jesus said he would rise from the dead. Mark and Matthew show the angel instructing the women to go tell the disciples he is risen and they can go meet him in Galilee (Mk 16:7; Mt 28:7). Luke and John do not include this instruction as their accounts focus mainly on Jerusalem. However John's gospel includes a section on Jesus meeting his disciples back on the shores of the Sea of Galilee (Jn 21:1–23, see chapter 2). Likewise, Luke's continuing narrative (Acts 1:3) asserts that Jesus made appearances over a forty-day period, plenty of time for several eighty-five-mile or 137-kilometer trips, the distance between Jerusalem and Capernaum, Jesus's operational base in Galilee.

### Response of Disciples to the News

Mark's reel of events cuts off before the women arrive at the place where the disciples are hiding. Matthew indicates the women head there but depicts no response or tomb run on the part of the disciples themselves. Luke shows the initial response of the men to the news reported by the women is disbelief, and the disciples scoff at the *"nonsense"* (Lk 24:11–12). They evince the cultural bias against women witnesses. Peter nevertheless gets up and runs to the tomb. He sees a pile of linen strips but no body and no angel. The gospel of John features an almost competitive apostolic footrace between Peter and another disciple (most likely

John, Jn 20:3–5). Likewise, they in turn go inside the tomb and find only linen strips and the cloth previously wrapped around the head of Jesus.

## Guards at the Tomb

Only Matthew's account describes the episode of the Jewish leaders insisting that the Roman governor, Pontius Pilate, deploy guards at the tomb (Mt 27:62–66). The guards are present when the women arrive at the tomb, but *"they shook and became like dead men"* due to the fear inspired in them by the angel (Mt 28: 2–4). They run away to the chief priests as soon as they can, apparently after the women leave to tell the disciples.

It makes sense that the guards would go to the chief priests rather than to their Roman commander. It might be in the interest of the priests to protect them because they would face death before the Romans for failing at their tomb-guarding assignment. The priests spare their lives as long as they agree to spread the story that the disciples stole the body (Mt 28:11–15; for more on this theory, see chapter 10). We have only one source for this episode, but it is plausible that the chief priests would want a guard posted at the tomb. It is also reasonable that the chief priests would want and be willing to pay for an explanation that accounts for the disappearance of the body.

## Appearances of Jesus to the Women

Two of the four gospels include an appearance by Jesus to one or two of the women. As seen before, Mark ends with the account of the women running from the tomb without any appearances by Jesus to them or to anyone else. Luke records other appearances by Jesus on that day but none to the women near the tomb. Matthew's account has two women who see Jesus on their way to tell the disciples. To use a cinematic term, it is brief and shot from a distance.

In contrast, John's account moves in for a close-up featuring a sequence of events that focuses on just one woman. She has a tender dialog with the risen Jesus. In both Matthew and John, a woman touches Jesus; they clasp his feet in Matthew and one holds onto him in John (Mt 28:9; Jn 20:17). These two accounts raise to an even higher level the role of women in the resurrection narratives. They make them the first witnesses not only of the empty tomb and the angelic news of Jesus being raised but also of the risen Jesus walking among them resurrected in his physical body after death (see more on these appearances in chapter 2).

---

### Found in the Ground: Magdala Tower, Harbor, Pools

Magdala, Galilee, Israel—Found in 2007. The findings included stone foundations of a tower (*migdal* is Hebrew for tower, with other names for the area, the Aramaic *magdala nunaya*, meaning fish tower, or the Greek term, *magdala tarichaeae*, meaning tower of fish salters, or often just Tarichaeae as the town name).

Also unearthed: an *L*-shaped harbor basin with a breakwater, six mooring stones for boats, a quay or wharf for unloading and loading cargo, and stone vats likely used to store fish in fresh water. This confirms Magdala was a key port on the lakeshore for storing and transporting fish. It is likely the disciples sold fish in this spot. It is possible they met Mary Magdalene when they went about their business in this town. (Lk 8:1–2)

---

## Jesus Sets Out the Welcome Mat for His Women Followers

Scholars of many stripes have pointed out that it was radical for his time for Jesus to welcome women among his followers. It was one thing for them to listen to his public teachings, but it was quite another for women to travel with him and his band of male disciples. It certainly could invite accusations of scandalous behavior.

Few if any precedents can be found for this dual-gender

community in the histories of Jewish rabbis, but in retrospect, it makes sense. Jesus intended to form a new community around himself, which he called the kingdom of God. This kingdom would include women and elevate them to a level of worth equal to that of men. Jesus made himself approachable by women. The gospels are full of accounts of women coming to Jesus for healing for themselves or for their loved ones or for spiritual guidance. Examples include a woman with a chronic bleeding condition (Mk 5:25-34), with a troubled daughter (Mk 7:25-30), with severe curvature of the spine (Lk 13:10-13), or with failed relationships (Jn 4:7-42). Most of these women go unnamed.

### Identifying the Women by Name Adds to Their Credibility

The accounts of the women at the cross and empty tomb could have come to us without their names, but naming them makes them more prominent and convincing as witnesses. If we, like the authors who report their actions, are to believe what they assert as witnesses, it is helpful to know as much as we can about them and what likely motivates them. The named women who follow Jesus can be grouped into two main categories: financial contributors and mothers of disciples.

### Affluent Women Financially Support Jesus's Ministry

Some women who followed and traveled with Jesus in Galilee are relatively affluent. They are credited by Luke as being financial supporters of Jesus and the disciples.

> *After this, Jesus traveled about from one town and village to another, proclaiming the good news of the kingdom of God. The Twelve were with him, and also some women who had been cured of evil spirits and diseases: Mary (called Magdalene) from whom seven demons had come out; Joanna the wife of Chuza, the manager of Herod's*

*household; Susanna; and many others. These women
were helping to support them out of their own means.
(Luke 8:1–3)*

The plural possessive term in the original Greek that Luke
uses in regard to their money carries the meaning that they
themselves control their own funds. Their motivation for traveling
with Jesus and for supporting his ministry seems to have been
driven by gratitude. They have received physical healing or
spiritual exorcisms from him.

Luke's account then identifies two of the three women listed
as contributors as also present at the empty tomb that Sunday
morning.

*When they came back from the tomb, they told all these
things to the Eleven and to all the others. It was Mary
Magdalene, Joanna, Mary the mother of James, and the
others with them who told this to the apostles.
(Luke 24:9–10)*

Mary the mother of James (described below) is the third
woman Luke names. Then he mentions there are others. This
means there are at least two more, making a total of at least five
women present to witness to the empty tomb.

From further evidence in the gospels, we can sketch out a
sense of the personal qualities of some of these women granting us
stronger witness profiles. We begin with the leader of the women.

### Mary Magdalene Is the Energetic Leader of the Women

Mary Magdalene figures prominently in all four gospels. Her
second name comes from the town where she lives, Magdala
(Aramaic for "tower," similar to the Hebrew *migdal*). It is on the
western side of the Sea of Galilee about six miles or ten kilometers
south down the lakeshore from Jesus's home base in Capernaum.
Magdala is a major port and trading center on the lake for fishermen

to bring their catch to market. Fish would be sold there or salted and stored for later sale or transport to other locations including Jerusalem (delivered and marketed at none other than the Fish Gate).

Mary Magdalene might have known some of the disciples through their fishing business before they joined Jesus, or she might have heard about Jesus's healings in Capernaum from the grapevine chatter since her town was not far away. Jesus may have spoken at the synagogue in her town. At some point, she seeks him out for spiritual help. She directly benefits from his ministry by having multiple evil spirits cast out of her. She becomes one of his followers and financial supporters (Lk 8:1-3).

The rest of the scenes in which Mary Magdalene appears take place in Jerusalem in the resurrection narratives. She is at the cross weeping over the sufferings of Jesus. She is with three other named women and many others (Mk 15:40-41). She leaves the site of the cross with one other female friend when the body of Jesus is taken down from the cross (Mk 15:40, 47). They sit across from the tomb entrance and watch how his body is laid to rest (Mt 27:61).

With two others, she buys and prepares spices to more fully anoint and wrap the body of Jesus. After waiting for the Sabbath

Found in the Ground:
**Magdala Synagogue and Stone**

Magdala, Galilee, Israel—Found in 2009. It is the first synagogue found in Magdala (an earlier find in the 1970s thought to be a small synagogue is now considered a latrine). Discovered in a central spot and less than a foot underneath the soil was a stone block with an image of a seven-branched menorah carved in relief. The findings confirm that synagogues are actively used in Galilee in the time of Jesus and are not anachronisms in the gospels as some critics once contended. It is possible though speculative that Mary Magdalene encounters Jesus at the synagogue and is healed here in her hometown. (Mk 1:39; Mt 4:23, 9:35; Lk 4:15, 44; Jn 18:20)

Index 1.6

day to pass, she rises early on the first day of the week probably with four or more other women to go to the tomb (Mk 16:1; Mt 28:1). She receives the angelic news that Jesus lives, and with the others, she runs to tell the disciples (Mt 28:8; Lk 24:9–10).

Two gospels report that Jesus appears to her personally that morning, and she holds onto him in worshipful joy (Mt 28:9; Jn 20:17). After these moments, she disappears in time; the author of Luke does not mention her in the succeeding volume of Acts, Paul does not identify her in his trove of letters, and no early church writings offer any reasonable accounts of what happens to her.

Yet these gospel accounts contain enough detail to sketch her portrait. In all but one scene in the gospels, Mary Magdalene is listed first among the other women (the exception in Jn 19:25 understandably puts Mary the mother of Jesus first). Being first on the list customarily indicates a leadership role (as Peter is first on the list of disciples in each of the first three gospels).

This quality is confirmed with the initiative she demonstrates. She tracks the route to the tomb (so she knows exactly where Jesus is buried), she goes shopping for spices, and she gathers a group of women to go with her to the tomb in the morning (Mk 15:47, 16:1–2; Lk 24:1).

She puts her treasure where her heart is; she contributes to Jesus's ministry in Galilee. Then when he meets his supposed demise, she spares no expense to ensure that his body is honorably prepared. She is energetic, even athletic. She is on the move after grueling hours beside the cross to the tomb late in the day, to the spice market, back again to the tomb early in the morning, then to tell the disciples the news (with two back-to-back wind sprints recorded in Jn 20:2, 18). She seems to be a feeling, expressive, and tactile person.

Jesus appears to her and her friend in Matthew, and they bow low and clasp his feet in worship (Mt 28:9). She weeps inconsolably in John (Jn 20:11). Then when Jesus appears, she holds onto him to the point that he gently asks her to get going to tell the disciples he will be ascending to heaven in the near future (Jn 20:17).

## Mary Magdalene Often Is Unfairly, Scurrilously Shamed

This expressiveness on the part of Mary Magdalene may explain why some imaginative types have been led to think that she and Jesus had a romantic relationship. There is no evidence in the gospels, in the complete New Testament, or in reliable historical accounts that there was any romantic involvement in the friendship of Jesus with Mary Magdalene or with any other woman. Mary's greeting to Jesus in the dialog in John shows her calling out to him using the Aramaic term *"Rabboni!"*, a respectful greeting that means "teacher" and shows a close relationship in the manner of student or disciple, not companion or lover (Jn 20:16).

From another angle, Mary Magdalene has been labeled by many commentators as a prostitute, but there is no direct evidence that justifies this shaming. The explanation often cited runs like this. She appears to be single unlike most named women in the gospels. She is not identified with a male relative—not a son, father, or husband. Mary Magdalene is from the town of Magdala. As a port and trading town, it is more prone to looser living than are the surrounding villages. Luke reports that she has multiple evil spirits cast out of her, and some people contend that prostitution can be a gateway to oppression by spirits (Lk 8:2). However, this is circumstantial, not direct evidence.

It is more likely that Mary Magdalene was a businesswoman. If her funds came from prostitution, it is doubtful the disciples could have accepted the money into their treasury without creating a scandal. Along with the business of storing and salting fish in Magdala, there were other businesses in town: dyeing cloth, tanning leather, and crafting leather goods.

The demonic oppression in the life of Mary Magdalene may have come because she appears to be an absorptive spiritual seeker. In Galilee with its mixed population of Jews, Greeks, Romans, and Assyrians there were many influences of pagan gods. North of the lake was a large, tempting shrine to the Roman goat-legged god of the pastures, Panias, built beside a gushing spring. Some of these influences may have led her astray from the faith of Israel into demonic oppression, that is, until she met Jesus and experienced his power that could with her permission secure her sudden and complete deliverance.

---

Historical Portal:
## Herod Is Not So Great as a Father

Herod the Great is the king of Israel when Jesus is born. He is in the last few years of his thirty-three-year reign. Herod is an Idumean, from the land of Edom. He displaces the Hasmonean dynasty descended from the Maccabees. He converts to Judaism, marries a Hasmonean princess, but he remains suspect by the Jews. He grows wealthy by taking advantage of Israel's strategic position as a land bridge between Egypt, Arabia, Syria, and Asia (Turkey) for trade and commerce. He builds the port city of Caesarea Maritima (where Paul is later held) in honor of the Emperor Augustus. In Jerusalem, he spectacularly expands the temple plaza and renovates the second temple itself, where Jesus and the disciples worship.

Paranoid and vindictive, Herod executes three of his sons. This led Emperor Augustus to famously joke, "Better to be Herod's pig than his son." (In Latin, "Melius est Herodis porcum esse quam filium.") The wit plays off the notion that Jews do not eat pork (though Herod actually was Idumean). One of the sons Herod kills is Aristobulus IV, the father of the later king Agrippa I (who executes James the disciple) and grandfather of the later king Agrippa II (who hears the charges against Paul). Herod Antipas, ruling Galilee at the time of Jesus, is a son of Herod the Great and follows the family pattern of brutality by needlessly executing John the Baptist.

---

## Joanna Operates in the Elite but Treacherous Royal Circle

Joanna is mentioned only by Luke. Her name means "God is gracious," the female equivalent of the male name John. She receives healing from Jesus and is credited with contributing to Jesus's ministry in Galilee (Lk 8:1-3). She is among those who travel with him to Jerusalem. Luke names her among the five or more women who go to the tomb early Sunday morning and discover it empty (Lk 24:10). A striking quality of Joanna is her commitment to the Jesus movement despite her living in proximity to a violent and powerful opponent of Jesus.

Luke tells us that she is married to Chuza (Lk 8:3), an executive manager in the royal household of the ruler of Galilee in northwestern Israel. This ruler also controls the region of Perea, east of the Jordan starting south of Galilee and reaching to the midpoint of the Dead Sea shore, a region where John the Baptist preached. The ruler is Herod Antipas, a son of Herod the Great.

Herod Antipas ends up ruling for more than forty years (4 BC–AD 39). In the short time covered by the gospels, he reveals himself as one who takes after the murderous tendencies of his father. He is responsible for the death of John the Baptist, a cousin of Jesus.

Later, Jesus is informed by friendly Pharisees that Herod Antipas has put out a hit on him and wants him dead as well. *"That fox,"* quips Jesus, referring to Antipas as a sly and cunning animal, will not succeed with his plot. Jesus is heading to Jerusalem, which lies outside Herod's domain, for it is under Roman and priestly control, and *"surely no prophet can die outside Jerusalem"* (Lk 13:33).

Ironically, Herod Antipas will get the chance he always wanted to interrogate Jesus not in Galilee but in Jerusalem at the Passover feast. The Roman governor Pilate hopes to recuse himself and let Antipas judge Jesus. Antipas lets loose with a flurry of questions. He demands that Jesus work a miracle in front of him.[17] Jesus remains completely silent. The chief priests

---

[17] This scene with Herod Antipas interrogating Jesus is cleverly dramatized in the rock opera musical *Jesus Christ Superstar* by Andrew Lloyd Weber and Tim Rice. The composer and lyricist imagine an ornery Antipas singing and coaxing Jesus to perform a miracle. "Prove to me that you're no fool, Walk across my swimming pool, If you do that for me, Then I'll let you go free, C'mon King of the Jews." Andrew Lloyd Weber and Tim Rice, "King Herod's Song," *Universal Music Publishing Group*, Warner/Chappell Music, Inc., 1970.

keep up their volleys of accusations against him. Luke reports that Herod himself along with his soldiers ridicule and mock Jesus (Lk 23:6–12). They are the ones who dress Jesus in *"an elegant robe,"* the color of purple, probably a hand-me-down from Herod Antipas's closet (Mk 15:17; Lk 23:11; Jn 19:2). Not making any progress and not wanting to be responsible, Herod sends Jesus back to Pilate.

This is the kind of pompous, sneering, and violent person Joanna has to deal with in Herod Antipas as her husband's boss. By aligning herself with Jesus and his community, Joanna takes enormous risks. She risks her husband's job and with it her financial security and social prominence. She risks the loss of her marriage should her husband disagree and divorce her, and she even risks her life. It is not beyond the Herodian kings to put their family members to death, so they surely would not hesitate to execute nonfamily members of their households for even the slightest charge of disloyalty.

In light of her two brief mentions in Luke's gospel (Lk 8:3, 24:10), Joanna not only displays enduring gratitude and generosity toward Jesus and his ministry, she also shows a courageous willingness to put everything on the line including her own life due not to any faith in King Herod but to her faith in Jesus and the kingdom of God he offers.

### Susanna Is Credited as a Ministry Contributor

Susanna is mentioned only once in the NT by Luke (Lk 8:3). Her name means "lily." Like Mary Magdalene, she is not identified in relation to a male (son, father, or husband). She is likely single or widowed. She has received healing from Jesus and is willing and able from her own means to contribute financially to his ministry in Galilee. It is not clear whether she went with the entourage to Jerusalem for the Passover feast. However, Luke allows for at least five women going to the tomb on Sunday morning, so Susanna easily might have been among them (Lk 24:10).

## Some Mothers Accompany the Traveling Team of Disciples

Other women who follow Jesus include mothers of his disciples. The disciples are likely in their twenties or early thirties. (Jesus himself probably is in his early thirties.) Consequently, their mothers are most likely in their mid- to late-forties or early fifties. Traveling as they do first in Galilee and then on the longer trek to the Passover feast in Jerusalem, where painful events will take place, they exhibit courage, faith, dedication, and sustained energy. Two mothers are named.

## Mary Mother of James, Sidekick to Mary Magdalene

Other than Mary the mother of Jesus and Mary Magdalene, a third woman named Mary plays a significant supporting part in the resurrection narratives. She stays close to Mary Magdalene at each key moment. Like Mary Magdalene, she is one of the women who had *"followed Jesus from Galilee to care for his needs"* (Mt 27:55). She is at the site of the cross *"watching from a distance"* (Mt 27:55–56; Mk 15:40; Jn 19:25). She and Mary Magdalene sit opposite the tomb and view how Jesus's body is laid to rest (Mt 27:61). In Mark, she buys spices with Mary Magdalene *"to anoint Jesus' body"* with at least one other woman. Then the three head out to the tomb (Mk 16:1).

Mark and Matthew place her at the tomb early Sunday where the women hear the angelic pronouncement that Jesus has risen. Matthew focuses on just these two Marys at the tomb. Then as they go on their way to tell the disciples, Jesus makes an appearance to the two, who bow low in worship and *"clasp his feet"* (Mt 28:9). She is among the five (or more) women Luke credits with going to the disciples to tell them the good news (Lk 24:10).

Other than Mary Magdalene, this Mary is the only other woman mentioned in the resurrection narratives in all four gospels. She is referred to with several different identifiers. In Mark, she is first cited as *"Mary the mother of James the younger and of Joseph"* (Mk 15:40) and then abbreviated as *"the mother of James"*

(Mk 16:1). In Matthew, she is *"the mother of James and Joseph"* (Mt 27:56), then simply as *"the other Mary"* (27:61). In Luke, she is *"the mother of James"* (Lk 24:10). The key term that emerges from these mentions is her status as the mother of James.

In the lists of the twelve disciples (in each of three gospels) are two men named James. To avoid confusion, Mark and Matthew distinguish each as the son of a different father. The James mentioned first on the lists is the brother of another disciple named John. Their father is known as Zebedee (Mk 3:16–17; Mt 4:21, 10:2). Later, their mother is mentioned as *"the mother of Zebedee's sons."* She is listed among those at the cross along with Mary the mother of James and with Mary Magdalene in the same verse in Matthew (Mt 27:56). Therefore, this second Mary cannot be the mother of the first James, who is one of Zebedee's sons.

The James mentioned second in the lists is James the son of Alphaeus (Mk 3:18; Mt 10:3; Lk 6:15). Mary would be the mother of this James. As such (barring the unlikely event of a divorce), she therefore would be married to the father of this second James, a man we know is named Alphaeus from the gospel lists of disciples. The gospel of John, however, identifies this same Mary as *"the wife of Clopus"* (Jn 19:25). It would seem to be a contradiction except for a scholarly investigation that found both names, Alphaeus and Clopus, could be attempts to translate into Greek an underlying Aramaic name.[18]

To make things slightly more complicated, Luke gives the name of one of the two persons Jesus appears to on the road to Emmaus as Cleopas (Lk 24:18; for the story, see the outset of chapter 9). This name is very similar to the gospel of John's Clopas. It is possible though not proven that these names refer to

---

[18] It is Joseph Henry Thayer, author of *A Greek-English Lexicon of the New Testament* (1889), who identifies an underlying linguistic or etymological connection between the names Alphaeus and Clopus in the original Aramaic root. Both names are attempts to translate into Greek an underlying Aramaic name believed to be Hilfai. Since Greek has no *h* sound, some transliterators leave it off while others would add a *k* sound. See "Clopus," wikipedia.org, retrieved 8 Aug 2017.

the same person. If so, this would mean that Cleopas is married to Mary the mother of James and therefore the father of the second disciple James (and he would be endowed in the NT with the two additional monikers denoted above—Clopus and Alphaeus). If this is the case, this matching of names might solve the mystery of the second unnamed traveler on the road to Emmaus. While some have imagined it might be the wife of Cleopas, it is more likely that it is their younger son, Joseph, also known in Greek as Joses (Mk 15:40, 47; Mt 27:56).

Organizing the names and references in the gospels to Mary the mother of James certainly can introduce various speculations. What is abundantly clear, however, are her actions. They reveal her as a spiritual, caring, and loyal person who is ready to serve and full of physical energy and faith. She raises a strong spiritual man in her son James, whom Jesus selects. Tradition holds he goes to preach in Egypt. She is a faithful friend to Mary Magdalene (who unlike most of the other women does not seem to have a direct male or female relative in the band of believers).

This other Mary is consistent in her caring about Jesus. She is with him in Galilee, with him as he suffers on the cross, and present at the tomb to see where he is buried, and she is intent on gathering spices to properly anoint his body. At his sudden appearance to her and to Mary Magdalene (Mt 28:9), she readily worships him. On that eventful Sunday morning, she has the honor of telling her son James among the other disciples the amazing news of Jesus's resurrection. If it is indeed her husband and second son on the Emmaus road, they also are there with the disciples to hear the news she delivers (Lk 24:22-23).

### A Relative Comforts Mary at the Cross

The second mother of a disciple who is named in the gospels is Salome, whose name is derived from the Hebrew *shalom,* "peace." Salome in the Jesus community is not to be confused with another Salome in history, a royal living in Galilee about the same time. She appears in Matthew but is not named in the

NT though she is named in the related account of Josephus (see chapter 5).

Mark mentions Salome the follower of Jesus by name as one of the three women watching from a distance at the site of the cross along with Mary Magdalene and Mary the mother of James. *"In Galilee these women had followed him and cared for his needs,"* Mark writes making it no doubt more painful for them to watch Jesus suffer. Mark adds, *"Many other women who had come up with him to Jerusalem were also there,"* yet these women are the only three he names (Mk 15:40–41).

The gospel of John places four individual women at the site.

> *Near the cross of Jesus stood his mother, his mother's sister, Mary the wife of Clopas, and Mary Magdalene. (John 19:25)*

To unpack who's who, we need to read the verse closely. In Greek, there are no commas. This leads some traditions to hold that *"his mother's sister"* describes Mary the wife of Clopas; that would mean that John places just three, not four, women at the cross. The interpretation followed here takes the verse to mean that the group consists of four women based on the parallel passage in Mark.

Placing John's list of four at the cross beside Mark's list of three (which does not mention Mary, Jesus's mother), the lists line up if we deduce that Salome is Mary's sister (Jn 9:25; Mk 15:40). The word *sister* in Greek can carry the meaning of cousin or relative, so it is best to say they are closely related. Note that it is not altogether surprising that the gospel of John, unlike Mark's gospel, avoids referring to Salome by name when it takes pains not to refer to her son John the disciple by name.

Her relationship with Mary the mother of Jesus illuminates one detour that she takes. It explains why Salome does not trail along with Mary Magdalene and Mary the mother of James to watch Joseph of Arimathea and his helpers lay the body of Jesus in the tomb. If Salome is a relative, it is likely she went home alongside the heartbroken Mary after the soul-crushing moment of watching Jesus suffer crucifixion. Instead of going to the tomb at twilight, Salome sought to accompany and comfort Mary in her hour of deep mourning and loss.

Later, Salome rejoins the two other Marys in Mark's resurrection narrative to buy spices in their effort to properly embalm the body of Jesus (Mk 16:1). In Mark's account, the three head to the tomb early in the morning on the first day of the week. Salome is among the women who enter the tomb and hear the news from the angelic messenger. They then rush from the tomb ostensibly heading out to tell the disciples Jesus has risen.

### Salome Acts Fiercer Than Your Average Fishwife

Matthew's list of women at the cross refers to Salome only in passing but reveals much about her. After naming Mary Magdalene and Mary the mother of James, the account identifies a third woman as *"the mother of Zebedee's sons"* (Mt 27:56). The sons of Zebedee are two of the three disciples in Jesus's inner circle, James and John (the third is Peter). They work in their father Zebedee's fishing operation on the Sea of Galilee. When from the lakeshore Jesus calls to them to come join him as his disciples, they *"left their father Zebedee in the boat with the hired men and followed him"* (Mk 1:19–20). That there were hired men in addition to the grown sons shows that the fishing business of Zebedee is prosperous. They also are partners with Peter in the business (Lk 5:10). Jesus challenges them by saying that he will transform them from fishing for fish to fishing for people (Mk 1: 16–18; Mt 4:19; Lk 5:9–11).

### Jesus Affectionately Nicknames Salome's Two Sons

As the mother of two early disciples and a relative of the mother of Jesus, Salome is there for the early days of Jesus's ministry. She has clearly raised her sons well if Jesus selects them as his disciples and as members of his inner circle. Jesus certainly bore an affection for them. He nicknamed them *boanerges*, Greek for "sons of thunder" (Mk 3:17). The nickname probably derives from their quick tempers shown when they wish to call down vengeance on villagers who reject their leader (Lk 9:51–56). Such strong-minded sons are likely to have been raised by a powerful mother.

According to an account in Matthew, Salome is full of faith that Jesus will rule a kingdom in the future (Mt 20:20–28). She combines that faith with her fierce love for and confidence in her sons. This combination leads her to go to Jesus with a large request. She asks if each of her sons might sit on thrones on either side of Jesus in his coming kingdom. A parallel account in Mark has the two sons making the request (Mk 10:35–45). Both accounts have Jesus replying not to their mother but directly to the sons, so it is likely that the three are there together making the request. He asks if they are able to drink the cup that he must drink. They readily agree not realizing to what degree Jesus is speaking of his suffering. Jesus tells them that the seating arrangement at his throne is *"not for me to grant"* but will be determined on another basis (Mk 10:40).

The other disciples overhear the request. They are irked at the chutzpah of the two brothers. Jesus uses the teachable moment to explain how greatness comes through serving others. This dynamic he will exemplify to the extreme in his own near future as he forewarns them: *"For even the Son of Man did not come to be served, but to serve, and to give his life as a ransom for many"* (Mk 10:45).

### Salome's Sons Endure Dramatically Different Destinies

Salome's son John would live the longest of the disciples. He helps lead the Jerusalem church for two decades in Jerusalem along with Peter and James the brother of Jesus. Later, he serves as the primary source for the gospel that bears his name as well as for at least one and traditionally three NT letters. He also customarily is credited with the book of Revelation written on the island of Patmos in the Aegean Sea, where he is exiled in his later years.

While one son of Salome outlives all the other disciples, her other son is the first of the original twelve disciples to be martyred. About ten to twelve years after comforting her relative Mary at the cross, Salome would bear her own grievous loss—her son James is summarily executed by Herod Agrippa I, grandson of Herod the Great and nephew of Herod Antipas. James perishes in this persecution of the early church, which Peter barely escapes (Acts 12:1–10, see chapter 5).

Salome is likely an exceptionally forceful person. She is the wife of a successful owner of a commercial fishing business. She raises assertive sons, who get along well with each other. She absorbs the teaching of Jesus about the kingdom of God, and she wants her sons to rule alongside him. She believes in Jesus as the Messiah. She applies her energy to serve the needs of Jesus and others in his band of disciples. She is there following Jesus at the grim end, at the cross, at the side of Mary his mother, comforting her when her son suffers so gravely. Then she is there at the glorious new beginning, at the site of the empty tomb and the reality-altering resurrection.

### Evidence is Solid for the Emptiness of the Tomb

In this first chapter we have looked in substantial detail at the line of evidence for the resurrection of Jesus that features women as the first witnesses to the empty tomb. Due to the cultural bias against women witnesses, this is extraordinarily strong evidence.

Yet the biblical accounts give additional pieces of evidence for the empty tomb; two major ones I will mention briefly here. Along with the women witnesses, a second source of evidence is the cover story the priests concoct that the disciples stole the body (Mt 28:11–15). Notice how this spin actually and ironically adds validation that the tomb was empty. If it were not empty, the priests would not have bothered to come up with an explanation for it. They simply would have scoffed and pointed to the corpse.

A third major piece of evidence is the way the disciples preach about Jesus in the city where he was buried and then they continue to reside there for years (see chapters 4 and 8). If the tomb were not empty, few if any of their fellow Jews would have listened to their utterly ridiculous idea: a rustic—and some said rebellious—rabbi had risen from the dead individually before the prophesied end-time resurrection of all righteous persons, and this strange and surprising event meant that he was the long-awaited Messiah. *Nonsense, just open the tomb and see his bones*, they would say in disbelief. *Besides, the Romans still run our country, nothing has changed.*

It should be clear that the tomb being found empty does not by itself establish that Jesus rose from the dead. It is a necessary but not sufficient factor. His tomb certainly would be empty if Jesus had risen, but other explanations for the body missing from the tomb have been attempted (see theories 1–5 in chapter 10). Some scholars who do not believe Jesus rose from the dead, nevertheless agree based on the historical evidence that the tomb indeed was empty.

Yet a few highly skeptical critics assert that there was no burial of the body of Jesus at all (see theory 6 in chapter 10). It is difficult to maintain this theory in the light of the overwhelming evidence for the burial. The burial account is multiply and independently attested (Mk 15:42-47, Jn 19:38-42). The tomb owner is named, is prominent and is in a position to exercise influence with the Roman governor (see prelude). Moreover, the account passes the criteria of embarrassment: a member of the generally hostile Sanhedrin takes responsibility to bury the body in place of the dejected, traumatized disciples. Furthermore, archaeological findings confirm the burial procedure described in the gospels was in vogue in the time of Jesus. Archaeology also confirms the fact that crucified persons could be buried in the honorable tomb zone in Jerusalem (see Found in the Ground, 1.1-3).

Judged by reasonable historical-critical standards, the evidence is strikingly well documented for the tomb burial of

Jesus and later for the tomb being empty. It was found empty early that springtime Sunday morning by a group of women who loved Jesus enough to care for his body even after he had died—only to become the first ones to discover that he did not appear to be quite so dead after all.

---

# 🎗️: CONCLUSION

### On Women Witnesses to the Empty Tomb

Led by Mary Magdalene, these women demonstrate love, faith, courage, caring, generosity, and unbridled passion for the kingdom of God. Seen not from the perspective of the patriarchal culture of their time but from their personal qualities, these women turn out to be highly credible witnesses of the resurrection events. Some like Joanna and Susanna contribute financially to the Jesus campaign in Galilee. Some like Mary the mother of James and Salome supply their sons as disciples to Jesus. Jesus selects these sons to be with him in the most intense times of his life and to be his witnesses to the world once he has risen. These women do not shrink from putting themselves or their sons at risk to follow Jesus. The fact that first-century culture does not readily endorse women as witnesses makes these gospel accounts that unabashedly feature them all the more credible and very unlikely to have been invented.

---

# CHAPTER

# LINE OF EVIDENCE

## SUMMARY

Nearly a dozen accounts of appearances that Jesus makes after his resurrection from the dead are recorded in the New Testament documents. Some critics scoff that these accounts are at worst made up and at best multiple hallucinations, mere figments of the imaginations of the original disciples or later generations of believers.

Yet the earliest list of appearances comes from one of the earliest sources in the New Testament. There are too many appearances to too many people individually or in small or large groups, to women and men, in too many different places and over too long a period to dismiss these accounts out of hand as invented or delusional.

Other critics recognize the multiple witnesses but contend that it was an amorphous spiritual presence of Jesus they sense, not an actual bodily resurrection, but the witness accounts do not allow much wiggle room. They claim Jesus rises physically from the dead with details. His physical appearances start to make even more sense when they reveal specific purposes Jesus pursues. In these encounters, he prepares his chosen witnesses to spread boldly the good news of salvation through faith in him no matter the consequences.

# PRELUDE

## CHAPTER 2

C learly pessimistic by nature, Thomas is unfiltered when it comes to imagining worst-case scenarios. He is not the only disciple who feels his fear escalating as he follows his teacher on the journey from Galilee to Jerusalem. Being from rural Galilee, he probably is not at all impressed with the big city and its manipulative leaders. By this time, he along with several other disciples seriously worry that Jesus is walking into a trap and will meet a fatal end.

Figuring they are safer on the east side of the Jordan River, they try to talk Jesus out of crossing back to the west side into Judea and heading over to see an ailing friend in Bethany, just two miles or three kilometers outside Jerusalem. *"But Rabbi," they said, "a short while ago the Jews there tried to stone you, and yet you are going back?"* (Jn 11:8). Jesus insists he is going even if his friend already has died. Thomas hears the discussion and cannot help uttering his own sense of resignation and defeat: *"Let us also go, that we may die with him"* (Jn 11:16). He is wrong about that. None of the disciples would die that week. But as they feared, Jesus would.

Even though Thomas sees it coming, the humiliating suffering of Jesus breaks his heart. With Jesus gone, he apparently withdraws from the rest of the disciples. When the women report the empty tomb on Sunday morning and later when Jesus appears that same evening to the disciples huddled behind locked doors, Thomas is nowhere to be found.

Some of the disciples go looking for him. When they find him, they tell him that they saw Jesus risen from the dead. His skeptical response? *"Unless I see the nail marks in his hands and put my finger where the nails were, and put my hand into his side, I will not believe"* (Jn 20:25). Thomas is not one to be taken for a fool or one to accept the word of others at face value. He would not get his hopes up only to be disappointed again. He would trust only his own eyes and hands before he could consider changing his inconsolable mind. About a week later, he would have another chance to reconsider.

## CHAPTER 2

---

# APPEARANCE REPORTS INVOLVE
# MULTIPLE WITNESSES

---

I n most cases when investigating the life of Jesus, the place to start is with the accounts in Mark, the go-to gospel; it is generally considered the earliest full narrative. It is used by both Matthew and Luke as a source of episodes and structure (see *Background Guide,* resource 1). However, when it comes to the aftermath of the resurrection, the gospel of Mark in its earliest manuscripts leaves us hanging, wanting more.

> *Trembling and bewildered, the women went out and fled
> from the tomb. They said nothing to anyone, because
> they were afraid. (Mark 16:8)*

Full stop. End of book. That is how our earliest manuscripts of Mark finish the narrative. (Later manuscripts try to rectify this abrupt halt with the addition of vv. 9–20 in Mark 16 as most Bible versions note.)[19]

---

[19] Adding verses 9–20 in Mark 16 to later manuscripts is an understandable but somewhat ungainly attempt to make up for the lack of appearances in the earlier versions. The style is matter of fact and less earthy than that of Mark. No appearances are mentioned that are not in other gospels (see

Readers of the original Mark manuscript hear the *"young man"* (further identified as an angel in the other gospels) declare that Jesus has risen from the dead.

> *"Don't be alarmed," he said. "You are looking for Jesus the Nazarene, who was crucified. He has risen! He is not here. See the place where they laid him." (Mark 16:6)*

Mark's earliest readers hear the news of Jesus rising, but they do not hear any accounts of Jesus appearing in person to his followers. Perhaps the word of the angel as heard and reported by the women would have been enough for them to believe in Jesus as their risen Messiah. Yet it would have left them with many questions. Is he still on earth, or did he go straight to heaven? If he stays around, in what form is his body? Or does he become a ghost? What is on his mind? Does he give any further teachings or instructions? Are there specific people he wants to see personally after his resurrection? When he eventually leaves, how does he go? On the surface, the account in Mark even seems to leave open whether the women ever get around to telling the disciples what the angel had announced.

To be sure, by ending so abruptly, the account captures the emotional shock of the moment.[20] The women had bought and prepared spices expecting to apply them to the corpse of Jesus.

---

Mk 16:9–11 from Jn 20:14–18; Mk 16:12–13 from Lk 24:13–35; Mk 16:14 from Lk 24:33–48; Mk 16:15–16 from Mt 28:18–20; Mk 16:17–18 ostensibly from Lk 10:18–20, Acts 28:3–5, 8; Mk 16:19–20 from Lk 24:50–53). When we remember how the gospels circulated independently for several centuries, we can see why these additions were made. It helps the reader who has access only to Mark weigh evidence for Jesus's resurrection from the other available sources.

[20] Some scholars assert that the lack of appearances in Mark may be a literary intention and effect. Other scholars hold that early in its transmission, the ending of Mark was lost through a broken scroll as sometimes happens at either the beginning or end of a scroll-based document. See George Eldon Ladd, *I Believe in the Resurrection of Jesus* (Grand Rapids, MI: Wm. B. Eerdmans, 1975), 79–84.

Their main concern on the way was how the stone could be moved to let them enter. Instead, they run up and find the stone already rolled away and the tomb empty. Then an angel tells them Jesus is not there—a startling turn of events to be sure.

### Time Frame of Appearances Clarified in Sequel

While the original account from Mark leaves off there, other witnesses step up in other gospel accounts to round out the picture with more evidence for the resurrection of Jesus.

Luke, consistent with his interest in the way Jesus leaves earth, provides a vital point for this investigation. In the opening note to the patron for his second book, the sequel to his gospel, he specifies a longer time for Jesus's post-resurrection actions.

> *In my former book, Theophilus, I wrote about all that Jesus began to do and to teach until the day he was taken up to heaven, after giving instructions through the Holy Spirit to the apostles he had chosen. After his suffering, he presented himself to them and gave many convincing proofs that he was alive. He appeared to them over a period of forty days and spoke about the kingdom of God. (Acts 1:1–3)*

More than a month gives Jesus time to make multiple cameo appearances according to his purposes. All the gospels other than Mark include appearances of Jesus after his resurrection. Again, similar to documentary filmmakers, the writers tend to select their own episodes to cover with some overlap. In Acts, Luke assures us they had many from which to choose, *"many convincing proofs."* Matthew includes two appearances, one unique to his gospel. Luke includes four appearances, two unique. John includes four appearances, two unique. Distinct appearances cited in the gospels add up to eight.

## Early Letter Includes Even Earlier List of Appearances

Yet another source for appearances of Jesus arrives in the first letter of Paul to Christians in Corinth. Most scholars date Paul's letter earlier than the writings of any of the four gospels, about AD 55 (see chapter 7). Paul is reminding the young church that the resurrection is the essential truth of their faith and that it is grounded on eyewitnesses.

> *For what I received I passed on to you as of first importance: that Christ died for our sins according to the Scriptures, that he was buried, that he was raised on the third day according to the Scriptures, and that he appeared to Cephas, and then to the Twelve. After that, he appeared to more than five hundred of the brothers and sisters at the same time, most of whom are still living, though some have fallen asleep. Then he appeared to James, then to all the apostles, and last of all he appeared to me also, as to one abnormally born.*
> *(1 Corinthians 15:3–8)*

The account of Paul's personal encounter with the risen Jesus is left for a later chapter (see chapter 6). In itself, it gives further evidence for the resurrection of Jesus. But since Paul's encounter occurs after Jesus leaves the earth in bodily form, we are not counting it with these other appearances that occur after Jesus dies but before he ascends. Subtracting this postdeparture appearance, Paul documents five other appearances: to Cephas, the Aramaic name for Peter; to the twelve disciples (meaning the original crew though at the first group dinner appearance it actually was fewer than twelve in number after deleting the betrayer Judas, who commits suicide, and the skeptic Thomas, who misses the first meeting but joins them a week later; see Jn 20:24–26); to at least five hundred believers both women and men; to James, almost certainly not either of the disciples with that name, who would be included in *"the Twelve,"* but most likely the brother of Jesus from his own immediate family; to *"all the apostles"* probably numbering in the range of seventy to eighty and most likely including those Jesus sent out two by two on an organized Galilean outreach (Lk 10:1–17).

Paul notes that he *"received"* the account of the death, burial, resurrection, and appearances of Jesus Christ (see chapter 7). Where and from whom would he have received this? It is highly probable that he receives this early creed in Jerusalem from the leading disciples. He recounts that three years after his conversion in Damascus, he returns to Jerusalem (Gal. 1:18). He is now a changed man from his former life as a persecutor. He stays fifteen days with Peter and sees one other leader, *"James, the Lord's brother"* (Gal. 1:19).

Note how both men are on the master list of people to whom Jesus appears. They also are likely to have been among the larger groups Paul cites that see Jesus after his resurrection. As the core leaders, they most likely standardized this list of appearances for use by other apostles like Paul in their preaching of Jesus (see chapter 7).

Of the five appearances Paul lists (other than his own), two are mentioned in the gospels: the appearance to Peter and the appearance to the full group of disciples known as *"the Twelve,"* or after one betrays Jesus, *"the Eleven"* (Lk 8:1, 9:1, 22:3, 24:33–36). The appearances not mentioned in the gospels but given by Paul are these three: to James, to five hundred believers, and to *"all"* the apostles. Adding these three to the eight distinct appearances compiled from the gospels brings the total of recorded appearances in the NT (after the resurrection but before the ascension) to eleven.

## Personal Appearances Listed in Approximate Order

The first four appearances occur on the day Jesus is first recognized as risen, the first day of the week, our Sunday. After those appearances, it is not easy to determine the exact sequence before the final appearance commonly called the ascension. Yet treading carefully, we can approximate the order over Luke's forty-day period. Locations are not exact, but indicators either place Jesus in Jerusalem or in his home region of Galilee.

Certain discrepancies arise in the accounts, and these discrepancies cannot be avoided if we take each account seriously. But as we have seen before, discrepancies in details do not invalidate agreement on the major events; they may in fact show sources are independent and therefore more reliably corroborate each other on the main points. The important thing to keep in mind is that a range of witnesses, and writers cataloging the witnesses, agree that Jesus is seen alive and well in bodily form after his resurrection.

According to the gospels, Jesus makes his first four appearances on the same day, all in or near Jerusalem. The rest occur over a forty-day interim until the last appearance when Jesus ascends to heaven from the Mount of Olives. Below, each of the eleven recorded appearances is numbered and named with the sources that include them. (A single chart later sums up these accounts.) We will follow the evidence given for each appearance. For the ones that are narrated with details, we can in a sense look over the shoulders of the witnesses to absorb what they experienced.

### Appearance 1: To the Women at the Tomb (Matthew, John)

As seen earlier, all four gospels place one or more women at the empty tomb of Jesus early on Sunday morning. They hear an angel declare that Jesus has risen from the dead. He bids them to go and tell the disciples the shocking news.

After that, two accounts take different angles. Matthew and John report that Jesus initiates a meeting near the tomb. In Matthew's account, he "*suddenly*" stops Mary Magdalene and "*the other*" Mary on their way to tell the disciples. He greets them, they fall to the ground in worship, and they "*clasped his feet*" (Mt 28:9–10). Jesus sends them on their way and reminds them of what the angel just said—that they should tell the disciples to meet him in Galilee.

While Matthew relates a brief meeting between Jesus and the two women, John concentrates his account on one woman, Mary Magdalene. John does not mention other women with her but does not exclude that possibility. In fact, when Mary Magdalene reaches the disciples, she is quoted by John as saying, *"We don't know where they have put him"* (Jn 20:2). The plural *"we"* implies that this tradition from John likely included other women originally. Yet the gospel edits out any other women in order to focus the picture on Mary Magdalene's emotional response to Jesus. Mary sees the empty tomb and runs to the disciples. Peter and John run back to the tomb with her. They return to where they were staying, but she lingers weeping. In John's rendering, at this point, Mary leans over to look into the shadowy tomb. She sees two angels.

> *They asked her, "Woman, why are you crying?" "They have taken my Lord away," she said, "and I don't know where they have put him." At this, she turned around and saw Jesus standing there, but she did not realize that it was Jesus. He asked her, "Woman, why are you crying? Who is it you are looking for?"*
>
> *Thinking he was the gardener, she said, "Sir if you have carried him away, tell me where you have put him, and I will get him." Jesus said to her, "Mary." She turned toward him and cried out in Aramaic, "Rabboni!" (which means "Teacher"). Jesus said, "Do not hold on to me, for I have not yet ascended to the Father. Go instead to my brothers and tell them, 'I am ascending to my Father and your Father, to my God and your God.'" (John 20:13–18)*

The angels and Jesus inquire about her tears. With a likely wink in his eye, Jesus asks her whom she seeks before calling her by name. Mary apparently touches Jesus and probably gives him a big hug (otherwise, his asking her to release her grip makes less sense). After all, a moment ago, she had thought he was dead. He asks her not to cling to him but to go tell the disciples, his *"brothers,"* that he will ascend soon to the Father. Briefly in Matthew and more at length in John, Jesus suddenly appears to Mary. He speaks to her. Then with relief, celebrating, she holds onto him until he sends her off with the news of his rising.

Why is this first appearance not on the master list received by Paul from the leading disciples in Jerusalem? As we saw earlier, it might have been just too embarrassing for the disciples to list this appearance to the women. Culturally, it would have undercut their initial message if it features women witnesses, who are not trusted in court proceedings in that patriarchal culture (see chapter 1).

Later, when the gospel authors research and write, they may be less concerned with getting the movement started and more concerned with delivering a full, comprehensive account of the appearances. So they give Mary Magdalene and Mary the mother of James their due.

### Appearance 2: To Peter (Paul, Luke)

Later that Sunday morning or in the afternoon, Jesus appears to Peter. There is no narrative account of this meeting in the NT. However, the fact of the meeting is mentioned in two reliable contexts. Paul's list in his letter to Christians in Corinth puts Peter first, before the rest of the disciples see Jesus that evening (1 Cor. 15:5). Then Luke reports how the two road travelers (see next appearance), who finally join the disciples in Jerusalem Sunday evening, hear from them that Peter has already seen Jesus (Lk 24:33–34). Given the schedule of Peter on Sunday, the meeting must have taken place in Jerusalem, and not eighty-five miles or 137 kilometers away in Capernaum or thereabouts in northern Galilee like the later appearance beside the lake (Jn 21:15–19).

## Appearance 3: To Travelers on the Road to Emmaus (Luke)

Found in the Ground:
**Emmaus Village**

Emmaus—The site for the village of Emmaus has probably been found, but dispute continues over which it is among three competing sites: Emmaus-Nicopolis, Emmaus-Qubeibeh, or Emmaus Moza or Motza. Each site reflects the meaning of Emmaus, featuring a "warm spring or well." Each sits along a major ancient road. Each is at least seven miles or eleven kilometers (sixty Roman stadia) away from Jerusalem as Luke indicates. (Lk 24:13)

Index 2.1

On the same Sunday when the women first find the tomb empty, Jesus makes a third appearance to two travelers leaving Jerusalem for a village seven miles or eleven kilometers down the road. Only one of them is identified by name. Their destination is Emmaus, a village. It is well past midafternoon. As the two walk, they are having an intense conversation. Jesus strides up probably from behind them and starts walking alongside them. He asks what they are discussing. They abruptly stop; their dejection is clear.

*One of them, named Cleopas, asked him, "Are you the only one visiting Jerusalem who does not know the things that have happened there in these days?" "What things?" he asked.*

*"About Jesus of Nazareth," they replied. "He was a prophet, powerful in word and deed before God and all the people. The chief priests and our rulers handed him over to be sentenced to death, and they crucified him; but we had hoped that he was the one who was going to redeem Israel. And what is more, it is the third day since all this took place. In addition, some of our women amazed us. They went to the tomb early this morning but didn't find his body. They came and told us that they*

> *had seen a vision of angels, who said he was alive. Then*
> *some of our companions went to the tomb and found it*
> *just as the women had said, but they did not see Jesus."*
> *(Luke 24:18–24)*

They do not yet believe what the women heard from the angels—that Jesus is alive. Rather, they seem to be focusing on Jesus's death, the tomb, and his missing body. They remain enmeshed in sorrow that their hopes of a national, political redeemer Messiah have been crushed. The stranger on the road then unloads on them.

> *He said to them, "How foolish you are, and how slow*
> *to believe all that the prophets have spoken! Did not the*
> *Messiah have to suffer these things and then enter his*
> *glory?" And beginning with Moses and all the Prophets,*
> *he explained to them what was said in all the Scriptures*
> *concerning himself. (Luke 24:25–27)*

They try to absorb what he is saying about a Messiah who suffers (see chapter 9). They come to their village, but Jesus continues down the road. They want to hear more and invite him to stay at their home. It is dinnertime, and they sit at a table. Jesus takes the bread, gives thanks, breaks it, and gives it to the two people. Only then do they recognize that it is Jesus risen from the dead who has been walking and talking with them. At that moment, he disappears. They are left in awe. As Luke records it, *They asked each other, "Were not our hearts burning within us while he talked with us on the road and opened the Scriptures to us?"* (Lk 24:32). It is dusk, but they get up from the table, make a U-turn, and head back to Jerusalem. They join the disciples to tell them how Jesus appeared to them on the road and in the breaking of the bread. (For an educated guess on the identity of the second traveler, see chapter 1.)

## Appearance 4: To Ten Disciples (Paul, Luke, John)

In their gospels, John and Luke record the appearance of Jesus to his disciples on that first Sunday evening after he rises. This is likely the appearance *"to the Twelve"* cited in Paul's list. Obviously at this point, Judas is not present (Mk 14:10; Mt 27:1-8). In light of this, the ever-precise Luke changes the shorthand term to *"the Eleven"* (Lk 24:33). According to John, still another original disciple also went missing at this meeting (Jn 20:24). So there were at least ten original disciples present probably with other entourage members including women. The two Emmaus road travelers burst in with their news, the disciples in turn inform them of the appearance to Peter, and then altogether they experience an extended appearance themselves.

> *While they were still talking about this, Jesus himself stood among them and said to them, "Peace be with you."*
>
> *They were startled and frightened, thinking they saw a ghost. He said to them, "Why are you troubled, and why do doubts rise in your minds? Look at my hands and my feet. It is I myself! Touch me and see; a ghost does not have flesh and bones, as you see I have."*
>
> *When he had said this, he showed them his hands and feet. And while they still did not believe it because of joy and amazement, he asked them, "Do you have anything here to eat?" They gave him a piece of broiled fish, and he took it and ate it in their presence.*
>
> *He said to them, "This is what I told you while I was still with you: Everything must be fulfilled that is written about me in the Law of Moses, the Prophets and the Psalms."*
>
> *Then he opened their minds so they could understand the Scriptures. He told them, "This is what is written:*

*The Messiah will suffer and rise from the dead on the third day, and repentance for the forgiveness of sins will be preached in his name to all nations, beginning at Jerusalem. You are witnesses of these things. I am going to send you what my Father has promised; but stay in the city until you have been clothed with power from on high." (Luke 24:36–49)*

Historical Portal:
**Hands and Nails**

Roman victims were nailed through the wrist bones, not the small hand bones, which would rip quickly from the body's weight. The Hebrew definition of hands included the wrists and lower forearms. Some victims had their arms roped to the cross instead, but not Jesus. (Jn 20:25)

Of all the appearances, this one to the disciples on Sunday evening reveals the most about Jesus. It deals with the question of whether Jesus, after his resurrection, becomes a ghost. He puts that question to rest by answering it directly. Jesus knows they can see him, but he wants them to touch him because you cannot touch a ghost. He also deals with whether he might be a human impostor.

He tells them to look at his hands and feet, which bear the marks of the nails hammered through them when he was stretched out on the cross. Then in case his followers have more doubts about whether his body is flesh and blood, Jesus asks them for something to eat. They offer him a piece of fish, and he eats it while they watch.

Once he has put them at ease that it is really he, he teaches them; he *"opened their minds so they could understand the Scriptures."* Specifically, he wants them to understand what was written about him. They need to see how he fulfilled the predictions in the books of Moses, the prophets, and the Psalms (see chapter 9). They need to understand it so they can be his witnesses. They must tell not just Israel but all nations about God's forgiveness resulting from the suffering and rising Jesus has gone through the past week. Finally, he tells them to wait for more power to come from the Spirit before they begin their mission.

### Appearance 5: To the Disciples and Thomas (John)

John reports a sequel appearance after the first Sunday evening with the disciples. In this account, Thomas misses the meeting the week before probably out of personal heartbreak and despair at what happened to his teacher and hero Jesus (see prelude for this chapter).

> *Now Thomas (also known as Didymus), one of the Twelve, was not with the disciples when Jesus came. So the other disciples told him, "We have seen the Lord!" But he said to them, "Unless I see the nail marks in his hands and put my finger where the nails were, and put my hand into his side, I will not believe."*
>
> *A week later his disciples were in the house again, and Thomas was with them. Though the doors were locked, Jesus came and stood among them and said, "Peace be with you!" Then he said to Thomas, "Put your finger here; see my hands. Reach out your hand and put it into my side. Stop doubting and believe."*
>
> *Thomas said to him, "My Lord and my God!" Then Jesus told him, "Because you have seen me, you have believed; blessed are those who have not seen and yet have believed." (John 20:24–29)*

As he had with the other disciples in the prior meeting, Jesus invites Thomas to touch not only his hands (again, the term includes wrists and forearms) but also his side, where the soldier's spear struck him and where water mixed with blood poured out signaling he had died (Jn 19:34–35). It may have been slightly awkward to pull open his cloak for Thomas to reach his side, but that was what Thomas had vowed to his fellow disciples must happen before he would believe.

It is enough. His skeptic's heart is not merely convinced but cathartically overwhelmed. Thomas responds, *"My Lord and my God!"* With that powerful expression, the main body of John's gospel concludes three verses later. Added on to the main body, however, is chapter 21, which narrates a further appearance of Jesus.

### Appearance 6: To Seven Disciples by the Sea of Galilee (John)

After covering the appearance to Mary Magdalene at the empty tomb, John describes two appearances of Jesus to his disciples a week apart in Jerusalem. Then John describes a third appearance to his male disciples, this time in Galilee near the lakeshore (Jn 21:14, making four appearances in total recorded in his gospel).

The appearance as described by John involves three parts all featuring the disciple Peter: a fishing story, a reconciliation and reinstatement of Peter, and a clarification of a false rumor about one other disciple. Six disciples are with Peter—Thomas, James, John, Nathanael (also thought to be called Bartholomew), and two more who are not named (probably Andrew, Peter's brother, and Philip, who comes from Peter's hometown of Bethsaida, Jn 1:44).

The story carries substantial detail and shows how John appreciates the challenge of fishing as an occupation. The account seems to replay an episode reported by the other three gospels early in the mission of Jesus when he is recruiting his disciples (Mk 1:16–20; Mt 4:18–22; Lk 5:1–11). It is possible it happened a second time. However, this first episode sets the scene for the lakeshore appearance; it may be a case of the writer similar to a documentary filmmaker using footage of an event out of its original order.

The second episode in the lakeside meeting is the central focus. It recounts a tender moment after a breakfast apparently cooked by Jesus over a fire he has built. Jesus asks Peter three times whether Peter loves him. Peter replies, *"You know that I love you"* all three times. In effect, the three rounds of questions and answers cancel out the three times Peter denies Jesus on the night of his arrest (Mk 14:66–72; see prelude for chapter 4). Peter is restored. Unlike the fish story of the bulging nets, this account requires a setting after the resurrection.

The third part of the appearance involves Peter asking about another disciple. Jesus chides him for comparing oneself to others. He wants Peter to focus on following Jesus himself. The writer (either John or a close collaborator) raises this incident to debunk a widespread misunderstanding.

Rumor has it that Jesus has predicted one disciple would remain alive on earth until he returns, but the author corrects the record. Jesus had issued a rhetorical question, not a specific prediction. Essentially, the writer of this section of John intends to protect the integrity of Jesus. This way, in the event the long-living John dies before Jesus returns, Jesus will not be charged wrongfully with false prophecy. This third part of the appearance account conceivably could have happened before but more likely occurs after the resurrection, and it fits with the other Peter-oriented episodes.

The core of this appearance in Galilee is the interaction Jesus initiates with Peter. It makes complete sense that Jesus would want a leisurely interaction in Peter's environment to revisit the sensitive subject of his denials. His intention seems to be twofold: to take away Peter's guilt and shame and to reinvigorate Peter's natural leadership ability, now motivated by love for his Lord. Jesus wants a confident and powerful Peter ready for the challenges ahead of spreading the news and extending the salvation community throughout Israel and to all other nations.

### Appearance 7: To the Disciples on the Mountain (Matthew)

Matthew ends his gospel with this appearance of Jesus to the eleven disciples in Galilee. It is not clear exactly when during the forty days of appearances the disciples go back to Galilee. According to John, they remain in Jerusalem at least one week after the resurrection. This enables the eleventh disciple, Thomas, to see Jesus for himself and return to the fold. Then later, according to Luke, they return to Jerusalem before Jesus ascends to heaven from the Mount of Olives.

In the meantime, five recorded appearances occur. Two of these definitely take place in Galilee, the one we saw by the lake with Peter along with six other disciples, and this second one on a mountain with all eleven.

> Then the eleven disciples went to Galilee, to the mountain where Jesus had told them to go. When they saw him, they worshiped him; but some doubted.
>
> Then Jesus came to them and said, "All authority in heaven and on earth has been given to me. Therefore go and make disciples of all nations, baptizing them in the name of the Father and of the Son and of the Holy Spirit, and teaching them to obey everything I have commanded you. And surely I am with you always, to the very end of the age." (Matthew 28:16–20)

Remarkably, Matthew acknowledges that some of the original disciples still harbor doubts about Jesus—presumably about whether he is the Messiah. Perhaps this uncertainty in some disciples is noted because in Matthew this is the first and sole appearance to the eleven. Also, Matthew may be alluding to the case of the skeptical Thomas depicted in detail in John. However, from other sources, we know that Jesus appears to the disciples on that first Sunday evening after he has risen and several other times, so one might think that the disciples would have had their doubts ironed out by now.

At any rate, in Matthew's account, Jesus seems to allay these doubts with his assertion that he has been given complete authority in heaven and on earth. On the strength of that authority, the disciples *"therefore"* can boldly go and make disciples of all nations. Jesus commits to being with them always in spirit until the current age ends and a new age begins. (From other teachings, it can be deduced that he as the Messiah will rule visibly and directly over the nations from his capital in Jerusalem, Zech. 14:9.)

This commanding moment is known traditionally as "the Great Commission." The time is now for the disciples to replicate themselves in all nations, baptize and teach others, and trust Jesus to be with them spiritually. This passage in Matthew sounds somewhat like the account in Luke that describes the ascension in Jerusalem. However, Matthew ends his book with this challenging commission and the promise of the presence of Jesus—with no further comment, no mention of the ascension. In a way, Matthew's emphasis is not on Jesus's ascent upward to heaven but on Jesus in spirit empowering his disciples outward on earth.

### Appearance 8: To Five Hundred Men and Women (Paul)

With the danger of persecution lurking in Jerusalem, a group of five hundred might have been able to gather safely only in Galilee. It may have comprised followers who had experienced large gatherings along the lakeshore when Jesus was teaching and healing. Women and men are mentioned equally by Paul, for he uses the term *"brothers and sisters"* (1 Cor. 15:6). He allows that some already have died (he writes about twenty-five years later), but most remain alive to verify this appearance of Jesus, should any of Paul's parishioners have further questions from these eyewitnesses.

### Appearance 9: To James (Paul)

Like the brief mentions of the personal appearance to Peter, there is no narrative in the NT covering the appearance to James. Jesus had two original disciples going by the name of James:

James the brother of John, and James the son of the woman named Mary who figures in the grieving at the cross and the rejoicing at the empty tomb (see chapter 1). Neither of these is likely to be the James Paul cites. His list already includes the full array of disciples present at one appearance.

As seen earlier, Paul receives the list on his visit to Jerusalem, where he stays with Peter for fifteen days and sees only one other disciple, *"James, the Lord's brother"* (Gal. 1:18–19). In both the letters of Paul and the accounts in Luke, James serves as a core leader of the Jerusalem church (Gal. 2:9, 12; Acts 15:13, 21:18). James probably was one of the brothers with Jesus's mother who together worried that Jesus was going too far with his healings and exorcisms and might be going out of his mind (Mk 3:21–35).

As it happens, Jesus appearing personally to his brother provides a plausible explanation for a difficult issue: how a potentially rival family member can overcome the natural prejudice against another family member claiming to be the Messiah. Not every family has that issue, but in James, we see a man working past that prejudice and arriving at a strong and vital faith.

Luke reports that the rest of the brothers of Jesus and his mother (perhaps his sisters as well) join the believers after the ascension. They gather with them regularly for prayer, and they likely were present for the giving of the Spirit on Pentecost (Acts 1:14–15, 2:1).

### Appearance 10: To All the Apostles (Paul)

The term *apostle* covers more than the original disciples. In Greek, it means "one who is sent." Some associate it with the idea of evangelizing and church planting in fresh territory. Paul must be using it to include more than the original disciples since he has already put them on his list. This group may include the seventy-two followers whom Jesus sends out two-by-two to go village to village in a late outreach campaign in Galilee before he heads to Jerusalem (Lk 10:17). If so, this appearance likely occurred in Galilee.

### Appearance 11: To the Disciples on the Mount of Olives (Luke)

The four gospels pay much more attention to the resurrection of Jesus than they do to the ascension. Only Luke specifically includes the episode in his gospel (Lk 24:50–53) though he retells it in his sequel with further details (Acts 1:1–11). This event is the end of Jesus's journey on earth. He does not die a second time or dematerialize, but according to the gospel account, he is *"taken up into heaven."* The gospel account is brief, only four verses long. Jesus blesses his disciples, but none of his words are recorded. The sight of him being uplifted through the sky leads them to worship and fills them with great joy.

For the time being, they meet in the temple praising God. Without actually saying so directly, Luke's gospel account gives the impression that the ascension of Jesus follows directly after his Sunday evening appearance to the original disciples. If that were actually the case, this scenario would allow time only for the first four appearances on our list (to Mary Magdalene at the tomb, to Peter, to the travelers to Emmaus, and to the disciples gathered for Sunday supper) plus this final departure from *"the vicinity of Bethany."*

Things clear up when we turn to the second book written by the same author, Luke, the book called Acts. While he ends his gospel with the ascension, he begins his book on the apostles with the same event. Evidently, during the interim between writing the two books, Luke has acquired more detail. Luke clarifies in the third verse of the second book that the ascension does not occur on the Sunday when Jesus makes his first four appearances. Rather, he ascends forty days later after he has had enough time to convince and train his disciples.

> *After his suffering, he presented himself to them and gave many convincing proofs that he was alive. He*

> *appeared to them over a period of forty days and spoke*
> *about the kingdom of God. (Acts 1:3)*

The forty-day period gives plenty of time for all the recorded appearances to take place. No doubt there were many more appearances that never made the cut to be included in the gospels or to be on the official list Paul receives from the Jerusalem-based leaders.

Having summarized and clarified matters in the prior book, Luke in Acts zeroes in *"on one occasion, while he was eating with them"* that turns out to be a more detailed description of the ramp-up to the ascension.

> *On one occasion, while he was eating with them, he gave*
> *them this command: "Do not leave Jerusalem, but wait*
> *for the gift my Father promised, which you have heard*
> *me speak about. For John baptized with water, but in a*
> *few days you will be baptized with the Holy Spirit."*
>
> *Then they gathered around him and asked him, "Lord*
> *are you at this time going to restore the kingdom to*
> *Israel?"*
>
> *He said to them: "It is not for you to know the times*
> *or dates the Father has set by his own authority. But*
> *you will receive power when the Holy Spirit comes on*
> *you; and you will be my witnesses in Jerusalem, and*
> *in all Judea and Samaria, and to the ends of the earth."*
> *(Acts 1:4–8)*

Jesus reveals that in just a few days, the Holy Spirit will come upon them and empower them. That is the next big thing to come, not the political liberation of the nation of Israel and direct worldwide rule by God from Jerusalem. Rather, they are to carry the message of Jesus starting in Jerusalem and extending to the ends of the earth. In his last moments on earth, Jesus assigns the disciples their mission and promises the arrival of the Holy Spirit to empower them. Then he ascends through the clouds.

> *After he said this, he was taken up before their very eyes, and a cloud hid him from their sight. They were looking intently up into the sky as he was going, when suddenly two men dressed in white stood beside them.*
>
> *"Men of Galilee," they said, "why do you stand here looking into the sky? This same Jesus, who has been taken from you into heaven, will come back in the same way you have seen him go into heaven."*
>
> *Then the apostles returned to Jerusalem from the hill called the Mount of Olives, a Sabbath day's walk from the city. (Acts 1:9–12)*

They watch Jesus ascend to the skies and are met by angels who bear a further revelation. Jesus will return, and return in the same way that he left, from the skies. In his gospel, Luke recounts the ascension event happening *"in the vicinity of Bethany"* (Lk 24:50). Now in Acts, he refines the location to the Mount of Olives. This elevation lies across a valley to the east of Jerusalem and the temple complex, about a one-kilometer walk (five-eighths of a mile) from the temple. The town of Bethany is another two kilometers (a mile and a quarter) farther down the road.

This place is momentous for Jesus. On this mount (2,710 feet, 826 meters), Jesus camps with his disciples during the days leading up to the Passover feast. It is where he prays under the olive trees in the Garden of Gethsemane (the name means "oil press", also see chapter 9). It is where he is arrested the night before he is crucified. The Mount of Olives is both the point of departure for Jesus at his first coming, and a critical destination for Jesus in his second coming—according to a prophecy given five hundred years earlier by the prophet Zechariah (Zech. 14:4).

The Messiah will return to the mount in victory after defeating all enemies to set up his throne in Jerusalem.

### RECORDED APPEARANCES OF JESUS RISEN

| # | Witness(es) | Location | Timing | Sources | Reference(s) |
|---|---|---|---|---|---|
| 1. | Mary Magdalene Mary mother of James | Tomb in Jerusalem | Sunday Morning | John Matthew | Jn 20:10–18 Mt 28:8–10 |
| 2. | Peter | Probably Jerusalem | Sunday | Paul Luke | 1 Cor. 15:5 Lk 24:34 |
| 3. | Cleopas Second Traveler | Road to Emmaus | Sunday Afternoon | Luke | Lk 24:13–32 |
| 4. | Ten Disciples | House in Jerusalem | Sunday Evening | Paul Luke John | 1 Cor. 15:5 Lk 24:36–43 Jn 20:19–20 |
| 5. | Ten Disciples and Thomas | House in Jerusalem | Next Sun. Evening | John | Jn 20:24–29 |
| 6. | Peter, John, Thomas, and four Disciples | Lakeshore in Galilee | During the 40 Days | John | Jn 21:1–19 |
| 7. | Eleven Disciples | Mountain in Galilee | During the 40 Days | Matthew | Mt 28:16–20 |
| 8. | 500 Believers | Probably Galilee | During the 40 Days | Paul | 1 Cor. 15:6 |
| 9. | James | Probably Galilee | During the 40 Days | Paul | 1 Cor. 15:7 |
| 10. | All Apostles (likely seventy plus) | Probably Galilee | During the 40 Days | Paul | 1 Cor. 15:7 |
| 11. | Eleven Disciples | Mount of Olives, Jerusalem | End of the 40 Days | Luke | Lk 24:50–51 Acts 1:1–13 |

These eleven distinct appearances reported in the NT underscore the many witnesses produced for the risen Jesus over the weeks he appeared and before the Spirit was given. These witnesses could tell others what they experienced with Jesus in the forty days between his resurrection and ascension. From their accounts preserved by the writers, we can assess the nature of his resurrection body and deduce what he accomplished in his appearances.

## Witnesses Consistently Report a Physical Body of Jesus

The appearance accounts in the gospels are emphatic that after Jesus is raised, he retains a human body. He is not a ghost he tells the disciples gathered the first Sunday evening; he is flesh and blood. He shows them his hands and feet with scars from the nails. He invites them to touch him. Then if they still doubt, he eats a piece of fish in their presence (Lk 24:36–49). From this appearance and from the others recorded with narrative details, we can identify the following attributes about the body of Jesus after his resurrection.

### He Walks

He keeps up with the road travelers to Emmaus, and he meets the fishing crew along the lakeshore (Lk 24:15; Jn 21:4, 13).

### He Eats

He asks the disciples for something to eat his first day back and eats with them later as well. His resurrection body continues to digest food (Lk 24:41–43; Jn 21:12, Acts 1:4).

### He Retains His Scars

The scars identify him as the one who has suffered, not an impostor pretending to be Jesus (Lk 24:37–40; Jn 20:20, 27).

## He Can Be Touched

Touching of Jesus occurs often in the appearances. Mary Magdalene holds on tightly to Jesus in John, and along with Mary the mother of James clasps his feet in Matthew. That same Sunday evening, Jesus tells his disciples to touch him. A week later, doubting Thomas is invited to touch him in the hands and side and probably does (Mt 28:9; Lk 24:39; Jn 20:17, 27).

## He Handles Objects

He breaks a loaf of bread with the road travelers, he holds the broiled fish Sunday evening, he apparently builds a fire by the lake to cook fresh fish, and he serves bread before sitting down with Peter (Lk 24:30, 42-43; Jn 21:9, 13).

## He Speaks and Teaches

His voice is recognized, he teaches the scriptures, and he challenges and commissions his followers to spread his message of salvation through faith in him (Lk 24:36-45; Mt 28:18; Jn 20:21-23, 21:19).

### Resurrection Body is Tangible Yet Altered

Yet there is an element of mystery to the resurrection body of Jesus as well. First, he is able to appear and disappear in the twinkling of an eye, and locked doors do not stop him from entering (Lk 24:31, 36; Jn 20:26).

Second, something about him has slightly changed that makes his followers have difficulty recognizing him initially, at least his first day back on Sunday. Mary Magdalene mistakes him for the gardener at the tomb site. The two travelers walk probably more than an hour with him, listen to his exposition of scripture, but still fail to recognize him until he breaks bread with them in their home. The disciples think he is a ghost at first when they see him Sunday evening (Luke 24:37).

One explanation for the difficulty in recognizing Jesus: he likely loses weight during his suffering and possibly loses color in his complexion from the massive loss of blood or from the time spent in the tomb. Yet a resurrection body would likely be restored to full functionality as Jesus displays high energy on the road and in the evening meeting. So this slightly altered look causing double takes before his friends recognize him remains an unknown; it hints at deeper dimensions of spirit-body integration in the life to come.

The resurrected body of Jesus is changed in some way, but it still bears the scars of his suffering. He has a recognizable face and presumably the same tone of voice. His slightly altered appearance may resemble what the apostle Paul was getting at when he endeavored to describe the bodies of resurrected believers in the end days based on revelations given to him.[21] People will not be disembodied spirits; they will have new bodies not subject to death.[22] Paul compares a human body that is buried

---

[21] The deservedly renowned NT scholar E. P. Sanders, while accepting that the disciples had some form of experience of Jesus after his death, makes the point that the body of Jesus appeared to them to be in some way transformed. He connects that physical transformation with the effort by Paul to describe the resurrection body that believers stand to inherit in heaven when they are raised (1 Cor. 15:35–57, see addition 4). See E. P. Sanders, *The Historical Figure of Jesus* (London: Penguin Group, 1993), 278–81.

[22] The noted author and bishop N. T. Wright argues forcefully for the physical resurrection of Jesus as a logical historical conclusion based on the Jewish cultural context of the era. Like most Jews, the early apostles believed in a physical resurrection of righteous persons at the end of the age. (Jesus himself takes this context for granted at one point in Luke 20:34–36.) The disciples claimed that Jesus had risen from the dead and that a new age had begun. By saying that he rose, Wright contends, they could not have meant in their context that the soul of Jesus had up and gone to heaven leaving his body behind, nor could they have meant that they were having existential feelings of his aura or presence despite his body lying in the tomb or later his bones being boxed up in an ossuary.

and raised to a seed planted in soil that emerges; the body of the plant is different from the body of a seed that was sown in the earth. (For the full text of this inspiring passage, see addition 4.)

> *So will it be with the resurrection of the dead. The body that is sown is perishable, it is raised imperishable; it is sown in dishonor, it is raised in glory; it is sown in weakness, it is raised in power; it is sown a natural body, it is raised a spiritual body. (1 Corinthians 15:42–44b)*

This confidence in God's plan to raise believers in new heaven-bound bodies leads Paul to assert how the OT bore the same hope as shown in an end-times vision of the prophet Isaiah who foresees death vanquished (Isa. 25:8).

> *When the perishable has been clothed with the imperishable, and the mortal with immortality, then the saying that is written will come true: "Death has been swallowed up in victory." (1 Corinthians 15:54)*

In conveying that this long-held hope has now been guaranteed by Jesus, Paul echoes the prophet Hosea (Hos. 13:14) as he triumphantly taunts death.

> *Where, O death, is your victory? Where, O death, is your sting? (1 Corinthians 15:55)*

Life after physical death is no longer a complete unknown. Paul asserts that the appearances of Jesus culminating in the ascension prove that he conquers death. Jesus enters a new kind of still embodied life available as well to those who trust in him.

---

Properly understood, the first-century Jewish mind-set basically rules out these out-of-context interpretations of the apostles' announcement. See N. T. Wright, *The Challenge of Jesus* (Downers Grove, IL: InterVarsity Press, 1999), 134–37. Also see Wright's magisterial work *The Resurrection of the Son of God* (Minneapolis, MN: Fortress Press, 2003).

Through him, the ancient hope of human resurrection in the last days will be fulfilled.

## Specific Purposes Jesus Pursues in His Appearances

Investigating the eleven recorded appearances one by one reveals that there is a lot more going on in these events than meets the eye at first. They are not simple celebrity sightings as if Jesus were a rock star supposedly dead but rumored to be living in disguise. The appearances are not as much sightings as they are interactions. The gospel writers capture a sense that Jesus has purposes he intends to achieve. Although some of the appearances are mentioned only in passing or just listed, more than half are narrated with revealing details.[23] At least five purposes become clear in these episodes.

### Purpose 1: To Prove He Lives and Is Not Dead and Gone

Jesus proves to his followers that he has been raised to life. Luke specifically mentions in Acts that Jesus *"gave many convincing proofs that he was alive"* (Acts 1:3). The multiple appearances indicate that Jesus wants his followers to see him up close and personal after his resurrection. He wants them to experience him in his renewed form themselves and not depend solely on the word of the angels at the tomb that he is alive.

Once they see him, he wants them to touch him or eat with him and then listen to him. In the Sunday evening meeting with the disciples, Jesus specifically denies that he is a ghost, a mere

---

[23] These are the seven narrated appearances (as opposed to four other simply listed appearances) using our numberings in this chapter: 1) to Mary Magdalene/Mary the mother of James, 3) to the two travelers on the Emmaus road, 4) to the ten disciples Sunday evening, 5) to the ten disciples and Thomas the next Sunday evening, 6) to Peter and six other disciples by the Sea of Galilee, 7) to the eleven disciples on the mountain in Galilee, 11) to the disciples when Jesus ascends from the Mount of Olives.

spirit or presence. He has flesh and blood as before (Lk 24:39). *"Look at my hands and feet. It is I myself!"* Jesus assures them he is the same person they have known and followed. Yet he seems to understand that it is normal to doubt that he would be raised to life again, so he goes to them to mingle and to prove that he lives.

### Purpose 2: To Teach the Scriptures

Jesus opens up the scriptures about himself so the apostles can understand and preach the message that he is the Messiah. On the first day of his appearances, at first with the two dejected travelers and then with the almost full house of disciples that evening, Jesus intensively walks them through the writings of Moses, the prophets, and the psalmists. His emphasis is that their writings predict that the Messiah will suffer as Jesus did. This is the key he gives them to open the scriptures in a new way.

In none of these appearances do the writers cite the specific passages Jesus taught them about a suffering and rising Messiah, which certainly would be valuable. (There are other ways to figure this out, a challenge taken up in chapter 9). Yet the point comes across in the appearances of Jesus. The suffering of the Messiah secures the forgiveness of sins proven by the way God raises Jesus from the dead. All nations now can receive this forgiveness and connect with God through his Messiah (Lk 24:46–47).

### Purpose 3: To Resolve Personal Issues

Jesus prepares the leaders for his mission and addresses personal issues with several key people. With Mary Magdalene, clearly a leader among the women, he comforts and reassures her at the empty tomb. With Peter, he restores his confidence and leadership mantle beside the shores of the lake. With Thomas, Jesus meets him where he is. He addresses his disciple's doubts as he displays the fresh crucifixion scars on his hands and feet.

With his family member James, he brings him to faith, which enables him to lead others.

### Purpose 4: To Provide the Vision

Jesus casts his vision and assigns his followers to the mission. This is perhaps best put in Matthew's rendering—the mission is to *"go and make disciples of all nations"* (Mt 28:19-20). The strategy is through teaching and baptizing. The essence is, *"You will be my witnesses"* (Acts 1:8, see also Lk 24:48, Acts 2:32, 5:32). They are to go into the world to tell others what Jesus has done based on what they have seen and experienced, or will soon—his ministry, healings, death, burial, resurrection, appearances, his forthcoming ascension and giving of the Spirit.

### Purpose 5: To Ready Them for the Spirit's Indwelling Them

Jesus announces and promises the arrival of the Holy Spirit to empower his disciples and all believers. In his interactions with his disciples during his ministry, Jesus taught them about the Holy Spirit. Now, with his departure in bodily form from earth imminent, he stresses the vital coming of the Spirit within them to fill and empower them. He does not want them completely mystified when the Spirit comes; he wants to assure them this personally transforming event is part of the plan. What he spoke of earlier now will be their experience in the present. The Spirit will pour God's love into and out of them (Jn 7:38-39), will teach them (Jn 14:26, 16:13-15), will help them sense the presence of Jesus with them (Mt 28:20), and will enable them to fulfill their mission—to live out the new life by the Spirit (Jn 6:63) and to reach as many people as possible with the good news of God's grace through Jesus (Acts 1:8, Mk 13:10-11).

# 2: <u>CONCLUSION</u>

### *On Multiple Appearances*

It would be much harder to believe in the resurrection if there were no appearance accounts. Jesus might very well have burst out of the tomb alive, but if no one saw him before he left earth, the resurrection would be a much bigger stretch to accept on faith.

Historically, that is not the case. The witness accounts of appearances from John, Luke, Matthew, and Paul are independent sources asserting the same claim: Jesus returned physically from the dead. Matthew and Luke do not depend on Mark's account here because Mark does not document any appearances (as far as we can tell from available early manuscripts). Moreover, the appearances in Matthew and Luke are independent of each other as they cover different appearances on our list.

From this data, the witnesses who interact with Jesus alive after he had died included individuals, his gathered disciples, his larger entourage, and more than five hundred people, women and men, who saw him at the same time. He was slightly different yet recognizable, and he bore the scars of his excruciating death. His followers could touch him, talk with him, walk with him, eat with him, and be taught by him. Then they were commissioned by him to tell the world how his death and resurrection had secured—for anyone from any nation—a relationship with God starting then and there on earth and extending forever into eternity.

# CHAPTER

# 3

# LINE OF EVIDENCE

## SUMMARY

If Jesus predicts his death and resurrection, this evidence weighs against the theory that the disciples invent the idea of an individual resurrection (as opposed to a group resurrection, which many in Israel believed would happen in the end times). Instead, this resurrection of a single person is an assertion of Jesus himself. He forewarns his disciples about his suffering and rising, but they do not seem to grasp it in advance. They still are attached to the belief that he will soon restore Israel to greatness and rule the nations as a royal Messiah.

If these predictions of his suffering and rising can be traced to Jesus himself with reasonable probability, it negates the view that there is *retrojection,* or later invention, by the disciples or the New Testament writers. Jesus as a prophet and as a close reader of the Old Testament is telling them what will happen in advance. Then events remarkably play out in his life as he predicts.

# PRELUDE

## CHAPTER 3

She does not seem to care what other people think of her. There is no record that she said a word (nor is there any indication this woman had a sketchy reputation as is the case in a separately described episode in Luke 7:37-38). She enters the house in Bethany of the host named Simon. She may have been his neighbor. She knows Jesus would be there as a dinner guest.

In those days, the custom in upscale homes is to have a three-sided, U-shaped table (the Romans called it a *triclinium*). Guests recline on flat dinner couches or dinner beds. They would lean on one arm while the other arm was free to partake of the food, with their feet jutting away from the table. Servants wait on guests from the open side of the table. It is likely she enters from that open side. She carries with her a white alabaster flask filled with expensive perfume. She breaks it open. The fragrance is released in the room where everyone can sniff it. She pours the ointment over the head of Jesus (Mk 14:3; Mt 26:7).

The reaction from some of the disciples of Jesus, who are invited along with him, is outrage. They say the expensive perfume is being wasted. It should have been sold and the proceeds given to poor people. The woman says nothing. With the remaining perfume, she goes around the table and the dinner couches to where she finds the feet of Jesus (Jn 12:3). She anoints his feet and spreads the perfume around his toes and ankles with her long hair.

Jesus sees how her uninhibited devotion captures the attention of the entire dinner party. Amid the consternation she causes, she can hear Jesus defending her.

*"Leave her alone," said Jesus. "Why are you bothering her? She has done a beautiful thing to me. The poor you will always have with you, and you can help them any time you want. But you will not always have me. She did what she could. She poured perfume on my body beforehand to prepare for my burial." (Mark 14:6–8)*

Jesus values her assertive caring and devotion and especially here her sense of timing. In fact, he may have known this woman well. (John identifies her as Mary sister of Martha and Lazarus, all friends of Jesus, Jn 12:1–3.) She gives him another prime opportunity to prepare his circle for what is ahead. Her bold action lets him again predict the torturous fate about to happen to him less than a week later, a short walk up the road from Bethany, in Jerusalem.

## CHAPTER 3

---

# JESUS PREDICTS HIS DEATH AND RESURRECTION

---

e join the action as Jesus and his disciples arrive in the town of Bethsaida, on the northern shore of the Sea of Galilee. They probably arrive by fishing boat. For several of the disciples, this was their hometown where they were raised (Peter, Andrew, Philip, Jn 1:44). They might expect to remain a while, but Jesus wants to stay on the move.

They walk north through small villages along the eastern side of the Jordan River. Jesus seems to be taking the disciples away from the crowds for a retreat into the fresh air of the green, waterbrooked northern hills. He intentionally may be avoiding the clutches of the ruler of his home province of Galilee, who has killed his cousin. Some sympathetic Pharisees have warned him that the ruler, Herod Antipas, wants to kill him too (Lk 13:31). They are outside the reach of Herod's police as long as they stay on the river's east side, which was run by a different ruler.

They reach the outskirts of this region's capital of Caesarea Philippi but stay in the smaller villages (Mk 8:21–22, 27).

Found in the Ground:
## Bethsaida Village and Harbor

Galilee, Israel—On the northeastern shore of the Jordan River, the
village of Bethsaida near the Sea of Galilee means "house of fishing"
(or to some scholars "house of hunting"). John reports Bethsaida
is the hometown of three disciples. Two sites compete for the village
of Bethsaida though they may be related as two parts of the same
settlement. The lower village lies close to the excavated harbor and
road and it is likely where the disciples go. This site supports the
account of the landing at Bethsaida harbor for the disciples' retreat
before their melancholic journey to Jerusalem. (Mk 8:13, 22, Jn 1:44)

Index 3.1

Found in the Ground:
## Caesarea Philippi and Panias Shrine

Banias, Golan Heights—Site found in 1838. At the bottom of the
foothills of Mount Hermon, this ancient shrine developed around a
spring to the pagan woodland god Pan. Beyond the shrine a city was
built that Herod the Great conquers. His son Philip expands the
city in honor of the emperor Augustus, hence the name Caesarea
Philippi during the time of Jesus. The location of the city and the
shrine supports the account of the disciples' retreat to villages on the
outskirts of the city. It is in this area that Jesus poses the question of
whether the crowds recognize his identity. (Mk 8:27; see also Lk 3:1)

Index 3.2

## On a Bucolic Discipleship Retreat, Jesus First Divulges His Fate

In private, Jesus asks his disciples, *"Who do people say I am?"*
(Mk 8:27). They have followed Jesus through many months of his

teaching and healing ministry in Galilee. Now, he asks for their sense of the crowd's reaction. Some see him as his cousin John the Baptist risen from the dead. Others see him as Elijah or one of the other prophets. Jesus bores in for their personal assessment.

> *"But what about you?" he asked. "Who do you say I am?" Peter answered, "You are the Messiah." Jesus warned them not to tell anyone about him. He then began to teach them that the Son of Man must suffer many things and be rejected by the elders, the chief priests, and the teachers of the law, and that he must be killed and after three days rise again. (Mark 8:29–31)*

Mark adds that he *"spoke plainly"* about this implying that up until then, Jesus did not speak this directly about his future (Mk 8:32).

About a week later as the northern retreat continues, Jesus takes a day hike with his three closest disciples (Peter and the two brothers, James and John). Jesus leads them to a high mountain, probably Mount Hermon. It rises to 9,232 feet or 2,814 meters, though it is not clear whether they reach the summit. They suddenly see Jesus's clothes turn a dazzling white (hence the traditional name for this episode, "the Transfiguration"). Then they see him talking with two men on either side of him. One they recognize as Elijah, the other as Moses. They

---

Interpretive Angle:
**Figures in Transfiguration**

Probably each of these persons on either side of Jesus during the transfiguration represent one of the two core text collections of the Israelite Tanakh (to Christians, the Old Testament), namely, the Law embodied by Moses and the Prophets embodied by Elijah. Both bodies of knowledge witness to the Messiah Jesus. A third category, the Psalms and wisdom literature, sometimes stands separately or is folded into the category of the Prophets as may be the case in this instance (Mk 9:2–8).

hear a voice from heaven telling them Jesus is *"my Son"* and to listen to him. Everything returns to normal in a flash.

> *As they were coming down the mountain, Jesus gave them orders not to tell anyone what they had seen until the Son of Man had risen from the dead. They kept the matter to themselves, discussing what "rising from the dead" meant.* (Mark 9:9–10)

Scholars refer to this tendency of Jesus to ban public disclosure of his identity most pronounced in the gospel of Mark as "the messianic secret." Jesus makes an effort to keep the wraps on his true nature. It seems counterintuitive. Should not all the crowds be told who he really is? Perhaps his reasoning runs like this. His identity cannot be humanly comprehended until after people see both the sacrificial transaction in his impending death and the power of his resurrection. If the crowds hear beforehand, they will get in the way of his mission.

Somewhat in contrast to Mark, John records Jesus more readily revealing his identity in private, one-on-one conversations with individuals. These include interactions with the ruler who comes to him by night (Jn 3:1–15); with the much-married Samaritan woman

---

Found in the Ground:
**Pool of Siloam**

Jerusalem—Found in 2004. It started with two stone steps unearthed during a city maintenance project south of the temple mount. The two steps led to a wider excavation that uncovered a multilevel, stepped stone structure 225 feet or sixty-nine meters long in a trapezoidal shape. The finding confirms the accuracy of the setting in the gospel of John for the account of Jesus healing a man born blind. He spits on the ground, makes mud pies, applies them to the man's eyes, and sends him off to wash in the Pool of Siloam. After gaining his sight, the man evokes first consternation then vicious hostility from the opponents of Jesus. (Jn 9:1–11)

Index 3.3

at the well (Jn 4:25-26); and with the man born blind, whom he heals with virtual mud pies on his eyes then tells the man to wash them away in the Pool of Siloam (Jn 9:1-39). How these private conversations are relayed and written down is a question often raised. John or his sources may have interviewed these individuals or he may have received from Jesus himself a recap of the conversations, either before or after the resurrection.

## Two More Predictions—Along the Lake and the Jericho Road

Back from the hike, the four from the mountain expedition rejoin the rest of the disciples in a village. Soon, the whole group is again on the move. They trek back west across the Jordan River to the northwestern shore of the lake and head south for Jesus's home base in the lakeside town of Capernaum. Jesus remains wary, seemingly in a hurry, for he is back in hostile territory. He is focused on informing the disciples a second time of the events to come.

> *They left that place and passed through Galilee. Jesus did not want anyone to know where they were, because he was teaching his disciples. He said to them, "The Son of Man is going to be delivered into the hands of men. They will kill him, and after three days he will rise."*
> *(Mark 9:30–31)*

Found in the Ground:
**Capernaum Synagogue**

Capernaum, Galilee, Israel—Found in 1866. The synagogue, built of limestone, dates to the fourth century based on coins and pottery found beneath the floor. The observed ruins however are built over a first-century building with black basalt for a foundation. The finding supports accounts of Jesus teaching in a synagogue in Capernaum, the town he selected as his base of operations (Mk 1:21; Lk 4:31–32; Jn 6:59).

Index 3.4

After a brief stay in Capernaum, Jesus leads his entourage to the south along the western side of the lake (Mk 9:33). He likely stays in Galilean territory by heading through the hills to the border of Samaria (Lk 17:11). The shorter way to Jerusalem would go through Samaria but he recalculates the route, turning to cross the Jordan River. They take the road south along the river in the territory known as Perea.[24] They cross the Jordan River from the east to the west near Jericho, the garrison city turned royal resort. Along the steep and winding road to Jerusalem, Jesus again for a third time predicts his death and resurrection.

*They were on their way up to Jerusalem, with Jesus leading the way, and the disciples were astonished, while those who followed were afraid. Again he took the Twelve aside and told them what was going to happen to him. "We are going up to Jerusalem," he said, "and the Son of Man will be delivered over to the chief priests and the teachers of the law. They will condemn him to death and*

---

[24] Luke in his gospel seems to send them south through Samaria along the inland route, not the river route (Lk 9:51, 13:22). If so, the minor discrepancy in the route need not alter the major agreement in the gospels that Jesus is heading for a denouement in Jerusalem. Other scholars think Luke refers to a prior journey of Jesus to Jerusalem, not the fateful one.

will hand him over to the Gentiles, who will mock him
and spit on him, flog him and kill him. Three days later
he will rise." (Mark 10:32–34)

---

Found in the Ground:
**Jericho in the Time of Jesus**

Jericho—Found in 1868. A fortress town in the OT accounts,
Jericho in the time of Jesus functions more as a resort town for the
aristocratic and priestly elites. Excavations have found remains of
Herod's winter palace, hippodrome, and aqueducts. The site supports
the account of the disciples' journey with Jesus through the Jordan
Valley, through Jericho, then up the steep incline to Jerusalem.
The site also explains the high degree of wealth obtained by one of
Jesus's direct converts, Zacchaeus. He collects taxes in prosperous
Jericho and according to Luke hosts Jesus on this final journey.
The road from Jericho to Jerusalem rises from about 820 feet or
250 meters below sea level to about 2,550 feet or 777 meters above
amounting to more than a 3,300-ft. or 1,000-m climb over less than
eighteen miles or twenty-nine kilometers. (Mk 10:46; Lk 19:1–10, 28)

Index 3.5

---

This north-south journey is the pivotal point in the first three
gospels between the ministry of Jesus in Galilee and the epic
events awaiting him in Jerusalem. In this context, it makes sense
that Jesus would try to prepare the disciples for these events
assuming he could anticipate what lay ahead. His predictions
organically fit into the overall narrative.[25]

---

[25] Matthew and Luke follow Mark in the lead-up to the arrival in Jerusalem
by including these three prediction episodes that Jesus conducts in private
with his disciples (Mk 8:31, 9:31, 10:32–33; Mt 16:21, 17:22–23, 20:17–18; Lk
9:22, 9:44, 18:31–33).

## How Jesus May Have Discerned the Events in His Future

How would Jesus know about his fate in advance? It could be as some say that he put to use his divine nature with its powers of foreknowledge. It could be just as well that he read the Hebrew scriptures closely to see what was written about him. For example, specific prophecies from Isaiah and Psalms give details about the brutality a figure suffers. It is similar to the way Jesus describes to his disciples the fate he will soon face: beating, spitting, mocking, disfiguring and rejection (Isa. 50:6, 52:14, 53:3, 7–8; Ps. 22:7–8). Other prophecies indicate resurrection to life again (Isa. 53:10–12, Ps. 22:24, 16:10). After he is raised, when he appears to his disciples, Jesus teaches them that the scriptures predict his suffering and rising (Lk 24:25–26, 44–46). However, the gospels do not include specific passages Jesus cites though they can be deduced (see chapter 9). For now in this chapter, we focus on the evidence that Jesus historically, in actuality, made predictions about his death and resurrection.

## The Predictions of Jesus Strike Skeptics as Impossible

Yet critics tend to challenge any predictions that the gospels credit to Jesus himself; they claim these predictions were invented and *retrojected*—inserted into the story after the fact. Critics who deny any supernatural reality rule out prophetic prediction and the idea of resurrection from the outset. Under those assumptions, there is little to discuss. But in this investigation, we allow for the possibility of both the resurrection event and its predictions. Whether these occur depends not on prior assumptions but on the evidence as given by the surviving texts, the credibility of the witnesses, other historical writings, and the supplementary power of archaeological findings.

## Cluelessness of the Disciples Adds Credibility

Weighing against retrojection of these predictions are the reactions of the disciples; for the most part, they just do not seem to get it. When they hear the third prediction pronounced near Jericho, some of them seem to realize the danger awaiting them in Jerusalem (Mk 10:32). But others like James and John are jockeying for positions and want to reserve seats on either side of the throne they anticipate Jesus will soon occupy (Mk 10:35–45). He has to inform them again that he did not come *"to be served, but to serve, and to give his life as a ransom for many"* (Mk 10:45).

After hearing his second prediction in Galilee on the way to Capernaum, the disciples again cannot absorb it. Mark comments on their guarded response.

> *But they did not understand what he meant and were afraid to ask him about it. (Mark 9:32)*

Looking at their reactions to the second and third predictions, we may employ the principle of historical assessment known as the criterion of embarrassment (see addition 3). Accounts that make the leading players in a movement look clueless are more likely to be true. The assumption is that people in control of the narrative will try to cultivate a proper image and delete events that tarnish it. So when what may be thought of as negative events or reactions are included in the accounts, it increases the probability that these are actual.

Applying this criterion gives the second and third predictions by Jesus increased authenticity. The disciples are not shown in a good light. This factor comes into play even more profoundly when we reassess the first prediction of Jesus. The negative reaction and the shadow cast on a single, major disciple make the level of embarrassment even more intense.

## Peter Receives the Mother of All Rebukes

The situation involves the lead disciple Peter. Expressive and impulsive, he is usually the first to plunge into things. As we saw earlier, he forthrightly answers the question about who Jesus is by saying, *"You are the Messiah"* (Mk 8:29). Jesus orders his disciples to keep it quiet for now. He briefs them for the first time about his upcoming death to be followed by his resurrection. Take a close look at the continuation of the episode in Mark.

> He spoke plainly about this, and Peter took him aside and began to rebuke him. But when Jesus turned and looked at his disciples, he rebuked Peter. "Get behind me, Satan!" he said. "You do not have in mind the concerns of God, but merely human concerns." (Mark 8:32–33)

This is Peter, the lead disciple in the gospel account, who also becomes a key leader in the early church. Here, he is accused by Jesus of essentially siding with Satan, the worst foe of Jesus. Pause here for a moment. The key future Christian leader is severely rebuked for thinking like the evil one. If this episode had been made up, if this episode had been retrojected, would the writers want to impugn the reputation of the leader whose faith is recorded elsewhere as being the rock on which Jesus would build his church? It is highly unlikely that this interaction between Jesus and Peter is imaginary; it is much more likely that it happened.

Peter is in character. He jumps up and protests and rebukes Jesus only to find himself on the receiving end of an even sterner rebuke for obvious reasons. He was thinking like the enemy, trying to talk Jesus out of going to the cross. The entire incident is predicated on the context of Jesus predicting his own death. Here, we tap into another one of these criteria measuring historicity. Because it is so embarrassing, the episode of Peter being rebuked by Jesus is highly probable (based on the criterion aptly called the criterion of embarrassment as noted above). Then we see that this highly probable incident is predicated on the prediction Jesus makes about his impending death. The criterion of predication kicks in here (again, see addition 3). So this means that the prediction itself becomes much more highly likely when a second probable event (Jesus rebuking Peter) depends or is predicated on it.

### The Public Predictions Jesus Makes Are Discreetly Veiled

As we just saw, the evidence for Jesus predicting his death and resurrection privately with his disciples is reasonable given the context of the journey to Jerusalem and the negative reactions of the disciples. Yet it is worth asking whether Jesus makes similar predictions in a public context. From the evidence in the gospels, he does make public predictions, but they are more veiled and therefore need to be uncovered carefully.

At several junctures, Jesus is approached by religious leaders (namely the Sadducees, the Pharisees, and legal teachers known as scribes; see chapter 4). They ask him to perform *"a sign"* (Mk 8:11–13; Mt 12:38–42, 16:1–4; Lk 11:29–32). At first glance, that seems redundant. Jesus has already performed many healings and exorcisms in the sight of crowds. In each case, Jesus responds defiantly; he is infuriated by their requests. In Mark, he sighs with exasperation at *"this generation"* and says, *"no sign will be given to it"* (Mk 8:12). The accounts of Matthew and Luke also indict the generation as *"wicked"* and say no sign shall be given it except for one major exception, the *"sign of Jonah"* (Mt 16:4; Lk 11:29).

What accounts for the fury Jesus directs at these requests for signs? In that culture, their requests amount to demands that likely register with Jesus as insistent, resistant, hardened unbelief in regard to him as a messenger from God. Moreover, their requests reveal how they want to control him. In their eyes, he must do more to satisfy their preconceptions. For them, the sign must qualify as a major spectacle; it has to reach the level of the Egyptian soldiers drowning in the raging sea or manna fluttering to earth in the wilderness (Jn 6:30–31). Only then will they deign to believe that the God of Abraham and Moses is working through this rustic country preacher, Jesus.

Behind their unbelief is likely their requirement that the Messiah be a secular, military figure who could topple Roman power and set up the kingdom of God on earth with its capital in Jerusalem. In that light, Jesus refuses to give them the kind of sign they want. In this respect, Mark is correct that no sign of the kind they want is given. Yet it sounds very much like Jesus to offer the nuanced exception of *"the sign of Jonah"* as he does in Matthew and Luke.

### A Foreshadow in the Oceangoing, Skin-Diving Prophet Jonah

The account of Jonah is captured in the Hebrew prophetic scriptures. He is most active as a prophet from 786 to 746 BC, during the reign of Jeroboam II in the northern kingdom. The kingdom of Israel with ten tribes had split from the southern kingdom of Judah, with two tribes, in 932–931 BC. Jonah comes from a village in lower Galilee called Gath-Hepher (2 Kings 14:25; Josh. 19:13). It is about five miles or eight kilometers north of Nazareth, the village where Jesus grows up about

Interpretive Angle:
**Jonah and the Ocean Creature**

Jesus takes the story of Jonah seriously. He asserts that the analogy of Jonah fits his destiny precisely. His insistence that he will rise three days after he dies apparently derives from his identifying with the elapsed time Jonah spends inside the ocean creature. Nowhere else in the Hebrew scriptures is a time frame of three days specified for an individual (Jonah 1:17). Note that the allusion in Hosea 6:2 concerns a group being revived or regathered, after their unfaithfulness and consequent judgment. It is possible Jesus could apply the analogy of Jonah's deep dive to himself while still considering it a literary legend as many scholars do, but it is more likely that Jesus treats the Jonah episode as a historical event embedded in Jewish history as a sign or foreshadowing of his messianic mission.

eight hundred years later. Jesus likely would have known the story of Jonah well.

Initially, Jonah refuses to preach salvation to a non-Hebrew city, Nineveh, in today's northern Iraq. Jonah takes a ship traveling in the opposite direction. In a storm, he is thrown overboard and is swallowed by a large (indeterminate) ocean creature, which usually is translated as a fish or a whale. In the belly of the creature, he fervently repents and prays. God arranges for the creature to vomit Jonah onto the shore. Jonah then obeys, and he preaches repentance to the Assyrians of Nineveh. Heathens in that city listen to his preaching and turn from their wicked ways to worship the God of Israel.

Scholars wrestle with the meaning of the sign of Jonah. Some see it as the act of preaching that leads to repentance. Jesus and Jonah both preach salvation—but Jonah's generation of Gentiles responds and repents while most of Jesus's generation of fellow Jews hardens and resists. In that way, the sign is the prophet's preaching, which leads to the conversion of Gentiles to worship the God of Israel. This idea may be included in what Jesus means. However, the gospel of Matthew, which mentions the sign of Jonah twice, gives a further explanation.

> *Then some of the Pharisees and teachers of the law said to him, "Teacher, we want to see a sign from you." He answered, "A wicked and adulterous generation asks for a sign! But none will be given it except the sign of the prophet Jonah. For as Jonah was three days and three nights in the belly of a huge fish, so the Son of Man will be three days and three nights in the heart of the earth." (Matthew 12:38–40)*

In Matthew's interpretation, the sign of Jonah, the sign that he is on a mission from God, is that his life is preserved in the fish and he is supernaturally spat up after three days. In a veiled but not altogether hidden manner, Jesus predicts that like Jonah, he will be buried for three days and brought back to life. Publicly, before the antagonistic Jewish leaders, he predicts his own death and resurrection through the symbolic allusion to the well-known episode of Jonah and the ocean creature.[26]

### The Temple Pun in Public Mystifies and Alarms the Accusers

The rushed trial of Jesus before the high priest brings out another instance in which Jesus publicly predicts his death and resurrection.

> *The chief priests and the whole Sanhedrin were looking for evidence against Jesus so that they could put him to death, but they did not find any. Many testified falsely against him, but their statements did not agree.*
>
> *Then someone stood up and gave this false testimony against him: "We heard him say, 'I will destroy this temple made with human hands and in three days will build another, not made with hands.'" Yet even then their testimony did not agree. (Mark 14:55–59)*

For the record, the hostile witnesses and biased priests never could nail down this line of questioning in their effort to accuse Jesus of seeking to destroy the temple. So the priests opt to allot Jesus the death penalty for blasphemy. They condemn him for

---

[26] Some scholars contend that Jonah dies in the creature and then is raised from the dead as he is spat up on the shore. In the book that bears his name, it states, *"From inside the fish Jonah prayed to the Lord his God"* (Jonah 2:1). To pray, he must be alive at that point. Yet it may be his last gasp. He speaks of crying to the Lord *"out of the belly of Sheol"* and that the Lord *"brought my life up from the pit."* Both terms in the OT refer to the realm of the dead. See Brant Pitre, *The Case for Jesus* (New York, NY: Image, 2016), 186–88. The heartrending prayer of Jonah can be interpreted either that he died and was revived or more probably that he was distressingly near death and rescued (Jonah 2:1–10). The allusion Jesus makes seems focused on the darkness Jonah endures and the elapsed time of three days rather than whether or not he actually expires.

saying in their hearing that he is the Messiah, who will sit at the right hand of the Mighty One (Mk 14:62 as described in Dan. 7:13–14 and Ps. 110:1). Note an important factor about the charge. This charge of blasphemy gives the priests the justification they are looking for to condemn Jesus to death in their Judaic legal system. However, at the trial before the Roman governor Pilate, on the pavement at his palace, the priests alter the charge; they change it to sedition or rebellion against Roman authority on the basis that Jesus claims to be an unauthorized king (Lk 23:2; Jn 19:7, 12, 15). They change the charge because at the time the occupying Romans reserved to their administration the power to apply the death penalty for civil laws (Jn 18:31). The Sanhedrin seems to have been able to enforce their religious laws with the death penalty in individual low-profile cases by stoning, at least by mobs if not officially (Acts 7:54–58, Jn 8:2–9; see a contrast in the case of the well-regarded, public figure James the brother of Jesus, *Antiquities* 20.9.1 and chapter 5). In the situation with Jesus, they do not want to take complete social responsibility for his demise due to his popularity as a prophet and healer. Since he stands as a direct threat to their authority and corruption, they want him dead to be sure but publicly and conclusively at the hands of the Romans (Mk 15:9–13, Jn 18:29–32).

---

Found in the Ground:
### Palace and Pavement Where Pilate Judged Jesus

Jerusalem—Site found in 1943. Foundation walls and sewage system for Herod's palace are found in 2000, below ground and underneath a former prison and citadel of the Turks. The palace sat on an elevated platform on the western side of the upper city. It was an earlier project by Herod of flattening and enlarging a plaza followed later by the more ambitious program to enlarge the temple mount complex. The site fits with the description in Josephus of Roman governors judging on the pavement outside the palace (*War* 2.14.8) and with John's reference to *"gabbatha,"* an Aramaic term for a stone pavement. The finding supports the detailed account of the Roman trial scene as reported in John. (Jn 18:28, 19:8–9, 13–16)

Index 3.6

---

Later, when Jesus is hanging on the cross, still conscious, still able painfully to push up from his feet to breathe, he suffers the added humiliation of being mercilessly mocked by these priests and other onlookers.

> *Those who passed by hurled insults at him, shaking their heads and saying, "So! You who are going to destroy the temple and build it in three days, come down from the cross and save yourself!" In the same way the chief priests and the teachers of the law mocked him among themselves. "He saved others," they said, "but he can't save himself! Let this Messiah, this king of Israel, come down now from the cross, that we may see and believe." Those crucified with him also heaped insults on him.* (Mark 15:29–32)

What has stuck in the minds of his mockers at the cross and his accusers at his trial is that Jesus threatened to take down the temple. Now in all the first three gospel accounts, there is no episode in which Jesus directly says that he will destroy the temple. The one quotation that comes closest goes like this.

> *As Jesus was leaving the temple, one of his disciples said to him, "Look, Teacher! What massive stones! What magnificent buildings!" "Do you see all these great buildings?" replied Jesus. "Not one stone here will be left on another; every one will be thrown down."*
> *(Mark 13:1–2)*

Jesus is making a prediction, but he is not saying he will destroy the temple himself. It is fair to say that he believes God will take direct action to bring down the temple. He certainly seems to believe that the corruption of the temple leadership plus their rejection of him make an impending judgment a foregone conclusion (Mt 23:37–39; Lk 13:34–35).

## Invading Roman Soldiers Take Down the Temple, Not Jesus

In about forty more years, in AD 70, the temple would be destroyed by marauding Roman troops. Under orders to level the temple, they demolish all the buildings leaving no stone unturned as Jesus had foreseen. It must be clarified that retaining walls built with large stones by Herod the Great to extend the temple plaza remain in place. One of these retaining walls is treasured to this day by worshipful Jews as the Western Wall.

Part of the incentive for the Roman soldiers to leave no stone on top of another was their quest for gold according to Josephus (*War* 6.1.2–7.4.1). In the heat of the fire, gold overlays in the temple facades melted into the gaps between stones, which had been fitted together precisely without mortar. Jesus accurately prophesies that no stone in the buildings is left untoppled. He says the temple will fall but does not say he will destroy it himself. He makes his prediction in an aside to his disciples, not in a public teaching (although it remains possible the comment was overheard by others in the temple precinct).

## The Riddle: Temple Has a Double Meaning

Extending our search to the gospel of John finds another episode that may account for this accusation against Jesus that he himself sought to destroy the temple. As explained earlier in the introduction, John as a documentary filmmaker puts a clip of the event of Jesus overturning the tables of the temple moneychangers near the outset of Jesus's ministry rather than at the end just prior to his arrest as in the other gospels. He frames the clip with the question repeatedly asked of Jesus: whether he can produce a sign or miracle that will satisfy the Jewish leadership that he has been sent by God.

> The Jews then responded to him, "What sign can you show us to prove your authority to do all this?" Jesus answered them, "Destroy this temple, and I will raise it again in three days." They replied, "It has taken forty-six years to build this temple, and you are going to raise it in three days?" But the temple he had spoken of was his body. After he was raised from the dead, his disciples recalled what he had said. Then they believed the scripture and the words that Jesus had spoken. (John 2:18–22)

As in prior attempts to cajole him into producing a sign on demand, Jesus refuses to comply. Yet he offers an alternative that turns out to be a veiled prediction of his death and resurrection. As John explains, Jesus speaks of his body figuratively as a temple (a place where God's Spirit dwells). He says the sign this generation will receive will come when they destroy his body, which in three days will rise to life again.

It is likely this public expression accounts for the false accusations at the trial. His accusers claim that Jesus said he would destroy the actual temple building and rebuild it in three days. Actually, he is making a public prediction that he will be killed and afterward rise from the dead, but the prediction is veiled. He employs a double meaning for the term *"this temple"*; it can mean the worship building or his body.

No wonder his accusers are confused. This charge of threatening to destroy the temple does not stick. It is not what leads to his being condemned to death by the priestly gathering (that would be the blasphemy charge). The pun on temple and the designation of a three-day burial period stand out as formulations that come straight from Jesus and are locked in the minds of his hostile listeners. Later at the nighttime interrogation, these listeners become compliant accusers for the ruling priests. Nevertheless, having these false accusations—that Jesus claimed he would himself destroy the temple building and reconstruct it in three days—recorded in the gospels provides great value. Ironically, these accuser memories offer solid evidence for a second public prediction of execution and resurrection that can be traced directly to Jesus.

There is a common theme to the sign of Jonah and to the sign of *"this temple"* of the body, two signs Jesus applies to his destiny. Both speak to the journey he will take through suffering, death, and burial to rising again. The sign that Jesus says his generation will be given to prove God is working through him is none other than the sign—a shocking moment of divine interference—that is Jesus in his body risen from the dead.

# ∃: CONCLUSION

### On the Predictions of Jesus

It is highly likely that Jesus predicts his own death and resurrection. He does so both in public even in the face of entrenched opposition and in private with his disciples even when they struggle to understand what he means. The disciples' responses to the three recorded private predictions make them look clueless; their bewilderment adds weight to the historical probability of Jesus's predictions. The responses of opponents to the two recorded public predictions reveal their rising anger and hostility toward Jesus when he does not meet their demands and threatens their sense of security. These reactions of opponents also add probability to the accounts. (Chapter 9 investigates the question of where in the OT Jesus likely derives his predictions.)

In this chapter, what is established for now is that he warned his disciples of his fate in private. In public, he hinted in a veiled way about what would happen to him. When Jesus himself is responsible for these predictions of his suffering and his rising, could the disciples really have created these scenarios? The evidence weighs strongly against any theory the critics purport that the disciples created the resurrection story out of whole cloth from their wounded and despairing but overactive imaginations.

# CHAPTER

# LINE OF EVIDENCE

## SUMMARY

A faith-based group from an agrarian region of Israel is hurting and demoralized when their leader suffers the death penalty at the behest of their Jewish religious authorities and the Roman occupiers. Yet within two months, their demeanor changes from weak and despairing to strong and bold. They end up changing the Mediterranean world. They replicate their faith in succeeding generations to the point that less than three hundred years later, the Roman emperor legitimizes and favors Christianity. That leader is Constantine, who issues the Edict of Milan in AD 313 that legalized the Christian faith.

In historical research, when an effect is this far-reaching, a cause is sought that can account for it. The New Testament narratives explain the change in the disciples by asserting two events: the resurrection of Jesus and the impartation of the Holy Spirit. Any other explanations must propose a sufficient cause for the change in the first disciples and their resulting worldwide, rippling effect continuing in our own day.

# PRELUDE

## CHAPTER 4

t is a cold, dark night. Yet she recognizes a rough-hewn man standing near the fire. He is in the courtyard of the high priest, who employs her as a servant. Inside the house, a sudden, late-night trial is going on for a man from Nazareth up north named Jesus. He is a roving rabbi with radical teachings. She has seen him before at the temple. She sees this other man silently mingling with those who are warming themselves around the fire in the flickering light including some of the temple guards.

She edges closer and looks right at him. She calls him out. *"You also were with the Nazarene, Jesus."* Peter denies it and leaves for the outer courtyard. She follows him to where he tries to hide among a different group of bystanders. Raising her voice, she presses her point. *"This man is one of them."* Peter again denies her charge. However, his very accent, to Jerusalem ears, gives away his unpolished, rural origins. She hears others chime in after her, *"Surely you are one of them, for you are a Galilean."* He swears he does not know the man under arrest. Then a rooster crows. Strangely to her eyes, this rugged rustic melts down in a crush of tears not at her taunts but at the sound of a rooster! (Mk 14:66–72.)

It would be about two months later when the servant girl of the high priest may very well have seen Peter again. He has been arrested the evening before, after the priests hear him preaching in the temple plaza. He claims that God has fulfilled his covenant to their founding father, Abraham, by raising Jesus from the dead to bless all the families of the earth. A huge crowd had gathered to listen after word had spread that Peter and another disciple John had healed a high-profile, paralyzed beggar at the temple gate. The ex-beggar had stood up and was walking around for everyone to see. So the next day, the priests hold a hearing with others from the high-priest families attending, likely accompanied by their inquisitive servant girl.

Assuming the servant girl hears Peter's brash speech before the high priest, would she recognize him from the cold, dark night by the fire? Would she see the transformation in him? Would she be curious to investigate this Jesus movement for herself? At any rate, more than almost any other person in the vicinity, she could testify to a most radical change in Peter.

The country bumpkin who had crumpled into a weeping, self-loathing mess that night in the outer court two months ago was now courageous, challenging, and fearless before the powerful citified priests. He and his ilk were turning Jerusalem upside down with their message. The Messiah had come, had been crucified, and now had been raised and exalted; in time, he would return and rule forever. Would she be among the thousands caught up in the preaching of this suddenly transformed fisherman no longer trying to net fish in the blue-green waters of Galilee but trying to save people in the dusty, tawny streets of Jerusalem?

# THE DISCIPLES CHANGE FROM FEARFUL TO BOLD

The boldest among the disciples, Peter, the leader, the one who vowed loudly he would go to his death with Jesus, flees instead from the courtyard of the high priest's palace on the night of Jesus's arrest. Fearing capture and worried about facing the same fate as Jesus, he denies his association with Jesus three times in a row. A rooster crows. Peter remembers Jesus telling him ahead of time about his denials, and Peter is reduced to tears. He is a crushed, ashamed, and broken man. By all accounts, he never shows up at the site of the cross. He is not around to help with the burial arrangements. He is in hiding.

It was not that long ago since his brother Andrew had brought Peter to Jesus (Jn 1:40–42). Not that long ago, Jesus had such earnest crowds pressing around him on the shore of the Sea of Galilee that he had climbed into Peter's fishing boat and asked him to put out into the water a little so he could teach the people (Lk 5:3). Later, as if to pay him for the boat rental, Jesus had told him where to fish, in deeper water. Soon, his nets along with those of his business partners James and John were bulging with the catch.

Found in the Ground:
**House and Courtyard of High Priest**

Jerusalem—Found in 1973. It is a Herodian mansion with ritual baths and a spacious courtyard near the temple, which is destroyed in AD 70. An investigation confirms the angle where Jesus from inside the house could see Peter outside in the courtyard. The site supports gospel accounts placing Jesus in the house of the high priest after his arrest in the garden and undergoing interrogation by the priests. It also supports accounts of Peter's denials under public pressure in the courtyard of the high priest. (Mk 14:53–72, 15:1; Mt 26:57–75, 27:1–2; Lk 22:54–71, 23:1–2; Jn 18:12–28)

Index 4.1

Found in the Ground:
**Ancient Galilee Fishing Boat**

Sea of Galilee, Israel—The wooden boat is found in the mud of the lake on the northwestern shore during a severe drought in 1986. It is 26.5 feet or 8.3 meters long. This boat, which was preserved for two millennia, likely plied the waters concurrently with the disciples. It probably passed by a boat carrying Jesus and his disciples on days when they would crisscross the lake to their destinations. This finding confirms gospel accounts (and mosaics) of fishing boats that are large enough for sleeping and for transporting twelve to fifteen people. (Mk 4:36–38, 6:30–32, 8:10–13; Jn 6:16–17)

Index 4.2

Jesus would call another nine disciples to join his campaign, but these three commercial fishermen would form his inner circle. He would base his ministry in the lakeside town where they lived, Capernaum. They would be the ones he would take into private homes for healings (Mk 5:37). They were the ones he took on a hike up a high mountain in northern Israel to reveal his power (Mk 9:2, see chapter 3). They were the ones he called to his side in the Garden of Gethsemane as he broke down in prayer and tears with the knowledge of his impending death (Mk 14:33). Unfortunately, they were not much good to Jesus that night once they fell asleep.

Peter had shared all these moments as one of the three closest to Jesus, but he also was the leader of the twelve disciples probably because he was a man of action as well as a man of quick expression. When Jesus asked all the disciples, *"Who do people say I am?"* it was Peter who spoke up triumphantly, *"You are the Messiah"* (Mk 8:27–30). Then when Jesus immediately warned them he would suffer, it was Peter who took him aside. *"Never, Lord!"* he said. *"This shall never happen to you!"*—only to trigger a stern rebuke from Jesus in return (Mt 16:22–23).

When a hard saying of Jesus about eating his flesh and drinking his blood turned many in the crowd away, Jesus asked his disciples if they would leave too. Peter was at his best, answering, *"Lord, to whom shall we go? You have the words of eternal life"* (Jn 6:68). Later, when Peter refused to let Jesus wash his feet, Jesus told him, *"Unless I wash you, you have no part with me."* Aghast, Peter walked it back, saying, *"Then Lord not just my feet but my hands and my head as well!"* (Jn 13:8–9). When temple guards came to the garden that night to arrest Jesus, Peter was right by his side. He alone drew a sword and injured the servant of the high priest (Jn 18:10, 26).

Found in the Ground:
Galilee Boat Harbors

Sea of Galilee, Israel—From 1970 to 2000, sixteen ancient ports on the lake were found. The ports include breakwaters, piers, promenades, along with boat anchors, mooring stones, and first-century fishing equipment including weights tied to fishing nets. Findings support the gospel accounts of fishing and boat travel. (Mk 1:19–20, 4:36, 5:21, 6:54, 8:10; Jn 6:17, 21:3–8)

Index 4.3

After all this contact with Jesus, for Peter to say that he has not been with him, that he does not know him, amounts to a grievous betrayal. There is one bitter irony. Simon was his given name, but Jesus had made a point of renaming him, signaling his destiny (Jn 1:42, Mt 16:18). His new name, "Peter," meant "Rock" in Greek (with other common variations today being Pierre, Pedro, Petros, Pietro, Pyotr, and in Aramaic, Cephas). It meant someone Jesus could count on, someone upon whom he could build his movement. A rock? Now, after his denials, he had to feel less like a rock and more like dust in the wind. The Jesus movement had come to a sudden halt. He had betrayed his teacher and friend in the cold, hard, stone courtyard of the high priest.

Peter's story might have ended right there. He might have returned to his house in Galilee disappointed in Jesus and disillusioned with himself. So much for what Jesus said about becoming a fisher of people (Mk 1:17; Mt 4:19–20; Lk 5:10–11). He would just fish for fish the rest of his life.

Interpretive Angle:
**Peter the Rock**

Some scholars suggest the "rock" Jesus will build upon refers to Peter's statement of faith or confession that Jesus is the Messiah—not so much Peter as an individual person who will be the core leader of his church. This idea could be true without altering the fact that Jesus nicknames his lead disciple what amounts to "Rocky" in our parlance today. The name denotes a person who is a tough and reliable fighter, one whom Jesus clearly intends to shoulder the leadership mantle. Peter's prior name of Simon, means "one who listens or obeys" from the Hebrew *shama*, "to hear" (see Deut. 6:9). This positive meaning may be why the gospels often put both names together (Mt 16:16, Mk 14:37, Lk 5:8, Jn 13:6-9, 36, 20:2, 6).

### The Holy Spirit Arrives Unless They Are Just Drunk

But let us fast-forward here to an event less than two months later. The Feast of Weeks is one of the three mandatory feasts per year requiring most males to travel to Jerusalem. It celebrates the wheat harvest in late May or early June. The band of disciples plus other followers who bring the estimate of the gathering to 120 were in one large house in Jerusalem (Acts 1:15, 2:1). A loud sound of rushing wind is heard by those inside the house. Passersby probably hear it too. The disciples file out of the house. Soon afterward, all those in Jesus's entourage start speaking in a variety of known languages. A crowd quickly forms. Jews from other nations gathered for the feast hear about the wonders of God working through Jesus in their own languages.

> Found in the Ground:
> **Peter's House in Capernaum**
>
> Capernaum, Galilee, Israel—Found in 1968. A normal house in the harbor town suddenly becomes a place of worship, a telltale sign someone important in the faith had occupied the original residence. The site supports accounts of Peter, who grew up in Bethsaida, living in Capernaum with his wife and mother-in-law and working as a commercial fisherman. (Mk 1:16–21, 29–31, 3:1–5; Mt 8:14–15, Lk 4:38–39)
>
> Index 4.4

There is such a gaggle of sound that some cynical types accuse them of being drunk, stupid Galileans—rustics going crazy in the big city. At that, Peter stands, and with the other eleven original disciples (minus Judas of course) backing him up begins to preach to the people (Acts 2:14). It is nine in the morning, he says. The people are not drunk. They are filled with the Spirit of God as the prophet Joel foretold (Joel 1). The very man they and their leaders put to death, Jesus, has been raised from the dead, is exalted at the right hand of God, has received from God the promised Holy Spirit, and has given the Spirit to these disciples.

What the bystanders see and hear is the Spirit pouring out

the truth to them. Taking passages from the Psalms, Peter proves to them that Jesus is both Lord and Messiah. He promises they will receive forgiveness and the Spirit of God if they will repent and be baptized.

This first street preaching by Peter is undeniably successful. Three thousand people accept the message and join up with the disciples that day (Acts 2:41).

### The Narrator for the Outreach Comes Well Qualified

How do we retrieve these accounts of Peter after the resurrection? The writer who brings us these records of the way that the disciples go out and preach the news of Jesus is Luke. He is the only one of the four gospel authors who writes a sequel, which covers what happens to a few key preachers (Peter, John, Stephen, Philip, Paul) over the next thirty years after Jesus physically departs the earth.

In his gospel, Luke mentions his research process. He knows other written accounts, and he has direct access to eyewitnesses and teachers (Lk 1:1–4, see *Background Guide,* resource 1). Probably Greek by ethnicity, Luke likely converts when he meets Paul about AD 50 (Acts 16:10). He travels with Paul extensively in Greco-Roman regions as well as later in Israel. His connection with Paul likely brought him into contact with Peter.

> Biblical Sidelight:
> **Passover Math**
>
> One way the math unspools is as follows. From the crucifixion to the resurrection, count three days. From the resurrection to the ascension, count forty days. From the ascension to the giving of the Spirit at Pentecost, count seven days. This totals fifty days. Pentecost or the Feast of Weeks comes seven weeks after Passover. Jesus dies on the Day of Preparation before Passover. (Mt 27:62; Mk 15:42; Lk 23:54; Jn 19:31)

Peter is still alive and based in Rome according to tradition when Luke accompanies Paul on his journey to Rome around AD

60 for his trial before the emperor (Acts 28:16). Moreover, Luke definitely had contact with an author close to Peter known as John Mark or just Mark. Peter speaks affectionately of Mark (1 Pet. 5:13) and knew and trusted Mark's family, who had a house in Jerusalem (Acts 12:12). Many scholars agree with early Christian writers who claim that the gospel of Mark is ostensibly the gospel of Peter as told to Mark. It is based on Peter's recollections and years of preaching.[27] At one point, Luke and Mark serve on the same ministry team led by Paul (Philemon 24). Historically, it is reasonable to assume that they exchanged notes since they both were interested in writing down events and teachings. Luke incorporates large swaths of Mark's gospel in his own making it all the more possible that Mark may have provided source material on Peter for Acts as well. Without technical recording devices in the first century, Luke may not have had the exact wording of speeches Peter gives, but it is likely Luke has the general flow and key references from the prophets that Peter uses at different turns.[28]

Now as we return to the streets of Jerusalem, obviously a new, confident Peter has emerged. He and his community of upstarts have received the Holy Spirit. He is moving freely throughout Jerusalem. As crowds along with tensions build, we will follow him around Judea and its environs to see what kind of witness to the resurrection Peter sustains.

One day, Peter and his business-turned-ministry partner John

---

[27] Richard Bauckham, *Jesus and the Eyewitnesses*, 155–81. Signs of Peter's content influence include grammatical constructions, point of view, self-deprecation, and transparency all framed by Mark's own emphasis on transformation and discipleship.

[28] For a full discussion of speeches in Acts, see F. F. Bruce, *The Speeches in the Acts of the Apostles* (London: Tyndale Press, 1942), 5–27, biblicalstudies. org.uk. Three decades later, Bruce revisited his essay in a *festschrift* or publication to honor a fellow scholar. See F. F. Bruce, "The Speeches in Acts—Thirty Years After," Robert Banks, ed., *Reconciliation and Hope. New Testament Essays on Atonement and Eschatology Presented to L.L. Morris on his 60th Birthday* (Carlisle, UK: Paternoster Press, 1974), 53–68. Also available at biblicalstudies.org.uk.

go up to the temple to pray about three in the afternoon and see a paralyzed beggar at the temple gate who has begged at that spot for many years. People know him. He reaches out to Peter and John for money. Peter, now back in his true character as a man of action, is ready to upset the status quo. He commands the man to walk in the name of Jesus. It works. He stands up and walks and even starts jumping around praising God. Inside the gates, a crowd forms along the eastern wall of the temple complex. It is a covered area held up by pillars, known as Solomon's Colonnade (or Portico or Porch). It faces the front of the temple. This was familiar ground. Jesus liked to teach here especially in wintertime when the roof would keep his listeners dry in the rain (Jn 10:23). The crowd wants to know how Peter and John healed the man. Peter denies it was his own power or godliness that brought healing. He points them to Jesus, but he pulls no punches when it comes to their complicity in the wrongdoing that led to his execution.

> *"You disowned the Holy and Righteous One and asked that a murderer be released to you. You killed the author of life, but God raised him from the dead. We are witnesses of this. By faith in the name of Jesus, this man whom you see and know was made strong." (Acts 3:14–16)*

He says the crucifixion was the way God fulfilled what the prophets foretold, that the Messiah would suffer (Acts 3:17-25). The people acted in ignorance, but now, they must repent and turn to God so that their sins may be *"wiped out"* (*"blotted out"* in some translations). Later, Jesus will return *"to restore everything,"* meaning to set up the kingdom of God on earth and rule from Israel. He refers to Jesus as fulfilling Moses's prediction of a prophet like himself. Samuel and other prophets foretold *"these days."* The people are seeing the promise to Abraham— that through his offspring, all peoples will be blessed—kept by God in their own day through the death and resurrection of Jesus. It is almost evening, but Peter is just getting wound up when the priests and the captain of the guard abruptly arrive, make the arrest, and put Peter and John in jail overnight. What Peter manages to proclaim before they cut him off is enough to persuade another two thousand Jewish believers bringing the total to five thousand according to Luke's account (Acts 4:4).

### Religious Authorities Harass the Apostles to No Avail

The true test awaits Peter and John the next morning. Preaching to the public is one thing, but now they are brought before the high priest Joseph Caiaphas and his ruling family. This is the same high priestly cohort that convinced the Romans to crucify Jesus. They want to know where Peter and John have acquired their power to heal this long-time paralyzed beggar. Peter could not be more direct.

> Then Peter, filled with the Holy Spirit, said to them: "Rulers and elders of the people! If we are being called to account today for an act of kindness shown to a man who was lame and are being asked how he was healed, then know this, you and all the people of Israel: It is by the name of Jesus Christ of Nazareth, whom you crucified but whom God raised from the dead, that this man stands before you healed. Jesus is 'the stone you builders rejected, which has become the cornerstone.' Salvation is found in no one else, for there is no other name under heaven given to mankind by which we must be saved." (Acts 4:8–12)

The priestly cohort is between a rock and a hard place. They would like to do away with these disciples, but they cannot kill or even punish them because the crowds are thrilled with the healing. The people praise God for working through Peter and John, so the priests cannot appear to be opposing God. In a major reversal, they are not intimidating Peter and John; it is the other way around.

> When they saw the courage of Peter and John and realized that they were unschooled, ordinary men, they

*were astonished and they took note that these men had
been with Jesus. (Acts 4:13)*

The rulers cannot agree on a punishment or even how to
proceed except to tell the disciples to cease and desist. The
preachers do not obey the order because they are operating under
a higher authority.

> *Then they called them in again and commanded them
> not to speak or teach at all in the name of Jesus. But
> Peter and John replied, "Which is right in God's eyes:
> to listen to you, or to him? You be the judges! As for us,
> we cannot help speaking about what we have seen and
> heard." (Acts 4:18–20)*

These rugged fishermen from the backwoods province of
Galilee stand up to the leading priests in Jerusalem and leave
them befuddled. Less than three months earlier, Peter was
shrinking away from the taunts of the high priest's servant girl.
Now, he is calling out the high priest himself. He tells him their
attempted takedown of Jesus did not work. Jesus is risen and has
all authority way beyond the temple system. Salvation comes only
through him.

The authorities end up letting them go. The backcountry
preachers head to the house where the rest of the disciples are
gathered. They praise God together and pray for even more
boldness and healings (Acts 4:29–30). As the stirring days unfold,
they share their possessions, and some sell their real estate to
supply those in need.

Found in the Ground:
## Bone Box of High Priest

Jerusalem—Found in 1990. The artifact is a limestone bone box or ossuary with an inscription on the outside of the box, "Joseph, son of Caiaphas." The bones inside are identified as those of a sixty-year-old male.

Joseph, son of Caiaphas, called in the NT simply Caiaphas, presides and leads the questioning of Jesus at the Jewish trial at night before the assembled teachers and elders. He also leads the interrogations of the apostles when they preach in the temple plaza about two months after the resurrection. The finding supports gospel accounts in which Caiaphas is identified by name as a key official or specifically as the ruling high priest. (Mt 26:3, 57; Lk 3:2; Jn 11:49, 18:13–14, 24, 28; Acts 4:6)

Index 4.5

### *Peter and John Are Happy to Get Themselves Arrested Again*

Crowds gather as word spreads about the healing power. The only problem is their high visibility in the face of the authorities. The high priest again arraigns the apostles.

*"We gave you strict orders not to teach in this name," he said, "Yet you have filled Jerusalem with your teaching and are determined to make us guilty of this man's blood." Peter and the other apostles replied: "We must obey God rather than human beings! The God of our ancestors raised Jesus from the dead—whom you killed by hanging him on a cross. God exalted him to his own right hand as Prince and Savior that he might bring Israel to repentance and forgive their sins. We are witnesses of*

*these things, and so is the Holy Spirit, whom God has*
*given to those who obey him." (Acts 5:28–32)*

Peter's words incite fury in the high priest and his family. They are jealous of the disciples' healing power and ability to attract crowds. Now, the priests are publicly accused of opposing God's purpose in Jesus. Further, they are told they do not have the Spirit of God working in them. They and their temple are no longer the center of the way God relates to humanity. Jesus in effect has displaced them. This explains why they now want to levy the death penalty on these subversive apostates.

### A Leading Pharisee Intervenes, Cautioning "Not So Fast"

One of the members of the council, a renowned teacher, averts the wrath of the council with a simple argument. He refers to two other revolutionaries who were killed. Not long after their demise, their followers scattered and the movements disappeared. Then he concludes this way.

> *"Therefore, in the present case I advise you: Leave these*
> *men alone! Let them go! For if their purpose or activity*
> *is of human origin, it will fail. But if it is from God, you*
> *will not be able to stop these men; you will only find*
> *yourselves fighting against God." (Acts 5:38–39)*

This teacher who persuades the council is a Pharisee named Gamaliel. His party of the Pharisees was one of the two main theological/political groups. They tried to stay true to the ways of God as revealed in the OT scriptures and keep the written and traditional (or oral) laws meticulously (their name came from the Aramaic word for "set apart" or "separated").

The other main group was the Sadducees (their name derived from Zadok, who aided King David and became the first high priest in Solomon's newly built temple, 2 Sam. 8:17, 1 Kings 1:39).

They controlled the temple systems and revenues and tended to be less scriptural and less spiritual than the Pharisees were.

It was the Pharisees who engaged more directly in discussions with Jesus in Galilee and Jerusalem. Their interest in Jesus emerged from their focus on God's will and ways. They were keenly listening to what Jesus taught whether they were angry at him when he reinterpreted the laws or whether they were latching on to his vision for the kingdom of God as were Nicodemus and Joseph of Arimathea (Jn 3:1–16, 19:38–39; Mk 15:43; Lk 23:50–51). The Sadducees were less interested in Jesus until he appeared to threaten their temple system.

Both groups were represented on the governing council called the Sanhedrin, which comprised seventy-one leaders with the Sadducaic high priest usually presiding over the council. Gamaliel was one of the Pharisees with status high enough to go toe to toe with the Sadducees. He is a renowned teacher in Jewish history, and to study under him is the reason Paul the apostle then known as Saul of Tarsus originally comes to Jerusalem (Acts 22:3, see chapter 6).

In the interrogation of Peter and John, Gamaliel's advice carries the day. However, many council members are still incensed enough to require that the apostles be whipped or *"flogged."* Then they are ordered again to be silent. Not going to happen.

---

Historical Portal:
**Gamaliel the Pharisee Sage**

He is mentioned in the Talmud and Mishnah. As a grandson of the acclaimed rabbi Hillel, he occupies a leading position in the Sanhedrin, the highest legal and government council in Israel. He dies about AD 52. As leader of the Hillel school, he sought to render legal ordinances with a view to the repair of the world (*tikkun ha-'olam*). His teachings included kindness toward non-Jews and protection of women undergoing divorce. The evidence supports the account of Gamaliel's relatively lenient approach to the disciples' preaching when they were brought before the Sanhedrin. (Acts 5:34–39)

> *The apostles left the Sanhedrin, rejoicing because they*
> *had been counted worthy of suffering disgrace for the*
> *Name. Day after day, in the temple courts and from house*
> *to house, they never stopped teaching and proclaiming*
> *the good news that Jesus is the Messiah. (Acts 5:41–42)*

The brush with suffering on the part of the apostles does not dissuade them; rather, it impels them all the more to get the message out because they sense they are following in the footsteps of Jesus when they encounter opposition. As he did, they too are doing the will of God.

Of the two scenarios Gamaliel had laid out, it was the second that history shows clearly unfolded. The Jesus movement does not sputter; the news of the resurrected Messiah sent by the God of Abraham, Isaac, and Jacob to save humanity in a new kingdom of God turns out to be an unstoppable force. The attempts to suppress the message of Jesus in its early days are pointless. The disciples have been transformed permanently. They spend the rest of their lives spreading the word that salvation from death and separation from God is found in no one except Jesus the Messiah.

### The Change Explained to a Roman Officer's Household

Yet the question remains, which factors gave the disciples so much momentum so suddenly? It is an indisputable historical fact that they changed radically from timid rustics to brave firebrands. How did they change so quickly from despairing to daring?

In the accounts featuring Peter (with John and other apostles at times as supporting actors), we see the transformation clearly. They swing from despairing, disappointed followers to bold, courageous proclaimers of the message of Jesus. The narratives viewed so far in this chapter give evidence that the change occurred as shown by courageous preaching, but how it occurred in the hearts and minds of the disciples is another question worth considering.

For insight on that question, we go to Luke's account of Peter's talk in the Roman port city of Caesarea Maritima on the west coast of Israel. A *"god-fearing"* Italian commander in the Roman army named Cornelius hears Peter is visiting the nearby coastal town of Joppa.[29] He requests that Peter come and speak to an entourage of his close friends and relatives, all of them non-Jewish people. It is an open and friendly audience for Peter. He recounts how Jesus began in Galilee healing so many because he was anointed by God with the Holy Spirit and with power. Then he describes what happened not only to Jesus but also to the disciples. He reveals how they were changed in the process and their confidence exponentially increased through at least nine factors all figuring in his account.

> Found in the Ground:
> **Italian Regiment Inscription**
>
> Caesarea Maritima, Israel—Dated to AD 69. Inscription indicates that a military force stationed in the city was known as the Second Italian Cohort of Roman Citizen Volunteers. Most scholars assume that it is likely that the cohort was there for many years prior to the inscription date. The finding supports the account of Peter being sent for by a centurion based in Caesarea Maritima, named Cornelius, who assembles his entire diverse household to hear Peter speak about Jesus.(Acts 11:14)
>
> Index 4.6

### *Factor 1: Resurrection*

*"We are witnesses of everything he did in the country of the Jews and in Jerusalem. They killed him by hanging him on a cross, but God raised him from the dead on the third day..." (Acts 10:39–40)*

---

[29] The biblical Joppa is known today as Jaffa. It has become virtually a borough of Tel Aviv as the city now surrounds it.

God raises Jesus from the dead, clearly the most obvious factor. This is the shocking, mind-altering, world-shaking event that propels everything else in the hearts of the disciples to change the world.

## Factor 2: Appearances

> *"... and caused him to be seen. He was not seen by all the people, but by witnesses whom God had already chosen—by us who ate and drank with him after he rose from the dead." (Acts 10:40–41)*

The appearances (see chapter 2) have a huge effect on the disciples' faith. They do not simply believe others (the first witnesses, the women in chapter 1) but they see and touch Jesus for themselves. They see Jesus eating and drinking and clearly alive with a recognizable human body. For those who received individual personal appearances from Jesus, the effect would have been potentially stronger as it was with Peter and James the brother of Jesus, who believed and rose to lead the Jerusalem church (see chapter 5).

## Factor 3: Mission

> *"He commanded us to preach to the people..."*
> *(Acts 10:42)*

The disciples have a sense of mission, a clear task given to them to spread the message of Jesus. That message, as Peter later puts it in a letter, is *"He himself bore our sins in his body on the tree"*(1 Pet. 2:24)—so that *"in his great mercy"* God gives believers *"new birth into a living hope through the resurrection of Jesus Christ from the dead."* God shields them and keeps in heaven *"an eternal inheritance"* guaranteed for them as they look forward to Jesus returning to earth in power (1 Pet. 1:3-5).

## Factor 4: Exaltation

*"... and to testify that he is the one whom God appointed as judge of the living and the dead."* (Acts 10:42)

Jesus has risen and is with God in heaven, but it is core to the disciples' confidence that he has been exalted to a place of authority. In one appearance in Galilee as recorded in Matthew, he tells them specifically, *"All authority in heaven and earth has been given to me"* (Mt 28:18). He has been appointed as judge of all humanity. So if you are forgiven by him, it is guaranteed you will escape judgment and be saved. This is good news for all persons no matter the sins they have committed. So by spreading that kind of positive and relieving news, they will make more disciples.

## Factor 5: Fulfillments

*"All the prophets testify about him..."* (Acts 10:43)

The disciples drew tremendous confidence from their search of the OT scriptures, which turned up multiple prophesies that were fulfilled in Jesus. Jesus himself makes a focused effort in several of his resurrection appearances to walk through the Bible with his disciples and shine light on the OT accounts that apply to him (see chapter 9).

## Factor 6: Forgiveness

*"... that everyone who believes in him receives forgiveness of sins through his name."* (Acts 10:43)

The message itself heartens the disciples because they themselves need this forgiveness. It also makes the news so good to bring to others. Simply put, the gospel offers complete forgiveness in Jesus for all who believe.

Today, we can miss the power of this shock for the first-century Jew. Forgiveness before now had come only through the temple system. Jews had to participate regularly in the sacrifices. Non-Jews could participate in worship from a distance, but their status with God was indirect. Now, forgiveness comes straight through Jesus. Can non-Jews come to God now through Jesus on the same basis as believing Jews? Apparently so, as seen in the next factor.

### Factor 7: Giving of the Spirit

> While Peter was still speaking these words, the Holy Spirit came on all who heard the message. The circumcised believers who had come with Peter were astonished that the gift of the Holy Spirit had been poured out even on the Gentiles. For they heard them speaking in tongues and praising God. (Acts 10:44–46)

In the OT, the Spirit of God would come on select people, usually prophets or kings, and this might be lifelong or temporary. Now that Jesus is risen, Peter sees the Spirit being poured out in Jerusalem on all Jewish believers in Jesus. No matter whether people are small or great, old or young, male or female, they are receiving the Holy Spirit as Peter cites the prediction of the prophet Joel in his preaching on Pentecost to explain what is happening (Acts 2:16–21). Up to this point, Peter may not have expected non-Jews to receive the Spirit. In this account of his speaking with Cornelius, he stops with the offer of forgiveness (Acts 10:43) not assuming they will be given the gift of the Spirit. But the Spirit is revealing to Peter and the other believers that God is not to be ethnically limited when faith in Jesus is present in any human being. This epic event dramatically enlarges Peter's view of the new kingdom of God ordained by Jesus. Members of the Roman household, non-Jews, express their receiving the Spirit in the same way the disciples did on the street in Jerusalem at Pentecost. They praise God in languages they did not know as Peter attests.[30]

## Factor 8: Inclusiveness

*"Surely no one can stand in the way of their being baptized with water. They have received the Holy Spirit just as we have." So he ordered that they be baptized in the name of Jesus Christ. (Acts 10:47-48)*

The giving of the Spirit now happens to all believers; this creates an inclusive message that emboldens the disciples. Once people believe, baptism is the entry point into the Jesus movement. It incorporates the concept of cleansing from sin (as in prior Jewish tradition), but it takes on a deeper meaning in the Jesus movement. It identifies believers with his death and resurrection and in a symbolic way reenacts it in the submersion version of baptism, the most common practice at the time. That each new recruit is baptized in Jesus's name signifies the full inclusion and equal membership of Gentiles and Jews alike in the new people of God.

## Factor 9: Community

*Then they asked Peter to stay with them for a few days. (Acts 10:48)*

---

[30] By no means is this interpretation naysaying the gift of speaking in tongues. The intent here is to follow closely the account in Acts. People hear and recognize their own languages being spoken in praise to God. The gift of tongues usually does not involve known languages. It is listed among the spiritual gifts that are allocated individually (1 Cor. 12:7-11). The apostle Paul himself has this gift (1 Cor. 14:18). For an excellent treatment of this sometimes controversial issue of tongues in the New Testament, see Michael Green, *I Believe in the Holy Spirit* (Grand Rapids, MI: Wm. B. Eerdmans, 1975), revised 1989, 2004.

Believing in Jesus and receiving forgiveness and this new life through the Spirit has the consequential effect of creating community. People have the desire to learn more about God, to connect with each other, and to worship and pray together (Acts 2:42–47). The Spirit goes to work to form a people. On the one hand, miraculous healings may be present, and on the other hand, the possibly even more miraculous selling of real estate to help others in need also may result as happened in Jerusalem in those early days (Acts 2:45). The sense of sharing with a community purpose has a magnetic effect to draw many people to Jesus.

Peter's talk to these Gentiles in the Roman household in Caesarea recaps the excitement he and his fellow Jewish apostles experience once the reality of the resurrection dawns on them. It explains how they become so confident in their message so quickly—a confidence bolstered even more when they see non-Jews as well astoundingly receiving the Spirit of God.

---

# 4: CONCLUSION

## On the Change in the Disciples

These accounts in the narrative of Acts demonstrate the radical change in the hearts of the disciples. Within two months, they are transformed from a ragtag bunch of depressives full of fearfulness and despair to a committed cadre impelled by conviction and courage. Any explanation other than the one the disciples give us in these reports—the heart-stopping shock of the resurrection—must account for their radical change of demeanor. It must account for their incentive to leave behind the comforts of home and go out and spread their discovery throughout their world—which is radically altered as a result of the way they live out their message.

# CHAPTER

# 5

# LINE OF EVIDENCE

## SUMMARY

# 5:

The disciples face dangerous cultural risks. It is a risk of life and death from multiple sources. There are three authorities with whom they must contend. The Jewish priestly hierarchy, the Roman procurator backed by heavily armed soldiers, and the Jewish kings or tetrarchs descended from the violent Herod the Great.

Under Jewish religious law, blasphemy is punishable with death by stoning. Blasphemy can be defined as speaking against the temple, against the Law of Moses, or making oneself out to be equal or in a special relationship with God.

The disciples in Jerusalem run the risk of arrest, incarceration, or death every time they preach in public. It is a theocracy, not a society of free speech or human rights. Their very hero was arrested, tortured, and killed. He was charged with blasphemy by the religious authorities and executed by the Roman power structure for sedition, or rebellion, for claiming to be a king unauthorized by Rome. If the disciples do not truly believe in the reality of the resurrection of Jesus, it is ridiculous for them to keep running this risk of punishment and death. Tragically, not all of them survive the threats.

# PRELUDE

## CHAPTER 5

I t has been a good while since our Jewish leaders rid the land of that deceiver from Nazareth. Clever man our high priest Joseph Caiaphas, Saul thinks, the way he stirred up the crowd to pressure the Roman governor to execute that nemesis Jesus just in time for a peaceful Passover week.

Saul is a young Jewish student from the Greek-speaking city of Tarsus in Cilicia, the southeastern part of modern Turkey. His family has noticed his intensity and intellectual gifts, so they have sent him to Jerusalem and enrolled him with the leading teacher of Jewish law, Gamaliel. Saul takes a special interest in fighting heretics and forcing them to return to true Jewish faith and practice.

Now what is this commotion in the streets near the temple? A burly mob of angry hotheads is dragging a man before the council of the high priest. Saul follows along to see what will result and to hear what the witnesses assert against this Jewish renegade.

> "This fellow never stops speaking against this holy place and against the law. For we have heard him say that this Jesus of Nazareth will destroy this place and change the customs Moses handed down to us." (Acts 6:13–14)

So the high priest inquires and allows the man to speak. The speaker takes the council back to the days of Abraham, to the days of Joseph, to the days of Moses and David, and finally he accuses the leaders of resisting God's purposes and killing God's prophets just as their forebears did.

143

*"Was there ever a prophet your ancestors did not persecute? They even killed those who predicted the coming of the Righteous One. And now you have betrayed and murdered him—you who have received the law that was given through angels but have not obeyed it!" (Acts 7:52–53)*

Saul viscerally objects. *He is accusing us of not keeping the law? Accusing us of betraying and murdering the Righteous One, the Messiah of God? That man he worships, that Jesus was an impostor!* Saul can feel his hot blood rising. *How dare this nonlocal, this Greek-speaking Jew accuse us?*

Many in the council start grinding their teeth in anger. Stephen keeps speaking. *"Look," he said, "I see heaven open and the Son of Man standing at the right hand of God"* (Acts 7:56). Blasphemy! The devout cover their ears and shout and drag Stephen out beyond the city walls, where they can stone him to death. Saul rushes along with them. There were plenty of men to throw stones, so he stands apart and collects the cloaks as the stone throwers fling them aside.

He watches Stephen get pummeled stone by stone into a bloodied, crumpled heap. *Good riddance,* he thinks. *This apostasy must be stopped, or like leprosy, it will eat away at our ancestral faith. We need to rid the city of any more of these Jesus sympathizers.* He vows to imprison as many of them as he can.

Yet standing within earshot, he hears the last words of Stephen—strangely spoken directly to that executed false messiah: *"Lord Jesus, receive my spirit"* (Acts 7:59). Then Stephen staggeringly asks the dead man to forgive those who are just about done killing him too. *These people are demented. They've lost their minds,* Saul decides. *And they're dangerously contagious. They threaten the law and the temple.* Enraged, he leaves to gather an enforcement brigade to arrest these apostates and keep this virulent heresy from spreading.

## CHAPTER 5

---

# THE DISCIPLES FACE PERILOUS
# CULTURAL RISKS

---

ven when he was walking the earth, following Jesus was
a risky occupation. It is less so at first when the crowds
are friendly in Galilee. They come from many villages to
experience healings, exorcisms, debates, and the occasional
mass picnic as well as his teachings filled with simplicity and
authority. He emphasizes the grace of God. He shows how God
cares for the downtrodden and outcast, how everyone is welcome
in the coming kingdom of God.

There are, however, rumblings against Jesus. Things do not
go well on his home visit to Nazareth. A mob almost murders
him in that hill town; some attempted to throw him off a cliff (Lk
4:16–30; see prelude for chapter 9). He receives other death threats
that he takes seriously. Some sympathetic Pharisees tip him off
that the ruler of Galilee, the tetrarch Herod Antipas, is plotting
to kill him (Lk 13:31). Antipas is a son of the brutal and paranoid
Herod the Great, who executes three of his other sons. Herod the
Great was the king of all Israel at the time Jesus was born though
he dies shortly afterward. Brutality runs in the family. Jesus has
reason to be concerned. His cousin, John the Baptist, has run

afoul of Antipas and been jailed by the temperamental ruler (Lk 3:19–20; Mt 4:12).

John's ministry had preceded Jesus's, and Jesus likely listened to John's preaching. Several of Jesus's disciples had started out with John until John directed them to Jesus. He told them Jesus was the *"Lamb of God"* who *"has surpassed me"* (Jn 1:29–30). When Jesus came to him for baptism, John famously refused; he said he was unworthy to untie his sandal, but Jesus insisted.

Later, Jesus receives word that a palace intrigue has led to John's beheading after a party boast by the king.[31] The frivolous murder affects Jesus deeply. He withdraws to a remote spot. No doubt he wants to grieve for his cousin and to process what it means for his own fate. He gets little time to himself; crowds follow him and interrupt his meditation (Mk 6:14–34; Mt 14:1–14).

---

[31] This account is recorded in Mk 6:14–29 and Mt 14:1–12 and verified in Lk 9:9 and Josephus, *Antiquities* 18.5.2. See also Linda L. Creighton, "The Seductive Salome has Inspired for Ages, A Deadly Dance," usnews.com, 25 Jan 2008, *U.S. News*, retrieved 18 Aug 2017.

---

Historical Portal:
## The Royal Murder of John the Baptist

The Galilean king Herod Antipas has arrested John the Baptist. He is keeping him in prison because John spoke out against the king for living with his brother's wife (prohibited in Lev. 18:16). His brother's wife, Herodias, has a daughter by her ex-husband (Mt 14:6). The daughter's name is Salome (the same as the mother of the disciples James and John), which we know not from the Bible but from Josephus (*Antiquities* 18.5.4).

At a feast, Salome dances so provocatively that in a bout of braggadocio, the king offers on oath to meet whatever request she desires. After consulting with her mother, she asks for the head of John the Baptist on a platter. Reluctantly the king agrees; he is unable to back down in front of the guests at the feast. When Jesus hears of this frivolous incident from John's disciples, he withdraws. He knows it foreshadows his own unjust death to come (Mt 14:3–13). Due to the story's salacious intrigue and rank injustice, literary works and operas have been written about Salome, most notably the drama by Irish playwright Oscar Wilde.

---

## Emboldened Disciples Face Same Threats Jesus Did

The same authorities who imprisoned and executed John and then convicted and crucified Jesus continue to threaten the disciples after the resurrection. The disciples are radically transformed by their contact with their risen Lord, but the controlling legal authorities have not changed. Essentially, there are three authorities whose wrath the disciples risk when they step out with their message. First, there is the Roman governor (also called a prefect) Pontius Pilate, who rules from AD 26 to 36. He is known for suppressing disorder harshly. In fact, he later loses his job over shedding too much blood in a Samaritan uprising (*Antiquities* 18.4.1–2). Second, there are the royal rulers of certain provinces of Israel not governed directly by Rome. These rulers include Antipas in Galilee and Perea, and Philip in Gaulinitis, who builds the city Caesarea Philippi in the north. Third, there is the temple priest contingent led by the wily manipulator Annas. He serves as high priest himself from AD 6 to 15. Even after he is dismissed, he controls the office for twenty-five years through his sons and his son-in-law, Joseph Caiaphas, who presides at the night trial of Jesus.

## Found in the Ground:
### The Floor Where Salome Danced

Machaerus, Jordan—The palace and citadel site atop a peak is found in 1807 with the lower city found in 1909. A pavement made of stone is the location where Salome dances and where the king, Herod Antipas, son of Herod the Great, sits and watches from one side from a central half-moon niche containing the royal throne. The outline on the floor for that niche still is visible today. He vows to give her whatever she requests; she asks for the head of John the Baptist on a platter. Already brought in chains to Machaerus, John the Baptist is held and beheaded probably in the lower city, where the exact place of his prison is yet to be located. The sites support the gospel accounts of the king's birthday party bravado gone horribly wrong. (Mk 6:14–28; Mt 14:6–11)

Index 5.1

## Apostolic Preaching and Healing Is Not Welcome

Peter and John run into trouble with the temple authorities when they preach—as did Jesus—in the temple complex. The high visibility healing of a well-known, forty-year-old paralysis victim brings out the crowd. Unlike at the Feast of Weeks (or Pentecost) when they were preaching in the streets of the city, now they are preaching right under the noses of the high priests. The captain of the temple guard arrests Peter and John and holds them in jail overnight.

At the hearing the next day, the high priests want to know by what power the disciples—now operating as active apostles—pull off the healing. They attribute the power behind the healing to the name of Jesus. The priests command them not *"to speak or teach at all in the name of Jesus"* (Acts 4:18). Peter and John admit they *"cannot help speaking of what we have seen and heard"* (Acts 4:20). The people are impressed and praise God for the healing. Any punishment of Peter and John by the priests would incite the crowd against them. So the Sanhedrin decides to let them go only with the warning to them that they must clam up.

> **Interpretive Angle:**
> **A Healing that Causes Strife**
>
> There is no debate on the part of the hostile leaders as recounted by Luke on whether the healing of the paralytic at the temple plaza occurred; the healed man who could not walk is standing in their midst. In the narrative itself, the healing catalyzes the entire arc of the account showing how the crowd swings to favor the apostles and to intimidate the priests. The episode makes little sense without the premise of the sudden healing. (Acts 4:13–18)

Undeterred, the apostles go back to their meeting place at a large home in the city and pray for more boldness and healings (Acts 4:29–31). Despite the warnings, the apostles continue to meet on the temple grounds often at Solomon's Colonnade opposite the temple entrance inside the eastern wall. It is a space with pillars and a roof but otherwise in the open air so people can casually drop by for a listen whether they are believers or not.

### The Irrepressible Preachers Face a Second Interrogation

Healings and exorcisms multiply. The high priests and their core contingent in the Sanhedrin, the Sadducees, are *"filled with jealousy"* according to Luke's account (Acts 5:17). They again arrest Peter and John along with other unnamed apostles.

At a second hearing before the Sanhedrin, Peter's speech infuriates them (Acts 5:33). He contends that Jesus is at the right hand of God, which means his authority outranks theirs as custodians of the temple. Peter claims that forgiveness now

## Interpretive Angle:
## The Pivotal Counsel of Gamaliel

Excerpts from Gamaliel's monologue as reported by Luke include two references to prior revolutionaries who epically failed. Scholars debate whether the reference to Theudas is an anachronism. Even if it is possible that Luke does not have access to the accurate information, the scene and argument to quell the outcry against the apostles on the part of Gamaliel still stands historically. The tension was searing enough that it makes sense it would take a Jewish authority figure with large sway to quiet the hate. This also fits with other accounts of the even-tempered nature of this highly regarded teacher.

comes only through Jesus, not the temple system. Then he says the Holy Spirit is given to those who obey Jesus, which clearly is not the case with them (Acts 5:32).

The fury of a solid section of the Sanhedrin rings out in calls for the death penalty for the apostles. When the allegation is solely a matter of religious law, the Sanhedrin even under Roman rule retains the power to stone to death a convicted violator. The risk was real that the apostles would meet a sudden end on earth. (On why the priests did not just stone Jesus themselves, or stir up a rent-a-mob to do it, see chapter 3.)

Interceding for them is an unlikely luminary, a respected Pharisee. He is the leading teacher of his time, Gamaliel. He asserts that the movement will run out of steam by itself if it is false. If on the outside chance it is from God, then it would be impossible to suppress. The hands-off argument wins the day (see also chapter 4).

However, this time, the Sanhedrin does not stop with just a warning to the apostles. They are flogged with whips and ordered again not to speak about Jesus before they are released. The risk of suffering for advocating the message has increased, but the indomitable apostles leave rejoicing *"because they had been counted worthy of suffering disgrace for the Name"* (Acts 5:41).

## Near Misses at Martyrdom for Some, Not for Others

Another follower of Jesus is not as fortunate when he encounters the Jewish authorities. His name is Stephen, a Greek name meaning "crown." He makes a brief entrance and exit, yet his is one of the most intense cameos in the NT narrative. It is not known at which point he joins the disciples. He is described as Greek speaking, which probably means it is his first language rather than Aramaic. Luke characterizes him as *"full of faith"* and *"of the Holy Spirit"* and someone through whom God is doing healings. He is one of seven spiritually minded deacons whom the apostles assign to manage the distribution of food to needy widows of multiple ethnicities among the thousands of believers the Jesus movement now comprises (Acts 6:5–7).

Stephen is well educated and articulate; he readily engages in debate with other Hellenistic, Greek-speaking Jews who are not believers. They probably have come to Jerusalem for a festival though none is specified in the account. Luke notes that these Jews are from outside Israel, from places like Cyrene (Libya), Alexandria (Egypt), Cilicia (southern Turkey, also home of Paul), and Asia (western Turkey).

Their debate gets heated. Stephen humiliates them with his arguments while they accuse him of the loaded charge of *"blasphemy."* He supposedly is preaching against the Law of Moses and against the temple. It gets physical, and the angry mob drags Stephen to the Sanhedrin for a hearing (Acts 6:8–12).

Apparently due to Stephen's rhetorical skill, the Sanhedrin sits attentively while he relates Israelite history stretching back to Abraham. Those in this audience supposedly know their faith history and could have been expected to cut him off sooner. Stephen's presentation is the longest recorded apostolic speech. The excerpts from the speech recounted by Luke show an approach different from the preaching of Peter in the streets on Pentecost. Peter proclaims Jesus as predicted by David in the book of Psalms. Stephen presents a broad sweep of history to draw an analogy between Moses and Jesus. This analogy shows the present Jewish leadership in a very bad light.

Stephen starts with Abraham. His focus is not on the promise that Abraham's offspring will bless all humanity (Gen. 22:18, 26:4–5); it is on the promise that his people will be in a foreign land for four hundred years and then be liberated (Gen. 15:13). Yet when God raises Moses to fulfill his promise, the Israelites reject him at first. Moses flees to remote pasturelands for forty years. Even after the people are liberated from Egypt and camping in the wilderness, they mutiny against Moses. They complain when he is gone too long in the cloud atop a mountain, where he goes to receive God's commandments. They form a statue, an idol, made from melted-down gold in the shape of a calf, a symbol of Baal, the god of rain and hence fertility in the Canaanite religions. It is a famous symbol in Israelite history of abandoning the one true God for other gods.

### Leaders Rage When Stephen Says They Defy Moses

Stephen focuses on these instances of misguided rejection of God's purposes. He then points out how Moses promised that God would raise up *"a prophet like me"* (Acts 7:37, referring to Deut. 18:15). Essentially, Stephen claims that God sent Moses to deliver the people of Israel but that generation rejected him; then Moses predicted the coming of Jesus as deliverer, and now, the Jewish leaders in this very council have rejected Jesus in this generation. The irony grows obvious: they claim to esteem Moses and all he taught, but they reject the very one Moses predicted would be sent to fulfill their nation's destiny.

In both cases, the generation rejects God's purposes and their own deliverance. Then Stephen brings up the point that God does not dwell in temples. *"However, the Most High does not live in houses made by human hands"* (Acts 7:48). This point seems to come out of the blue until Stephen uses the phrase *"made by human hands"* to describe the temple. It is similar to the term he uses to describe the golden calf. He implies that the temple system is now corrupt like the worship of the golden calf. *"They brought sacrifices to it and reveled in what their own hands had made"* (Acts 7:41). Assuming the leaders perceive the implication, it would raise their ire. Then Stephen deploys what seems to be a trigger word sure to rile them; he says they are just like their *"stiff-necked"* ancestors. This accusation engenders more anger.

Stephen adds to the charges. Those of the temple hierarchy resist the Holy Spirit, they persecute the prophets, they kill those who *"predicted the coming of the Righteous One,"* and then to cap it off, they betray and murder the Messiah himself. They may have received the law of God like no other nation, but they have not obeyed it. This series of charges is already enough to get Stephen stoned to death. His furious audience gnashes their teeth at him, but he does not back down in the face of virulent anger and accusation. He calls out, *"Look!" he said, "I see heaven open and the Son of Man standing at the right hand of God!"* (Acts 7:56). He asserts the recently executed Jesus now stands in the position of triumphal authority. This qualifies to the ears of the hearers as blasphemy—making a man equal with God. So they cover their ears as if not to hear. It is a gesture in the culture that convicts the perpetrator of blasphemy.

The rhythm of the narrative then crescendos with the crowd rushing to drag him outside the city to be stoned, and the Sanhedrin does not stand in its way. Unlike the prior hearings with Peter and John, the crowd in this case is on the side of applying the death penalty. The Sanhedrin follows the crowd.

To free their arms for better aim, the stone throwers shed their cloaks at the feet of a young, Greek-speaking OT scholar from Cilicia named Saul. He has come from a family of Pharisees to Jerusalem to study under Gamaliel. He is a student and an activist. He has no intention of following Gamaliel's earlier advice to the Sanhedrin to let the Jesus movement run out of steam by itself (see chapter 4).

Saul ignites a harsher and expanded persecution of Jesus followers. He targets not simply apostles or preachers, but all believers, not just men but also women; they are apprehended at the temple or in the street, hunted down, and dragged out of their homes to prison. For some, their fate is death. And this happens not just in Jerusalem. As they scatter to outlying areas, Saul organizes brigades with letters from the high priests to chase them down far and wide as far north as Damascus (225 miles or 360 kilometers). He hauls them back to stand trial and be punished in Jerusalem by imprisonment or death (Acts 8:1–3, 26:10; Gal. 1:13).

Although hundreds of believers flee to parts unknown, the account in Luke notes that for some reason, the leading apostles remain in Jerusalem despite the outbreak of persecution (see chapter 8). Possibly some limited immunity was granted to them based on the compromise proposed by Gamaliel at their hearing (Acts 5:38, see chapter 4).

### One Inner Circle Disciple Is Executed by a King

If there was some early level of immunity from the Sanhedrin contingent, it did not turn out to extend to other controlling authorities. Herod Antipas, the ruler who beheaded John the Baptist, is banished in AD 39 to Gaul (today's France) for disloyalty to the new emperor Caligula. A nephew of Antipas, Herod Agrippa I, grandson of Herod the Great and school chum of Caligula, takes over Galilee and Perea.[32]

In Acts, Luke records that during his reign, Agrippa I beheads one of the three disciples in Jesus's inner circle, James the brother of John. In an earlier episode on the way to Jerusalem, James and John famously asked Jesus if they could sit on thrones on either side of him when he comes to power in his kingdom. His reply was a sobering question: were they able to drink the cup he was to drink? (Mk 10:35–40). James certainly does drink the metaphorical cup of an early and untimely death; he is beheaded

---

[32] See "Herod Agrippa I, King of Judaea," brittanica.com, *Encyclopaedia Britannica*, n.d.

about ten or so years after Jesus is crucified in contrast to his brother John, who lives the longest of the original disciples.

To lose one of the original disciples was a serious setback. Apparently, Agrippa I is seeking to ingratiate himself with the Jewish leaders. To that end, he decides to take a step further and imprison Peter right before Passover in AD 44. He intends to hold a public trial after the holiday.

The entourage of apostles is fervent in prayer for Peter's deliverance from the tyrant. Despite being heavily guarded, Peter escapes through the divine intervention of an angel, and his guards are summarily executed by the king (Acts 12:6–19).

Before the year is out, Agrippa I keels over in public while accepting adulation from a crowd gathered for games in a stadium in Caesarea. He suffers a sudden, excruciating disease—divine punishment for his hubris according to the accounts in Acts (12:19–24) and in Josephus (*Antiquities* 19.8.2).

> Historical Portal:
> ## Agrippa I Gains a Grip on Galilee
>
> Rival relatives vie to reign over Galilee in AD 39. Herod Antipas tries to preempt the rise of his nephew, Herod Agrippa I, by denouncing him to the new emperor, Caligula. It backfires. Antipas is undermined by his nephew, who makes a counteraccusation of disloyalty to the empire based on a large arsenal Antipas has amassed. As a youth, Agrippa I had become a friend of Caligula in Rome. By successfully undercutting his uncle, he gains control over the territory of Galilee and Perea. He adds it to his eastern province of Gaulinitis, which he obtained in AD 34 after the death of Philip, another of his uncles.

---

Found in the Ground:
### Herodian Theater or Hippodrome

Caesarea Maritima, Israel—City site found in 1873. Herod Agrippa
I, grandson of Herod the Great, executes James, one of the twelve
disciples of Jesus, and imprisons and plans to execute Peter before
his harrowing escape (Acts 12:1–19). Luke narrates Agrippa's
comeuppance when he addresses a crowd gathered for games in
Caesarea. They worship him as a god; he does not deter them, and
he is struck with a fatal condition and dies shortly afterward. This
moment might be treated as fictional by some scholars if not for a
parallel account of the event in a secular history by the Jewish-Roman
writer Josephus (*Antiquities* 19.8.2). Josephus knew Agrippa
II personally and collected information from his histories directly
from him. This stadium or amphitheater held 20,000 spectators.
Remnants of it can be seen today, though recently, part of the area
reportedly has been used as a banana field. The site supports
Luke's account in Acts of the death of the king, who is the first ruler
to order the execution of an original disciple. (Acts 12:19–24)

Index 5.2

---

The death of James the brother of John, son of Zebedee and
Salome, is the only one recorded in the NT from among the
original disciples. This fact probably means that his death is
the first one from among that group aside from the betrayer
Judas, who commits suicide most likely before Jesus is raised
(Mt 27:5, Acts 1:18–19). Stephen nevertheless retains his place as
the first Christian martyr. Both history and tradition point to
more killings of the original disciples. However, most of their
martyrdoms happen much later after they have had the chance
to spread the message of Jesus to other regions.[33]

---

[33] Tradition finds nearly every one of the original disciples is martyred
eventually. Among these accounts are Thomas in India, Philip in Asia
Minor (southwestern Turkey), and Matthew in Persia or Ethiopia. See
Patrick J. Kiger, "How Did the Apostles Die?" 19 Feb 2015, channel.national

## Church Leader in Jerusalem Is Executed by a High Priest

One grievous, unjust end comes to another apostle, James the brother of Jesus. Not an original disciple, but a convert after the risen Jesus appears to him, James provides years of core leadership to the original Jerusalem church.

The NT evidence shows he is held in the same high esteem as Peter and John if not higher. He and Peter team up to lead a key council recorded in Acts that determines that non-Jews need not keep the laws of Moses (Acts 15:5–21). When Paul returns to Jerusalem for the last time, he reports to James as the leader of the other elders (Acts 21:18). The group requests that Paul ritually cleanse at the temple to prove his faith to help counter critics who claim Paul is teaching rebellion against the Mosaic law (see chapter 6).

When Peter leaves for Rome and John leaves for Ephesus sometime around twenty years after the crucifixion, James continues as the chief leader in Jerusalem. He is broadly accepted as the author of the NT book that bears his name. Yet the account of his death is not included in Acts or any other NT writings but comes through the writing of Josephus.

In AD 62, a high priest plots to kill James. It so happens that this rogue priest is the youngest and last of the five sons of the former high priest Annas. Annas himself serves as the first high priest under Roman rule during AD 6–15 but is deposed by the Roman governor at the time, Gratus. Thereafter, Annas rotates his sons through the priesthood to remain in control for at least twenty-five years. He even puts in the work rotation of his priestly pawns his son-in-law, Joseph Caiaphas, the official high priest at the night trial of Jesus.

Annas, however, was deeply involved in the machinations that put Jesus on the cross. Now it is about thirty years later.

geographic.com, *National Geographic;* and Ken Curtis, "Whatever Happened to the Twelve Apostles?" christianity.com, *Christianitymobile.com,* 28 April 2010; and Brian Kelly, "How Did the Apostles Die?" catholicism.org, *Saint Benedict Center,* 12 Apr 2016.

Annas has died, and so has his son-in-law Caiaphas. This man, the youngest son of Annas, is now the current high priest. He has been prevented by the Roman governor from acting against James. A gap suddenly occurs between the governors during a transition. This son of Annas, actually named Ananus, pounces during that time; he executes James by stoning him for supposedly breaking the Law of Moses despite the reputation of James among believers and nonbelievers alike for carefully keeping the religious law. James longed for the salvation of his fellow Jewish people; it was said his knees grew hardened like a camel's from praying on his floor for their salvation.[34]

Historical Portal:
**The Unjust Death of James**

The high priest strikes when the Roman governor Porcius Festus dies and the newly appointed one, Albinus, remains on the way. The account of the death of James the brother of Jesus comes from Josephus (*Antiquities* 20.9.1). Another account arrives from Hegesippus (AD 110–180) by way of Eusebius (*Church History* 2.23.6) but does not have as much scholarly endorsement. Hegesippus dramatizes the death of James with an account where he is thrown off the temple wall, then stoned, yet still barely alive, until he is clubbed on the head to death with a laundry rod. While the accounts differ on some deathly details, they are in accord on the injustice James suffers.

Many of the nonpriestly Jewish leaders object to this extrajudicial murder and make it known to the next Roman governor, who thus appoints a new high priest. Several years later in the days leading up to the Jewish revolt, Ananus himself is

---

[34] The report of the praying intensity of James comes from Eusebius (*Church History* 2.23.6), see Eusebius Pamphilius: "Church History, Chapter XXIII—The Martyrdom of James, who was called the Brother of the Lord." Christian Classics Ethereal Library, ccel.org, NPNV2-01.

killed; in AD 66, Jewish rebel leaders execute him for advocating peace with Rome (*War* 4.5.2).

## Outside Israel Roman Rulers Execute Apostles

Philip, an original disciple, is a fisherman with roots in Bethsaida on the Sea of Galilee similar to his fellow boaters and friends Peter, James and John. He is the one at the Last Supper with Jesus who is recorded by John to have asked Jesus, *"Lord, show us the Father"* (Jn 14:8).

Tradition holds Philip moves out to preach in Syria and Greece. In the end, he is beheaded and buried as a martyr in the spa city of Hierapolis in southwestern Turkey. Certain scholars think his tomb has been found, though some associate the location and martyrdom account with the other Philip, who is featured in Acts first as a deacon and later commonly known as Philip the Evangelist or Deacon (more on this Philip in chapter 9).

Found in the Ground:
## Tomb of One Philip or Another

Hierapolis, Turkey—Found in 2011. A shrine or *martyrium* has been known for ages marking the death of Philip. About forty yards away, a first-century Roman tomb was found below a Byzantine church built around it. Writings on the walls and the structure of the tomb reveal its first-century character and association with Philip. Philip is thought to have died about AD 80 as a martyr by beheading or crucifixion. No human remains were found, but that is not surprising due to traditions holding they were transported to Constantinople and then to Rome.

The question of which Philip migrated to Hierapolis has been confusing Christians since the early centuries. Is it Philip the Disciple and the Apostle mentioned in the gospels especially in John (6:5-7, 12:20-22), or is it Philip the Deacon and the Evangelist mentioned in Acts? (Acts 6:5, 8:5.) Both connected well with Greek speakers. Philip the Evangelist was a fellow deacon with the martyred Stephen, a father of four daughters known for their prophesying, and a host based in Caesarea for Paul and Luke on their last trip to Jerusalem (Acts 21:8-9). Whichever person it is who made his way to Hierapolis, the finding of a well-marked tomb of a first-century biblical figure is nothing short of remarkable.

Index 5.3

After two decades of evangelizing people and training disciples in Jerusalem, Peter relocates to Rome (according not to the NT but to tradition based on early church sources). Three months after a fire rages through Rome in October AD 64 on the occasion of the ten-year anniversary of Nero's ascending to the imperial throne, the milestone is celebrated with plentiful bloodshed; it probably includes Peter's crucifixion. Tradition holds that his last request is met: to be crucified upside down because he feels he is not worthy of dying the way his Lord did.

This high level of courage and willingness to suffer death on the part of the leading apostles is praised and used to inspire others by the second-generation apostle Clement of Rome. About the mid–AD 90s, during the dangerous reign of the emperor Domitian, he writes a letter to Christians at Corinth who face persecution. He hails heroes of the faith from the OT scriptures such as Joseph, Moses, and David. Then he comes to shining examples of their own day in the first century who not only suffered but also gave their lives for their faith.

> *But let us pass from ancient examples, and come unto those who have in times nearest to us, wrestled for the faith. Let us take the noble examples of our own generation. Through jealousy and envy the greatest and most just pillars of the church were persecuted, and came even unto death. Let us place before our eyes the good Apostles. Peter, through unjust envy, endured not one or two but many labors, and at last, having delivered his testimony, departed unto the place of glory due to him. (Clement of Rome 5, 1–4)[35]*

Paul also is executed in Rome during the reign of Nero; he probably was beheaded around AD 67.[36] (More of Paul's journey is covered in chapters 6 and 7.) Clement eulogizes him and holds him up to the suffering Corinthians as an example of endurance.

> *Paul too showed by example the prize that is given to patience: seven times was he cast into chains; he was banished; he was stoned; having become a herald, both in the East and in the West, he obtained the noble renown due to his faith; and having preached righteousness*

[35] Clement, *First Epistle to the Corinthians*, tr. Charles H. Hoole, 1885, earlychristianwritings.com, n.d, n.p.
[36] Dionysius of Corinth, in his Letter to Romans (c. AD 165–175) confirms Peter and Paul are martyred in Italy. Cited by Eusebius (c. AD 320), who also drew from Caius, *Disputation Against Proclus* (c. AD 198). For the full text, see Dionysius of Corinth, "Fragments from a Letter to the Roman Church" III, earlychristianwritings.com, Peter Kirby, ed. 2017, tr. Alexander Roberts and James Donaldson, c. 1900.

*to the whole world, and having come to the extremity*
*of the West, having borne witness before rulers, he*
*departed at length out of the world, and went to the holy*
*place, having become the greatest example of patience.*
*(Clement of Rome 5, 5–7)*[37]

In the end, most of the apostles—the more and less prominent alike—eventually suffer martyrdom but not before they get the word out, mentor more disciples, plant churches, write letters, and propel an unstoppable force that makes the message of Jesus sustainable and powerful in every generation thereafter.

---

[37] Clement, *Corinthians*.

# 5: CONCLUSION

## On the Risks the Disciples Take to Preach Jesus

The apostles fulfill their commission to get the word out. Nevertheless, in their Mediterranean world of authoritarian governments, it is a high-risk occupation to proclaim that Jesus is the Lord and Savior of humanity and that he will return to rule on earth as he does in heaven.

For three centuries, earthly authorities do not take kindly to the message. In the early decades, under the Jewish priesthood and Sanhedrin, the cultural risk that the disciples take is being charged with blasphemy. This was the charge made against Jesus by the high priest at the night trial, after which he tore his robes to signify the defendant was worthy of death. The disciples risk this charge every time they speak. Violators face the death penalty by stoning, or at least being cast out of their Jewish community with the spiritual threat that they likewise will forfeit an eternal destiny with God. Under the Jewish royal rulers, the charge can be most anything and the penalty is death by beheading. Under the Roman authorities, the charge is claiming there is a king greater than Caesar, or the charge is espousing atheism, defined as not worshiping Roman gods.

Executions usually are done by stoning, beheading or crucifixion, but the apostles do not flinch in the face of these cultural risks, these constant life-and-death situations. Their willingness to lay their lives on the line does not prove by itself that they were right about the resurrection of Jesus. What it does prove is that they died sincerely believing it to be true. Would this many people die for a hoax they had dreamed up themselves?

# CHAPTER

# LINE OF EVIDENCE

## SUMMARY

A brilliant, young student of Jewish law leaves his prosperous city in today's southwestern Turkey. He wants to study under a leading educator of the Pharisee persuasion in Jerusalem. After settling in the city, he gets intensely agitated when he sees an outbreak of a heretical sect of Jews. These false believers claim that the Jewish Messiah has come in Jesus, a low-income rabbi from the backwaters of the agrarian region of Galilee. The earnest student in his late twenties rallies an armed force and drags these heretics out of their homes, both women and men. He imprisons them, and some are put to death.

When many others flee north to Damascus, he gains authorization from the ruling priests to follow them and bring them back. His momentum suddenly stops. On the road to Damascus, he is blinded by a burst of light and disavows his prior ideology. He embraces Jesus as the Jewish Messiah. He goes on to found churches around the Mediterranean. His letters to these churches are preserved and make up a large part of the New Testament. This former enforcer of Jewish law becomes the most persistent evangelist for the other side, the good news of God's grace in Jesus.

When such a public opponent switches sides in a historical situation, a cause must be sufficient to explain such a radical and decisive change. His first-person accounts in letters along with reports and speech excerpts compiled by his travel companion Luke in the book of Acts make it clear why his reality is altered and he never turns back: Paul encounters a risen Jesus.

# PRELUDE

## CHAPTER 6

**H**e is a disciple of Jesus, though he lives in Damascus, about 225 miles or 360 kilometers north of Jerusalem. The city had been part of Israel during the reigns of two of its greatest kings, David and Solomon. Now in the early AD 30s, it is run by the Roman governor of Syria. There are many Jewish synagogues in Damascus, and Jesus believers still mingle with them freely.

Ananias seems accustomed to speaking with the risen Jesus personally in interactive prayer. He does not sound surprised when Jesus calls him by name. What alarms him is what the Lord asks him to do. He directs his servant to place his hands on a notorious and greatly feared persecutor of believers. This persecutor has enlisted with the high priest in Jerusalem to act as an enforcer of proper Jewish belief and customs. In effect, he becomes the high priest's hatchet man. He arrests and imprisons men and women in Jerusalem. He provokes such fear that many other believers have scattered to outer areas with some seeking safety in Damascus. Now, reports say this fierce enforcer is coming to Damascus to cart away Jewish believers for trial in Jerusalem. Fearing for his own life, Ananias seems desperate to inform the Lord that with all due respect he may not fully grasp the dire situation.

*"Lord," Ananias answered, "I have heard many reports about this man, and all the harm he has done to your*

*holy people in Jerusalem. And he has come here with authority from the chief priests to arrest all who call on your name." (Acts 9:13–14)*

The Lord has a different idea. This man is his *"chosen instrument"* to *"proclaim my name"* before non-Jews, Jews, and kings, so he tells Ananias, *"Go!"*

The interaction in prayer seems to calm and embolden Ananias. He follows directions. He goes to the designated house on the street called Straight, still a main thoroughfare in today's Damascus. He finds a recently blinded man—fasting, broken, not looking like such a fearsome enforcer. Ananias lays his hands on him calling him *"Brother Saul."* He tells him, *"The Lord—Jesus, who appeared to you on the road as you were coming here—has sent me so that you may see again and be filled with the Holy Spirit"* (Acts 9:17). Ananias ensures that Saul is baptized and introduces him to other disciples (Acts 9:1–19).

Within days, this energetic and articulate convert starts preaching in the Jewish synagogues that Jesus is the Messiah. In a short time, he causes serious controversy to the point that his life is threatened. He must flee. Believers sneak him out of Damascus at night by lowering him down the city wall in a large woven basket tied to a rope. Little did Ananias know the revolutionary impact this chosen instrument Saul, better known by his Roman name Paulus shortened to Paul, would make on the Mediterranean world of his own time and then, through his powerful letters to start-up churches, on many generations to come.

## CHAPTER 6

---

# A FIERCE ENFORCER
# SWITCHES SIDES

---

At least forty men have sworn a vow not to eat until they kill a leading missionary of the Jesus movement, the apostle Paul, formerly known as Saul of Tarsus. They are deadly serious. As Greek-speaking Jews, they come from the same areas and display the same hostility as did those who stoned Stephen to death about twenty-five years earlier.

Yet the mob cannot get to Paul easily. He is holed up in the robust stone fortress in Jerusalem called Antonia. It lies in the northwest corner of the temple mount in Jerusalem. The Romans use the fortress to keep the peace. They station about six hundred soldiers there, more at times when three annual pilgrimage feasts swell the population of the city. It is practically impregnable.

### A Diabolical Plot to Assassinate an Apostate

Nevertheless, these fasting vigilantes have a plan. They ask the priests to manipulate the Roman commander so that he brings Paul to the Sanhedrin for additional interrogation. They want to position him at a more vulnerable place in the temple complex. At that point, they will pounce. Imagine the irony—the young man who stood by approving the stoning of Stephen and then ignited a persecution that drove hundreds of Jesus people out of Jerusalem is now decades later in his early fifties the target himself. Once the hunter, he is now the hunted (Acts 7:57–58, 23:12–15).

---

### Historical Portal:
### The Antonia Fortress Guards the Temple Complex

The Antonia Fortress is named after the Roman general Mark Antony. He commanded the Roman legions in the east under Julius Caesar before he was assassinated. Antony schemes with his lover, Cleopatra, queen of Egypt, to wage a naval battle on the Ionian Sea at Actium. The battle is for primacy in the Roman republic against Octavian, Caesar's adopted son, and Antony's ex-brother-in-law. In 31 BC, the forces of Antony and Cleopatra are defeated, and Octavian proceeds to become Emperor Augustus.

Herod the Great built the fortress in Antony's honor just four years earlier in 35 BC. Wily politician that he was, Herod deftly switched his loyalty from Antony to Octavian after the naval battle. About one hundred years later in AD 66, the Romans will lose control of the fortress during the Jewish war. However, they know its floor plan well. An underground access point will be the linchpin that the Romans use finally to break the siege defenses of Jerusalem and invade and destroy the city in AD 70, a little more than a decade after the temple riot over Paul in the late AD 50s.

---

### *Paul's Switcheroo Is Significant Historical Evidence*

Looking at the perils of Paul in some detail puts us in touch with someone whose very life journey is a line of evidence for the resurrection. Paul is a witness to Jesus in his exalted existence. He encounters Jesus not during the resurrection week or in the following forty days of appearances but at least a year or two later. What is so historically significant about his life is the way he suddenly switches sides. He morphs from a fiery Pharisee out to imprison or kill Jewish believers in Jesus into the most irrepressible evangelist of Jesus to his fellow Jews to be sure, but especially to non-Jews, Gentiles. We need to figure out why he switches.

The historical information on Paul is well documented from first-century sources. Initially, it comes in Paul's own first-person letters written approximately between AD 48 and 62. Later, it comes in a sweeping account of Paul's ministry written by Luke, the same author of the gospel that customarily bears his name. Luke seems to have been converted by Paul probably in the town of Troas, on the western coast of today's Turkey. It was likely Luke's hometown. Luke himself then travels with Paul to Macedonia and Greece as shown by the way Luke changes the pronouns to employ the first-person plural "we" (Acts 16:10).

To offer a holistic picture of Paul's life and to help you assess his witness profile, I will turn largely to Luke's narrative in this chapter. It shows how Paul goes about his empire-shaking ministry, how he faces his opponents, and how he adjusts his preaching of the resurrection to his ethnically diverse listeners. Nevertheless, historically speaking, the best evidence for Paul's change of heart comes in his own words found in his letters. These letters qualify as primary sources. In historical work, primary sources usually are preferred over secondary sources. Luke's narrative proceeds as a secondary source up until he meets Paul in Troas. Once Luke includes himself as part of Paul's entourage, the narrative in effect changes to a first-person account and therefore becomes a primary source.

Yet Luke is writing less about himself than he is about the key protagonist—Paul—whose written words still serve as our best historical evidence for his radical, life-altering reorientation. We will look first at key parts of Paul's letters in which he reflects on his life change. Then we will follow in Acts the consequences his turnabout holds for the direction of his life, which alters the history of the Western World as we know it.

Paul addresses one of his earliest letters to churches in Galatia, in central Turkey. He is alarmed at reports that the churches are slipping back into a mentality that they must keep Jewish law to be part of the Jesus community. Those who are teaching this system in contrast to what Paul taught them denounce Paul as being a second-class apostle. They charge that he has garbled a gospel message that he obtained secondhand. Paul defends himself by showing how he gained his gospel straight from Jesus.

> *I want you to know, brothers and sisters, that the gospel I preached is not of human origin. I did not receive it from any man, nor was I taught it; rather, I received it by revelation from Jesus Christ. For you have heard of my previous way of life in Judaism, how intensely I persecuted the church of God and tried to destroy it. I was advancing in Judaism beyond many of my own age among my people and was extremely zealous for the traditions of my fathers. (Galatians 1:11–14)*

Paul explains how he had his own encounter with God and did not consult with other leading apostles for several years. He took his own path and eventually returned to his home region in southern Turkey. He had not come out publicly as a believer in his former city of Jerusalem.

> *I was personally unknown to the churches of Judea that are in Christ. They only heard the report: "The man who formerly persecuted us is now preaching the faith he once tried to destroy." And they praised God because of me. (Galatians 1:22–24)*

It took a while for believers to embrace Paul because he had earned such a bad reputation as a virulent foe of their community. Later in his ministry, Paul again brings up in a letter to believers in

Corinth how it happened that he switched sides. The Corinthians are doubting whether believers among them who die will be raised from the dead. Paul goes back to the basics of the faith and stipulates the reality of the death, burial, resurrection, and appearances of Jesus. He includes his own encounter with Jesus on the tail end of the list of appearances (1 Cor. 15:7-8). Almost instinctively and probably due to the constant undercutting of his authority by his critics, Paul takes off on a short tangent to justify his own apostleship and to brag perhaps just a bit.

> *For I am the least of the apostles and do not even deserve to be called an apostle, because I persecuted the church of God. But by the grace of God I am what I am, and his grace to me was not without effect. No, I worked harder than all of them—yet not I, but the grace of God that was with me. Whether, then, it is I or they, this is what we preach, and this is what you believed.*
> *(1 Corinthians 15:9-11)*

Paul then returns to the issue of whether dead humans will be raised. He argues that their resurrection is linked inextricably to Jesus's resurrection: if the dead are not raised, Jesus was not raised, and vice versa—if Jesus has been raised, they will be raised. (More detail concerning Paul's response on this assertion comes later in this chapter.)

Further, historical evidence of his switch comes in another letter from Paul when again he is under fire later in his life. He writes to believers in Philippi, on the Greek coast (c. AD 62). They are getting the message that they need to be circumcised to be saved or at least to be fully devoted, elite followers of Jesus. (Circumcision is the cutting of the male foreskin after a boy is born, usually eight days after in Jewish culture; see more on the circumcision issue in this chapter when Paul confronts his critics.) Paul will have none of this talk. All believers are spiritually circumcised. Their standing with God is based on receiving his grace in the work of Jesus through faith. There is no human performance involved. He would know.

Under the rules of Judaism, Paul, the persecutor formerly known as Saul, was the ultimate human performer. He calls external performance putting *"confidence in the flesh."* The term *flesh* carries the meaning here of human effort independent of God's power. He relates this meaning of *flesh* to another meaning associated with circumcision. When he blisteringly condemns *"those mutilators of the flesh"* (his graphic language for knife-wielding circumcisers), he speaks from experience because he was formerly one of them.

> *Watch out for those dogs, those evildoers, those mutilators of the flesh. For it is we who are the circumcision, we who serve God by his Spirit, who boast in Christ Jesus, and who put no confidence in the flesh—though I myself have reasons for such confidence. If someone else thinks they have reasons to put confidence in the flesh, I have more: circumcised on the eighth day, of the people of Israel, of the tribe of Benjamin, a Hebrew of Hebrews; in regard to the law, a Pharisee; as for zeal, persecuting the church; as for righteousness based on the law, faultless. But whatever were gains to me I now consider loss for the sake of Christ. What is more, I consider everything a loss because of the surpassing worth of knowing Christ Jesus my Lord, for whose sake I have lost all things. I consider them garbage, that I may gain Christ and be found in him, not having a righteousness of my own that comes from the law, but that which is through faith in Christ—the righteousness that comes from God on the basis of faith. (Philippians 3:2–9)*

Paul reaches back into his own biography from thirty years earlier to reinforce his core message that connecting with God in Jesus comes by faith, by trusting God, not by law keeping. These excerpts alone from Paul's letters are sufficient evidence to make the historical argument that the former enforcer of Jewish belief and practice suddenly switches sides and joins those he formerly persecuted. Paul's life change is an epic historical event that is exceedingly well documented. It adds substantially to the credibility of the claim that the resurrection of Jesus occurred in history. Paul's turnaround is difficult to explain if the bones of Jesus lie moldering in a stone ossuary in Jerusalem.

## NT Covers Paul's Trips and Speeches, Not Just Letters

It is valuable for the reader who is not that familiar with Paul and his intense personality to see how his radical switch played out over the succeeding decades. It is much simpler to trace the longer arc of his life not through his occasional letters but through the action-packed narrative of Paul's hazardous missionary work as recorded by Luke in Acts.

Before we plunge into the account, take note of one important factor. Luke recounts several excerpts from the speeches Paul makes as he travels to cities around the Mediterranean world. In this era as well as in preceding centuries, speeches figure prominently in the genre of Greco-Roman historical writing, and Luke adopts this standard technique. Unsurprisingly, critics try to assert that Luke himself makes up the speeches out of thin air. Without modern recording devices, these speech excerpts would not likely be rendered exactly word for word, yet it is highly likely that Luke captures the gist of Paul's orations.[38] Luke knows Paul, he travels with Paul, he is present on some of the occasions of the speeches, and he remains at Paul's side in Rome near the end (Philemon 24; Acts 16:10, 27:2, 28:16, 30). For those occasions where he was not present, he could easily have interviewed Paul to gain a sense of what was said in those moments. His personal interactions with Paul, his sophisticated style of writing, and the

---

[38] F. F. Bruce, *Speeches*. See chapter 4 for full reference, and *Background Guide*, resource 1 for more explanation on the role of speeches in the culture.

way archaeological discoveries have continued to support his accounts make Luke a highly reliable narrator and a solid source of historical evidence.

## An Effort to Follow Mosaic Law Goes Awry

> Bible Sidelight:
> **Purification Rite**
>
> It is not completely clear from the account, but the four men probably are following the purification rite for those who have committed to the Nazirite vow (Num. 6:13–21). The vow involves growing one's hair long and not shaving the face. In the event of breaking the vow by being near a dead body, one restarts the vow by shaving one's head and making detailed sacrifices.

We rejoin the action as reported by Luke where Paul has gotten himself into a life-threatening situation at the temple. It was not really Paul's plan to visit the temple precinct. He is asked to go there by the leader of the Jerusalem church, James the brother of Jesus. Four men in the church already were planning to take a purification rite. The seven-day rite involves shaving one's head on the day of cleansing and offering carefully prescribed sacrifices. James advises Paul to join them and to pay their expenses. (Fortunately, Paul has shaved his head before, so he has that hirsute detail down pat; Acts 18:18). James knows Paul's reputation is being sliced apart with heavy criticism. Those critics rail against Paul for not keeping the Law of Moses himself and for teaching Jews living among Gentiles that they do not need to keep it either. James hopes everyone will see that Paul remains obedient to the law. This will help keep the societal heat off the Jerusalem church.

This somewhat staged public moment at the temple turns precarious, however. Greek-speaking Jews from the province of Asia (today's Turkey), where Paul has gone on three missionary journeys, recognize him as a heretical teacher. They shout, *"This is the man who teaches everyone everywhere against our people and our law and this place"* (Acts 21:28). They accuse him falsely of bringing one of his Greek friends (Trophimus, Acts 21:28–29) to the temple and supposedly defiling it. The narrative in Acts recounts people running from all directions to help seize Paul, drag him from the temple courts, shut the gates behind him, and attempt to beat him to death. The Roman commander and his soldiers stream out of their fortress to break up the crowd, arrest Paul, and bind him with two chains. The crowd quiets for a moment, and the commander asks Paul what he has done to upset so many people.

The shouting starts all over again. He orders Paul to be taken into the fortress. The crowd presses the soldiers, yelling and jostling. As they reach the fortress steps, the mob surges at Paul, and the soldiers have to carry (all reportedly less than five feet of) him up the steps.[39] The crowd has a simple solution: *"Get rid of him!"* (Acts 21:36b).

> Found in the Ground:
> **Temple Warning Inscriptions**
>
> Jerusalem—These plaques function as Do Not Enter or Off Limits signs. The first one is found in 1871, the second in 1935. The most complete plaque reads that any trespasser "will invite death for himself" should he go beyond the three foot or one meter high boundary wall marking the point from which non-Jews could go no farther toward the temple (Acts 21:27–29). The signs are cited in Josephus (*War* 5.5.2, 6.2.4, *Antiquities* 15.11.3). These findings support the account in Acts of the false accusations against Paul for trespassing this boundary with his non-Jewish companion, Trophimus, from Ephesus. (Acts 21:27–30)
>
> Index 6.1

---

[39] The name Paulus means "small" or in some definitions "humble." A certain second-century otherwise unreliable account asserts that Paul was bowlegged and considered "homo tricubitalis," meaning he stood less than five feet tall. The description of Paul may reflect accurate oral tradition despite the spurious nature of the overall account known as *The Acts of Paul and Thecla*.

**Paul Never Lets a Good Riot Go to Waste**

Paul, always one to have his wits about him and to take advantage of an opportunity, asks the commander if he can speak to the crowd from the steps.

> *"I am a Jew, born in Tarsus of Cilicia, but brought up in this city. I studied under Gamaliel and was thoroughly trained in the law of our ancestors. I was just as zealous for God as any of you are today. I persecuted the followers of this Way to their death, arresting both men and women and throwing them into prison, as the high priest and all the Council can themselves testify. I even obtained letters from them to their associates in Damascus, and went there to bring these people as prisoners to Jerusalem to be punished."* (Acts 22:3–5)

Damascus was a major trading center where caravan routes crisscrossed from Arabia, Persia, Mesopotamia, Anatolia (Turkey) and northern Syria. The high priests who dispatched their rabid enforcer probably figured if they could stamp out the heresy in Damascus they could keep it from spreading to Jewish enclaves throughout the region. Yet the record shows there was a countervailing force wanting the exact opposite to happen.

Paul goes on to describe being blinded by a bright light on the road about noon and hearing Jesus say, *"Saul! Saul! Why do you persecute me?"* He is led to Ananias in Damascus along the street called Straight. Through Ananias, Paul regains his sight. He then tells the crowd how he had returned to Jerusalem several years later. He prays in the temple, falling into a trance. In the trance, he sees the Lord telling him that he must leave Jerusalem because the people will not accept his testimony. Paul protests. His fellow Jews will respond positively he contends because he was one of them in his zeal for the law.

Found in the Ground:
**The Damascus Street Called "Straight"**

Damascus, Syria—An ancient street in Damascus continues to be a main thoroughfare to this day and goes by the same name. The Romans arrive in the first century BC. They use the term "Via Recta" and add a theater at one end. The existing road supports account by Luke in Acts that names this street as the location where Paul was taken after his eyes were blinded on the road to Damascus. Here at the house of a disciple named Judas, Paul would meet a resident Jesus follower, Ananias, who would restore his sight and get Paul baptized. After meeting other disciples, Paul shortly began preaching in the synagogue and proving Jesus was the Messiah, until death threats drove him from the city. (Acts 9:10-25)

Index 6.2

*"'Lord,'" I replied, "'these people know that I went from one synagogue to another to imprison and beat those who believe in you. And when the blood of your martyr Stephen was shed, I stood there giving my approval and guarding the clothes of those who were killing him.'"* (Acts 22:19–20)

He is told nevertheless to go far away to the Gentiles. Conveying this temple dialogue with the risen Jesus sets off the rioters again. They cry, *"Rid the earth of him! He's not fit to live!"* (Acts 22:22). They shout, shed their outer cloaks, and toss dust in the air as if a stoning party is about to begin. The Romans yank Paul back into the fortress and away from the crowd.

The next day, the commander orders the Sanhedrin and the high priests to assemble to figure out the charges against the prisoner. But Paul has other ideas. He quickly strategizes how to divide and conquer this crowd.

> *Then Paul, knowing that some of them were Sadducees and the others Pharisees, called out in the Sanhedrin, "My brothers, I am a Pharisee, descended from Pharisees. I stand on trial because of the hope of the resurrection of the dead."*
>
> *When he said this, a dispute broke out between the Pharisees and the Sadducees, and the assembly was divided. (The Sadducees say that there is no resurrection, and that there are neither angels nor spirits, but the Pharisees believe all these things.) (Acts 23:6–8)*

The country's greatest deliberative body starts to get violent just like the masses in the temple crowd had. (See chapter 4 for more on the rivalry between the Pharisees and Sadducees.) The commander, now aware that Paul is a Roman citizen, fears that Paul will be torn to pieces by these supposedly sober-minded leaders. The soldiers escort him from the sundered Sanhedrin and return him to the fortress for his protection. Yet the danger of the ambush increases by the hour since the forty assassins, still lying in wait, have sworn not to eat until they kill Paul.

### Flashback to the Start of Paul's Unlikely Missionary Career

After Stephen was stoned, the persecution Saul fomented drove hundreds of Jewish believers out of Jerusalem to outlying regions and towns in today's Lebanon and Syria and to the island of Cyprus (Acts 8:1-3, 11:19). Some believers from Cyprus and Cyrene (Libya) land in Antioch.

Historical Portal:
No Trouble in River City for Believers

Antioch is a river city in northern Syria founded by one of the generals of Alexander the Great, Seleucus I Nicator. The city is on multiple trade routes for silk, spices, and many Persian products. The city's river is the Orontes. Its population reached a half million under the Roman emperor Augustus, but it declined due to its vulnerability to earthquakes and to the redirection of trade routes due to the Mongol invasions in the Far East. Jews enjoyed full status as citizens in the city. This made it easier for the Jewish believers to cross over beyond their synagogues to reach the Greek communities with the news of Jesus. Many people of various ethnicities believe. Antioch becomes the key missionary-sending church in outreach to non-Jews.

The church grows rapidly. For the first time, the people *"of the Way"* become known by the term *"Christians"* in Antioch (Acts 11:26).[40] The Jerusalem church leaders send one of their most reliable people to shepherd the Antioch community in Barnabas. He in turn wants to take on an assistant pastor. He decides to recruit the ex-persecutor formerly known as Saul, who is living in his hometown of Tarsus about 150 miles or 240 kilometers away.

After alienating the unbelieving Jews in Damascus soon after he converts and almost getting himself killed, Saul had fled to Arabia. Then after things quieted down, he had returned to Damascus. About three years later, he takes a two-week trip to Jerusalem to meet the core leaders (see chapter 7). Then he ends up in his own hometown of Tarsus, in the region of Cilicia, for a stretch of years amounting to almost a decade until Barnabas comes calling. Saul accepts the offer. The two of them teach the church community in Antioch for a year with growing numbers of believers (Acts 11:26).

---

[40] The term *the Way* for the early Jesus movement arises frequently in Luke's reports (Acts 9:2, 19:23, 22:4, 24:14–15).

## Journey One: City Missions Usually Start in Synagogues

The leaders in Antioch sense a new calling for Barnabas and Saul, who goes more by his Roman name Paul, in pagan lands (Acts 13:2, 9). They send them out as missionaries on a trip first heading to Cyprus, where Barnabas lived earlier (Acts 4:36). Then they go to a set of inland towns in southeastern Turkey. The primary strategy the missionaries adopt is to enter the Jewish synagogue in each town on the Sabbath. Usually, guests are invited to speak. Paul's longest recorded synagogue sermon comes on his visit to a town called Pisidian Antioch (not his base at Syrian Antioch) in today's central Turkey.

---

Found in the Ground:
### Inscriptions of Cyprus Official Who Believes

Cyprus—Two inscriptions with the name Sergius Paulus found c. 1877. A third inscription found in 1887 in Rome records that a Sergius Paulus was one of the managers of the riverbanks and the channel of the Tiber River, a position he could have held before or after serving as proconsul in Cyprus. It is written in Latin and dated to AD 47. These findings support the account in Acts of the first Roman ruler who comes to faith through Paul during his first missionary journey on Cyprus. (Acts 13:4–12)

Index 6.3

---

Paul walks them through their common Jewish history—God liberates them from Egypt, gives them land, installs judges, and meets their request for a king. For insubordination, God removes the first king in favor of the second one, King David. Using this context, Paul then introduces the attendees to David's descendant, Jesus. He explains how the rulers in Jerusalem killed him. Yet in so doing, they unwittingly fulfilled the predictions the prophets made, which are read in their synagogues weekly.

*"From this man's descendants God has brought to Israel the Savior Jesus, as he promised ... We tell you the good news: What God promised our ancestors he has fulfilled for us, their children, by raising up Jesus. As it is written in the second Psalm: 'You are my son; today I have become your father.' God raised him from the dead so that he will never be subject to decay. As God has said, 'I will give you the holy and sure blessings promised to David.' So it is also stated elsewhere: 'You will not let your holy one see decay.'" (Acts 13:23, 32–35)*

He cites Psalm 2:7, Isaiah 55:3, and Psalm 16:10 to show how the prophets foresaw that David's descendant would be raised from the dead. (Note Peter's similar approach in Acts 2:22–32; see chapter 4 and chapter 9 on OT prophecies.) Then he explains how the events apply to his listeners.

*"Therefore, my friends, I want you to know that through Jesus the forgiveness of sins is proclaimed to you. Through him everyone who believes is set free from every sin, a justification you were not able to obtain under the law of Moses." (Acts 13:38–39)*

No riot breaks out that day in Pisidian Antioch; it will take another week. The missionaries are invited back for the next Sabbath, where a larger crowd gathers. This time, some unbelieving Jews heatedly argue against them and *"heaped abuse"* on them (Acts 13:45). Then Paul and Barnabas answered them boldly.

*"We had to speak the word of God to you first. Since you reject it and do not consider yourselves worthy of eternal life, we now turn to the Gentiles. For this is what the Lord has commanded us: 'I have made you a light for the Gentiles, that you may bring salvation to the ends of the earth.'" (Acts 13:46–47 quoting Isaiah 49:6)*

While the many Greeks and other non-Jews embrace this

news along with many Jewish believers, the nonbelieving Jews turn against Barnabas and Paul and expel the two intruders from the city. This pattern repeats itself in other towns along their way. The itinerant missionaries speak in synagogues, win over many people both Jews and non-Jews, then face a vicious backlash (in Iconium, Lystra, and Derbe). At one stop, Paul is stoned and left for dead. Yet he regains consciousness, keeps calm, and carries on (Acts 14:19–20). Both Paul and Barnabas remain undaunted. They backtrack through the same towns that had driven them off and encourage the new believers. Then they head for a coastal port from which they sail for their home base, Antioch.

### To Circumcise or Not to Circumcise–That Is the Question

Back at their base, Paul and Barnabas continue to teach many new believers. A controversy arises whether new male believers must be circumcised to receive salvation through Jesus. Circumcision was the sign of entering into membership in God's salvation community of the nation of Israel. Many Jewish believers thought it should still apply. Obviously, it would hinder acceptance of the good news. In an age without anesthetics, if a man must undergo sensitive surgery to convert, he might think twice about it whereas women would not face any such impediment.

Bible Sidelight:
## The Agonizing Circumcision Question

Circumcision is the custom of cutting the foreskin of the penis shortly after birth (in Jewish tradition, it is done on the eighth day). For Israel, it is a physical indicator that one is in blood covenant with God and belongs to God's covenant people. The custom went back to their common ancestor Abraham (Gen. 17:9–11).

Circumcision is possible but far more painful for adult males. The issue had been building over the years, and it came to a decision point through the ministry of Paul to the nations of non-Jews, or Gentiles (often called Greeks for short). At the council, the consensus ruling favors Paul's contention that no circumcision is needed to be part of the new Jesus community; it has a new covenant on new terms. Membership is based on faith in Jesus's work in the cross and resurrection, not by performing works of the former covenant given through Moses to the ethnic people of Israel.

The larger issue was whether all new believers must follow all the Jewish laws handed down from Moses. A church-wide council is called in Jerusalem to sort it all out, so Paul and Barnabas must attend. Peter cites his experience with the entire household of the Roman officer Cornelius in Caesarea and how the Spirit came upon these Gentiles without their being circumcised (see chapter 4). Should they be required to bear the yoke of circumcision and law keeping? *"No! We believe it is through the grace of our Lord Jesus that we are saved, just as they are,"* Peter declares (Acts 15:11). We do not want to make things *"difficult"* for non-Jewish believers, agrees James the brother of Jesus, who serves as the presiding leader of the church. They write a letter to this effect adding several lifestyle suggestions on diet and sexuality ostensibly to enable Jews and non-Jews to live together in the same communities peacefully (Acts 15:19–21).

## Journey Two: Paul Sails West, the World Is Never the Same

The more sedentary, pastoral life of teaching in the Antioch church does not sit well with Paul. He decides to get back out on the road again for a second missionary journey. He takes Silas with him. Along the way, he adds Timothy in Lystra and Luke in Troas, not far from ancient Troy, in western Turkey (Acts 16:1–10). They do not go south to the cities of Asia (their word for western Turkey) but sail west from Troas to Greece and land in Samothrace. They travel by land through the Greek coastal cities along the western shore of the Aegean Sea. Paul will make these towns forever famous through the letters he later writes to these churches (namely Philippians, Thessalonians, and Corinthians). At Thessalonica, we see his strategy.

> Found in the Ground:
> **The Egnatian Way**
>
> Albania to Turkey—This was Rome's major road to link its capital city to its colonies in the east. The road began on the east side of the Adriatic Sea. It was almost opposite of the terminus of the Appian Way on the west side of the sea at Brindisi, so ships could take the fastest route. The road crossed over the Jablanica mountain ridge and lake country to the coastline of Greece first at Thessalonica and then north through Greece on to Byzantium, later Constantinople, now Istanbul. The finding of the route supports Paul's reported itinerary through Neopolis, Philippi, Amphipolis, Apollonia and Thessalonica traveling from east to west. (Acts 16:11–12, 17:1)
>
> Index 6.4

> As was his custom, Paul went into the synagogue, and on three Sabbath days he reasoned with them from the Scriptures, explaining and proving that the Messiah had to suffer and rise from the dead. "This Jesus I am proclaiming to you is the Messiah," he said. (Acts 17:2–3)

Many Jews in Thessalonica believe, but others form a mob and start a riot. They attack the home where Paul is staying. Paul is nowhere to be found, but he and Silas figure they had better leave town by night and head south for Berea.

Some of these unbelieving Jews from Thessalonica keep chasing Paul down the coast. He leaves Silas and Timothy behind in Berea while he makes a swift escape to Athens.

Interpretive Angle:
**Paul at Ares Rock or Mars Hill**

Some theories assert that Paul endures a judicial hearing in Athens. In earlier times, trials—especially murder trials—were held on this hill by ruling councils. Areopagus means Ares rock; it derives from the mythical scene set in this place that involved a legal trial of the Greek god of war Ares (Mars to the Romans) for murdering the son of the sea god, Poseidon. In Paul's era, the group does not appear to have official legal duties, but it holds a forum for philosophical discussions. There is no hint in the narrative that Paul is under arrest or being interrogated by a legal authority.

### Tough Audience in Athens

While he waits for his companions to join him in Athens, Paul speaks about Jesus and his resurrection not only in synagogues but also in the marketplace. Paul is ushered to a debating society that meets on the Areopagus, Mars Hill. With this non-Jewish and mainly Greek audience, Paul takes an approach markedly different from the one he uses in the synagogues. He does not refer to Jewish ancestors such as Abraham, Moses, or David. Instead, he starts with God as creator of humanity. He sees an altar with an inscription among their array of idols. It reads, To an Unknown God. That is Paul's opening.

*"So you are ignorant of the very thing you worship—and this is what I am going to proclaim to you. The God who made the world and everything in it is the Lord of heaven and earth and does not live in temples built by human hands. And he is not served by human hands, as if he*

*needed anything. Rather, he himself gives everyone life*
*and breath and everything else." (Acts 17:23b–25)*

God made all nations that they should seek him, he continues, quoting not the prophets but two poets. One is Epimenides, from the island of Crete, who wrote, *"For in him we live and move and have our being."* The other is from Paul's own home region of Cilicia. Aratus, a stoic, writes the line, *"We are his offspring."*[41] Paul leverages that line to dismiss inorganic idols.

*"Therefore since we are God's offspring, we should not*
*think that the divine being is like gold or silver or stone –*
*an image made by human design and skill. In the past*
*God overlooked such ignorance, but now he commands*
*all people everywhere to repent." (Acts 17:29–30)*

Here in Athens, it is not the coming of an expected messiah as in the case of the Jews that should lead these Greeks to repent; instead, it is the coming of a judge to deal out justice.

*"For he has set a day when he will judge the world with*
*justice by the man he has appointed. He has given proof of*
*this to everyone by raising him from the dead." (Acts 17:31)*

Paul takes a major theme from the prophets that the Messiah will judge the world. He makes this reality the incentive for Greeks to join the Jesus movement. This way, they will be sorting things out ahead of time with their future judge. How can we be sure Jesus will be the judge? Paul would reply because God raised him from the dead and exalted him to his right hand.

---

[41] Tarsus, the main city of Cilicia, Paul's hometown, is a commercial and educational center rivaling Alexandria and Rome. Among its population are many practitioners of the Stoic philosophy. Paul swings easily between Greek and Hebrew literature.

### Paul Weathers the Storm in Corinth and Avoids Legal Trouble

Still waiting for Silas and Timothy, Paul leaves Athens for Corinth. He supports himself by making tents during the week. Paul then goes to the synagogue on weekends to persuade people to believe in Jesus as the Messiah and judge. His companions join him.

---

Bible Sidelight:
**Priscilla and Aquila, Tentmakers with Paul**

Among Paul's companions in his first stay in Corinth are a striking, courageous Jewish couple named Priscilla and Aquila, from Italy. They are tentmakers like Paul. They leave Rome when the Emperor Claudius famously orders all Jews to leave (probably in AD 49 though some scholars place it in AD 41). They travel with Paul when he sails from Corinth. While Paul continues to Jerusalem, they settle in Ephesus, where they host a house church (1 Cor. 16:19). They mentor privately in their home a highly educated, traveling evangelist named Apollos, who wins public debates in synagogues on whether Jesus is the Messiah (Acts 18:26). Eventually, they return to Rome.

Writing about five years after his first visit during his second stay in Corinth, Paul ends his renowned letter to the Romans commending the couple. *"Greet Priscilla and Aquila, my coworkers in Christ Jesus. They risked their lives for me. Not only I but all the churches of the Gentiles are grateful to them"* (Rom. 16:3–4).

---

Unbelieving Jews continue to try to silence Paul. In Corinth, they drag him before the eminent proconsul of the entire region of Achaia, who summarily dismisses the case. Due to that outcome, Paul is protected in Corinth enough to stay there more than a year. From Corinth, he writes at least one and probably two letters to the Thessalonians. He makes his way back to Antioch via a short stop in Ephesus and a brief visit to Jerusalem (Acts 18:18–22).

## Journey Three: Extended Ephesus Stay, Riots, Revisits

After less than a year in Antioch, Paul again is back on the road. Embarking on his third major journey, he takes an inland northern route through today's central Turkey and bases himself in Ephesus in western Turkey for two or three years. Later, he again travels along the western Aegean Sea to the Greek coastal cities and then doubles back through them until he returns to Troas. Then he heads along the eastern Aegean (or Ionian) Sea to several port cities. Finally, he sails for Judea via Phoenicia and arrives at Caesarea and then Jerusalem.

Found in the Ground:
**Temple of Artemis**

Ephesus, Turkey—Site found in 1863. Artemis (the Greek name, with Diana the Roman name) is the goddess of the hunt, wild animals, forests, and wilderness; she came to be associated with childbirth and motherhood. The temple was four times the size of the Parthenon in Athens befitting a city that competed with Antioch to be the third largest in the Roman world after Rome and Alexandria. The site confirms the rationale for the rioting against Paul when his preaching threatens the shrine. (Acts 19:27)

Index 6.5

Found in the Ground:
**Statues of Artemis**

Ephesus, Turkey—Found in 1956. The statues are dated to the second century, fifty to a hundred years after Paul's time in Ephesus. Representing the goddess of the hunt, the statues have oval pendants clustered to form a necklace or sash around each figure. The pendants were once thought to be breasts, or ostrich eggs, or fruit. Now they are considered more likely to be bull or (even more probably) stag testicles, trophies of her silver bow and arrow indicating the divine feminine dominance of virility. The finding supports the account in Acts that records the broad popularity throughout the region achieved by proponents of the Artemis religion. (Acts 19:27–28)

Index 6.6

In his extended tenure at Ephesus, Paul stays busy preaching first at the synagogues. When strong opposition grows, he relocates to a large secular lecture hall (Acts 19:8–10); the change of venue reduces Jewish opposition.

Found in the Ground:
**Commercial Shops and Agora**

Ephesus, Turkey—Diagonally across the main street from the theater in a large square, these shop units filled three sides, an early mall or agora of sorts. The site confirms the account in Acts that many shop owners in Ephesus felt threatened by Paul's preaching against the religion of Artemis. Their trade in crafting mini shrines of silver would be severely hurt if people were to believe gods made of hands were powerless souvenirs. (Acts 19:23–27)

Index 6.7

Later, Greek opposition breaks out among the silversmiths of

Ephesus. They (correctly) fear he will destroy their idol-making industry, a big business next to a wonder of the ancient world— the tourist and pilgrim destination of the expansive temple of Artemis. A union leader stirs up the craftspeople and then the whole town.

> He called them together, along with the workers in related trades, and said: "You know my friends, that we receive a good income from this business. And you see and hear how this fellow Paul has convinced and led astray large numbers of people here in Ephesus and in practically the whole province of Asia. He says that gods made by human hands are no gods at all. There is danger not only that our trade will lose its good name, but also that the temple of the great goddess Artemis will be discredited."
>
> (Acts 19:25–27b)

Angry activists rush into the city theater to protest Paul's presence in their community. Paul wants to address them. This time, his disciples and friendly provincial officials restrain him from entering the theater. It works; the gathering eventually disbands. Paul takes the hint. He leaves having already planned to move on. He visits the churches he had founded along the western Greek coast before he heads for Jerusalem (Acts 19:21–22, 20:1–3).

Well before the outbreak of opposition in Ephesus, Paul writes at least one letter while

Found in the Ground:
**Riotous Theater**

Ephesus, Turkey—A large, semicircular, limestone, open-air theater seated 25,000 people for dramas, religious services, public events, and bloody battle contests. The Roman design dates from AD 40. The site supports the account of shop owners and others gathering at the nearby theater to speak with government officials about the radical Paul, who was preaching against their goddess Artemis and jeopardizing their trade in silver souvenirs and trinkets honoring her. (Acts 19:8–10, 23–41)

Index 6.8

there to the Corinthian church. He responds to issues they were struggling with including feuds, lawsuits, sexual morals, and misuse of spiritual gifts. One major issue concerns the central hope for the resurrection of the dead. Paul treats it extremely seriously because it is a core belief that is at stake.

> *Now, brothers and sisters, I want to remind you of the gospel I preached to you, which you received and on which you have taken your stand. By this gospel you are saved, if you hold firmly to the word I preached to you. Otherwise, you have believed in vain.*
> *(1 Corinthians 15:1–2)*

Paul proceeds to pull out from his files a condensed creed.

> *For what I received I passed on to you as of first importance: that Christ died for our sins according to the Scriptures, that he was buried, that he was raised on the third day according to the Scriptures...*
> *(1 Corinthians 15:3–4)*

He does not invent this synopsis; he receives it almost certainly during his two-week Jerusalem visit to see Peter and James. (See chapter 7 for the historical significance of this early creed.) Then Paul gets to the issue at stake in their community. Some of them now believe that there will be no resurrection of the dead.

### Paul's Sufferings Are All in Vain if There Is No Resurrection

Emphatically, Paul states that Jesus being raised from the dead and believers being raised after death are interconnected. He argues you cannot have one without the other. He works through the logic backward. If they say there is no resurrection of believers, then Jesus has not been raised. If Jesus has not been raised, then *"our preaching is useless and so is your faith"*; it is *"futile."* In that case, Paul and the other apostles are *"false witnesses about*

*God, for we have testified about God that he raised Christ from the dead."* Worse yet, if Jesus has not been raised, *"you are still in your sins"* and those who have died believing wrongly in Jesus *"are lost."* Paul concludes, *"If only for this life we have hope in Christ, we are of all people most to be pitied"* (1 Cor. 15:12–19). If that were the case, Paul himself would deserve pity more than most. All that he has endured would make him a tragic figure if it were simply done for a lost cause.

In a later letter to the Corinthians, he describes his unenviable hardships. Slightly embarrassed to do so, he continues nevertheless to deter them from following legalistic teachers who are out to bring them under Mosaic law and undercut Paul's authority. So he establishes his credentials by listing the sufferings he endured.

> *Whatever anyone else dares to boast about—I am speaking as a fool—I also dare to boast about. Are they Hebrews? So am I. Are they Israelites? So am I. Are they servants of Christ? (I am out of my mind to talk like this.) I am more. I have worked much harder, been in prison more frequently, been flogged more severely, and been exposed to death again and again. Five times I received from the Jews the forty lashes minus one. Three times I was beaten with rods, once I was pelted with stones, three times I was shipwrecked, I spent a night and a day in the open sea, I have been constantly on the move. I have been in danger from rivers, in danger from bandits, in danger from my fellow Jews, in danger from Gentiles; in danger in the city, and in danger in the country, in danger at sea; and in danger from false believers. I have labored and toiled and have often gone without sleep; I have known hunger and thirst and have often gone without food; I have been cold and naked. Besides everything else, I face daily the pressure of my concern for all the churches. (2 Corinthians 11:21–28)*

Paul certainly would deserve to be pitied if he had suffered all these conditions for nothing, for a hoax or false belief, all a bucket of non-kosher hogwash. He begs to differ.

> *But Christ has indeed been raised from the dead, the firstfruits of those who have fallen asleep. For since death came through a man, the resurrection of the dead comes also through a man. For as in Adam all die, so in Christ all will be made alive. But each in turn: Christ, the firstfruits; then, when he comes, those who belong to him. (1 Corinthians 15:20–23)*

Paul cannot imagine a resurrection of one person without the resurrection of the whole group to follow. He reflects a strongly held tradition in Jewish culture (notwithstanding the odd denial of it by the priestly Sadducees) that the resurrection at the end of the age would be a group experience. Understood from this perspective, the shocking point of the resurrection of Jesus is less that a person came back to life than that a person was raised individually in advance rather than along with everyone else at the same time. Paul explains the new reality of a two-stage resurrection with an analogy to an agricultural harvest. As sure as the *"first fruits"* of a harvest show that the rest of the crop is on the way, so also does the resurrection of Jesus show that the rest of the believers will be resurrected as well.

Still on his third journey, Paul's hardships are not over. He travels along the eastern Aegean (or Ionian) islands stopping at one mainland port to bid a tearful farewell to his Ephesian leaders. These leaders may want to avoid antagonizing their local silversmith union any more than they have by meeting him outside of town at the port of Miletus. He then sails for Judea and arrives at Caesarea. From the coast, he travels east, uphill to Jerusalem. Once there, in the same city where he studied as a Pharisee as a young man, he is swarmed by the mob at the temple. He is arrested and confined for his own protection in the Antonia Fortress as we saw earlier.

## The Hated Traitor Dodges the Assassination Plot

Secretly, his would-be assassins lie in wait having sworn not to eat until Paul is killed. They want a priest to go to the commander and request to have Paul transferred to the Sanhedrin for further questioning. They scheme to set upon him on his pathway there. What they do not count on is that a nephew of Paul, the son of his sister who resides in Jerusalem, catches wind of the plan and goes to the fortress to tell Paul. Paul asks a centurion guarding him to take the young man to the commander, and his nephew relates the plot in detail. The commander warns him to tell no one he reported it.

---

Found in the Ground:
**Evidence for the Antonia Fortress**

Jerusalem—The fortress site is northwest of and adjacent to the temple complex. No ruins have been unearthed, only bedrock cuts indicating its foundation lines. The descriptions of the site come mainly from Josephus (War 1.21.1, 5.5.8). It was a barracks for a cohort of Roman soldiers in Jerusalem. A cohort usually consisted of 480 to 600 soldiers though some reached to 800. The fortress location served to repel enemy attacks that usually came from the north and to control the volatile temple mount crowds. The site layout and descriptions support the account of the near riot and rescue of Paul by Roman soldiers who lift him up on their shoulders and carry him as if in an ancient mosh pit. (Acts 21:27–40, 22:1–30, 23:10)

Index 6.9

---

The commander, Claudius Lysias, decides to send a message of first-century shock and awe to the conspirators. He will transfer Paul to the Roman capital back on the coast in Caesarea with a show of force: 200 soldiers, 70 horsemen, and 200 spearmen. They leave at nine that night; they are armed and dangerous in their red tunics overlaid with silver armor glinting in the torchlight. The detachment takes Paul, mounted on a horse, well beyond the city to Antipatris. This outpost is a fortress town, a caravan crossroads where the foothills give way to the coastal plain. Here, the infantry and spearmen halt. From there, the cavalry alone accompanies Paul the rest of the way to Caesarea. The assassination plot is foiled (Acts 23:16–35). Five days later, his accusers, the high priests, will follow him there for a hearing, but it ends inconclusively.

Paul remains confined in Caesarea for two years until the prior governor, Felix, is succeeded by the new official, Festus. The new governor aims to clean up the old docket. After his first two weeks on the job, he convenes a court to try Paul. Again, the priestly accusers arrive to bring their charges against him. Paul denies he has done anything wrong against Jewish law, the temple, or Caesar. The accusers want a change of venue to Jerusalem. Festus asks if Paul is willing as a Roman citizen to agree to that change. Paul, knowing security will be problematic in Jerusalem, refuses. Instead, he exercises his right as a Roman citizen to appeal directly to Caesar and to be tried in Rome. Festus realizes he must agree to Paul's choice. He also must file charges prior to sending Paul to Rome. However, none of the charges against Paul make any sense to him.

### Paul's Pointed Preaching Puts Jewish King on the Hot Seat

Within a few days, an ally for Festus arrives in the city. King Agrippa II and his sister Bernice come to greet the new governor. The former governor, Felix, was well known to these two royal siblings. He had married their sister Drusilla, acclaimed for her beauty. Drusilla would be one of the two most famous people to die in Pompeii from the sudden lava flow from Mount Vesuvius about twenty years later in AD 79. (The other famous person to perish there volcanically was the Roman historian and naturalist, Pliny the Elder.)

Agrippa II rules most of northern Israel, Galilee in the west, Gaulinitis in the east, and Perea, a more southerly section east of the Jordan River. Rome retains direct rule of Judea and Samaria. However, Agrippa II holds the mandate to manage the temple complex and has the power to appoint and depose the high priest. Agrippa II's father, Agrippa I, is the king who put to death James the disciple, the brother of John. Such violence is not too surprising considering that the great-grandfather of Agrippa II is Herod the Great.

---

Historical Portal:
Bernice Cuts Her Own Historical Figure

Bernice has been through two marriages, the last one to her uncle, and she resides at the court of her brother. Josephus reports the rumor that they live in an incestuous relationship (*Antiquities* 20.7.3). Notwithstanding that, she marries a king in Cilicia, Paul's home region. Later, she moves on to an affair with the future emperor Titus during the first Jewish-Roman War. Pushback from other leaders in Rome forces Titus to dismiss her before ascending to the throne in AD 79. The Roman writers Suetonius, Tacitus, and Juvenal all mention her. She is the subject of much fascination in literature, drama, ballet, and opera in Europe in the 1600s to the 1800s.

---

Festus convinces Agrippa II (known usually as just Agrippa) and Bernice to help him cut through the clutter to prepare the charges against Paul. He explains that at the prior hearing, he could not understand the accusers.

> "They had some points of dispute with him about their own religion and about a dead man named Jesus who Paul claimed was alive." (Acts 25:19)

At the highly formal gathering, Festus defers to Agrippa, who invites Paul to speak for himself. Our account comes through Luke. He might very well have been attending the hearing himself because he later travels with Paul by ship to Rome departing from this coastal location in Caesarea (Acts 27:1-2).

### Career Move to Persecutor Out of Loyalty to Jewish Faith

Paul takes a before-and-after approach; he wants them to know how he started out on the side of his accusers against this new belief. Yet he argues the belief is not really new; it is fully in line with the promises made to *"our ancestors"* in the Jewish scriptures.

> *"The Jewish people all know the way I have lived since I was a child, from the beginning of my life in my own country, and also in Jerusalem. They have known me for a long time and can testify, if they are willing, that I conformed to the strictest sect of our religion, living as a Pharisee." (Acts 26:4–5)*

His intensity in following the lifestyle of a Pharisee shows how closely he followed the promises. He hoped to please God in serving him so God would act decisively to liberate Israel from its political oppressors.

> *"And now it is because of my hope in what God has promised our ancestors that I am on trial today. This is the promise our twelve tribes are hoping to see fulfilled as they earnestly serve God day and night. King Agrippa, it is because of this hope that these Jews are accusing me. Why should any of you consider it incredible that God raises the dead?" (Acts 26:6–8)*

Paul ties the resurrection of the individual person, Jesus, into the Jewish hope of a future resurrection at the end of the age. He admits he did not understand this claim of an individual resurrection initially and opposed it intensively.

> *"I too was convinced that I ought to do all that was possible to oppose the name of Jesus of Nazareth. And that is just what I did in Jerusalem. On the authority of the chief priests I put many of the Lord's people in*

*prison, and when they were put to death, I cast my vote against them. Many a time I went from one synagogue to another to have them punished, and I tried to force them to blaspheme. I was so obsessed with persecuting them that I even hunted them down in foreign cities."*
*(Acts 26:9–11)*

### Paul Explains the Intervention That Led Him to Switch Sides

He establishes his credibility as an enforcer of the Jewish religion. Then he gives the account of why he made the radical move to switch sides. This official hearing allows Paul to go into more detail than the rushed speech he offered during the temple riot about two years earlier.

*"On one of these journeys I was going to Damascus with the authority and commission of the chief priests. About noon, King Agrippa, as I was on the road, I saw a light from heaven, brighter than the sun, blazing around me and my companions. We all fell to the ground, and I heard a voice saying to me in Aramaic, 'Saul, Saul why do you persecute me? It is hard for you to kick against the goads.' Then I asked, 'Who are you, Lord?' 'I am Jesus, whom you are persecuting,' the Lord replied."*
*(Acts 26:12–15)*

When this story is heard so often, it can lose some of its power. We need to put ourselves in Paul's shoes (or to be more exact his sandals). To an enforcer set on arresting heretics, hearing the heroic figure of the heretics call to him by name out of the blue in Aramaic would be a visceral, mind-boggling, cataclysmic jolt to his system. To be told by Jesus that he is exhausting himself *"to kick against the goads"* is for Paul a rude awakening. He suddenly sees himself as an unruly sheep or goat that will not let the wooden staff of his shepherd direct him along the right path. In that fateful moment, he is not just halted in his tracks by the voice of Jesus; he also is commissioned to be a witness to Jesus as Lord just as the believers he had intended to imprison were. Jesus promises him that he will be rescued repeatedly so he can fulfill the mission to bring many people to faith.

> *"'Now get up and stand on your feet. I have appeared to you to appoint you as a servant and as a witness of what you have seen and will see of me. I will rescue you from your own people and from the Gentiles. I am sending you to them to open their eyes and turn them from darkness to light, and from the power of Satan to God, so that they may receive forgiveness of sins and a place among those who are sanctified by faith in me.'"*
> *(Acts 26:16–18)*

Paul then explains how he has more or less followed orders and concentrated on spreading the message of Jesus first to Jews and then to non-Jews. This new message of forgiveness in Jesus comes from heaven, so Paul is carrying out what the God of Israel called him to do.

> *"So then, King Agrippa, I was not disobedient to the vision from heaven. First to those in Damascus, then to those in Jerusalem and in all Judea, and then to the Gentiles, I preached that they should repent and turn to God and demonstrate their repentance by their deeds."*
> *(Acts 26:19–20)*

He wants the king to know that he is causing people to turn to the God of Israel, a positive development among Jews and Gentiles. In that sense, it is ridiculous for the Jewish leaders to try to execute him when all he is doing is preaching that God is now doing what the OT Jewish prophets predicted he would do. God is fulfilling his promises about the Messiah's arrival, about the resurrection that has occurred, and about the ingathering of the Gentiles.

*"That is why some Jews seized me in the temple courts and tried to kill me. But God has helped me to this very day; so I stand here and testify to small and great alike. I am saying nothing beyond what the prophets and Moses said would happen—that the Messiah would suffer and, as the first to rise from the dead, would bring the message of light to his own people and to the Gentiles."* (Acts 26:21–23)

## Festus Gets Restless, Thinks Paul Has Gone Crazy

After the lengthy explanation, the Roman procurator Festus, who requested the hearing, seems to sense some discomfort on the part of his guest, King Agrippa.

---

Found in the Ground:
### Palace Where Paul Appeals to Caesar

Caesarea Maritima, Israel—Herod the Great's former seaside palace is where Paul is brought for his own safety when the Jerusalem priests demand he face a trial. He is held in custody for two years. Excavations reveal rooms where Paul may have been held in confinement, one of which had an ocean and harbor view to the north, where loaded merchant ships arrive. Excavated palace stone floors in the audience hall are likely the venue for Paul's hearing before the authorities in which he appeals to Caesar. Later he is sent to Rome by ship, about AD 59, arriving in AD 60. (Acts 25:11–14; 25)

Index 6.10

---

*At this point, Festus interrupted Paul's defense. "You are out of your mind, Paul!" he shouted. "Your great learning is driving you insane."* (Acts 26:24)

Paul respectfully deflects the charge of insanity, but he will not let Festus change the subject. Opportunistic evangelist that he is, he senses a chance to persuade the king to believe.

*"I am not insane, most excellent Festus," Paul replied. "What I am saying is true and reasonable. The king is familiar with these things, and I can speak freely to him. I am convinced that none of this has escaped his notice, because it was not done in a corner. King Agrippa, do you believe the prophets? I know you do."* (Acts 26:25–27)

---

### Historical Portal:
### Agrippa II, the Last King of the Herodian Line

Agrippa II eventually alienates the Jewish leadership with the high-handed way he manipulates his power to appoint the high priest. He fails to forestall the Jewish revolt of AD 66, when he himself is expelled by Jewish rebels from Jerusalem. In the first Jewish-Roman War (AD 66–73), he sides with the Romans, raises an army to help them recapture the Golan Heights in the north, and eventually retires in Rome. He dies there around AD 93–94 as the last ruler from the house of Herod the Great. The author Josephus and Agrippa II are contemporaries and friends, and Josephus relies on the king to supply records for his writings. They exchange more than sixty letters.

---

Paul puts the king on the hot seat (or should we say the hot throne), but the king wriggles out and fires a question back.

*Then Agrippa said to Paul, "Do you think that in such a short time you can persuade me to be a Christian?"*

*Paul replied, "Short time or long—I pray to God that not only you but all who are listening to me today may become what I am, except for these chains."* (Acts 26:28–29)

By that comment, Paul means that he hopes that each onlooker might not become a chained-up prisoner as he is presently but rather become a believer in Jesus as he is destined for a resurrection to eternal life with God. The hearing breaks up at that point. Agrippa tells Festus privately that Paul does not deserve death and could have been set free had he not appealed to Caesar (Acts 26:32).

Within months, Paul will take a wild voyage to Rome. It will include raging storms, a shipwreck, swimming for dear life, shaking off snakebites, and holding a health clinic on an island resort (Acts 27:11–28:16). He lands near today's Naples and travels on foot along the Appian Way to the capital city.

Once in Rome, probably in AD 60, he will spend two years under house arrest, but he will keep teaching his visitors and guards (Acts 28:30–31).

Luke's account in Acts ends there, but tradition holds that Paul is set free for three or four years. Possibly, he went on an escapade to Spain, for he had greatly anticipated that plan and had hoped the Roman believers

---

Found in the Ground:
**The Renowned Roman Road, The Appian Way**

Italy—The major Roman road in Italy is first built in 312 BC by Appius Claudius Caecus. The distance it eventually traversed was 350 miles or 563 kilometers from the Roman Forum to the southeastern port of Brundisium (modern Brindisi) on the Adriatic Sea. From there, ships would embark for Greece or the eastern Mediterranean.

The finding supports the account in Acts of Paul's landing by ship at Puetoli (modern Pozzuoli near Naples), the key Roman port for importing grain from Egypt. He then travels 170 miles or 274 kilometers along the Appian Way to Rome and is met by friends about 43 miles or 69 kilometers from Rome at the Forum of Appias. About twelve miles or twenty kilometers closer to Rome at the Three Taverns (or Three Inns or Shops) he is met by more friends. (Acts 28:13–16)

Index 6.11

would support it financially (Rom. 15:24, 28–29). He then faced imprisonment again.

During either his first or second imprisonment in Rome, Paul writes to the Philippians, the first church planted within what we regard today as the borders of Europe. To this group of believers for whom he bore a special affection, he reveals his enduring hope and inner modus operandi.

> *I want to know Christ—yes, to know the power of his resurrection and participation in his sufferings, becoming like him in his death, and so, somehow, attaining to the resurrection from the dead. Not that I have already obtained all this, or have already arrived at my goal, but I press on to take hold of that for which Christ Jesus took hold of me. (Philippians 3:10–12)*

Finally, Paul is martyred by the demented emperor Nero (who commits suicide in AD 68). Tradition holds Paul is beheaded in the period of AD 66–67 outside the gates of Rome on the Ostian Way, the road to a major seaport. Unlike Peter, he could not be crucified because he was a Roman citizen. In a letter sent to his understudy Timothy, Paul muses about how he would likely feel at the moment that he met his end in this life.

> *I have fought the good fight, I have finished the race, I have kept the faith. Now there is in store for me the crown of righteousness, which the Lord, the righteous Judge, will award to me on that day—and not only to me, but also to all who have longed for his appearing. (2 Timothy 4:7–8)*

# b: CONCLUSION

## On Paul Switching Sides

In his explanation to Agrippa and Festus, Paul could not have been more direct. He switches sides from the Pharisees to the Christians because the prophet he did not believe in, whose followers he was persecuting for betraying the true Jewish faith, suddenly called to him by name on that dusty Damascus road. He could no longer deny that something was afoot with this Jesus. He was alive, reigning in heaven as the Messiah, staging interventions in Aramaic, and sending hard-charging Paul in the opposite direction.

Any explanation of the resurrection must account for the historically verified radical turnaround in the life of Paul. Exactly what other than this clearly claimed encounter explains the change in this former violent persecutor? He is the enraged, determined enforcer who suddenly switches sides. He had too much to lose to give up all the status he had attained in Judaism for no good reason. He would have been too rational, too skeptical not to carefully validate his own experience on the Damascus road against the other appearances of Jesus to other leading apostles especially Peter and James.

Paul turns around and never looks back. As a fervent, traveling evangelist, he readily braves a much more dangerous future in the new way of Jesus—the crucified yet risen and ascended Savior, the power and wisdom of God (1 Cor. 1:24).

# CHAPTER

# 7

# LINE OF EVIDENCE

## SUMMARY

# 7:

If the reality of the death and resurrection of Jesus is proclaimed by the disciples soon after the events happen, there is not enough time for layers of fiction and folklore to form over the years if not generations into a farfetched legend. Categorizing the resurrection narrative as a myth is a convenient way for people to disregard the written records of the witness accounts. Supposedly, the fictional events form over years like sedimentary layers in geology. The problem with the resurrection evidence for this theory is that there simply was not enough time for legends to develop. Some of the evidence shows the resurrection was proclaimed within months, other evidence within a few years. Neither time frame permits an event of the magnitude of the resurrection to escalate into legend so quickly.

# PRELUDE

## CHAPTER 7

**H**is soldiers inform him a rabble is making its way from the synagogue through the stone-paved streets of Corinth to the forum where he judges cases. They constantly debate their religion there, and one of their own must have said something that lit their torch. He has seen this hubbub before. He does not enjoy this part of his job.

He is no ordinary civil magistrate. He is the proconsul of the entire province of the southern peninsula of Greece known then as the region of Achaia. He is a friend of Claudius, the Roman emperor. Now in his midfifties, he has risen through the ranks of the Roman government and knows how the system works.

His region includes the famous Temple of Apollo, which is falling into disrepair. He refuses to let it become a ruin on his watch when its host city of Delphi endures a population decline. He secures permission from the emperor to recruit leading families to resettle Delphi and rebuild its economy. Engravers inscribe a letter from Claudius mentioning Gallio's success on an outer wall of the temple. The inscription not so humbly highlights this ambitious official's contribution and connections.

Gallio is widely admired for his even-keeled disposition even by his own brother, a widely known playwright and self-help writer, Seneca the Younger (their father, a renowned lawyer, had the same name). His younger brother dedicates two of his how-to books to Gallio, one entitled *On Anger (De Ira)* and the other *On the Happy Life (De Vita Beata)*.

The synagogue mob arrives at the forum. Gallio sits on an upraised stone platform known as a *bema*. He can sense the anger and hostility rising to a fever pitch. It all is directed at a rather short and not very imposing man named Paul. *"'This man,' they charged, 'is persuading the people to worship God in ways contrary to the law'"* (Acts 18:13). Would Gallio have recalled in his mind the words of his brother Seneca from the book *On Anger*?

> *The cause of anger is the belief that we are injured; this belief, therefore, should not be lightly entertained. We ought not to fly into a rage even when the injury appears to be open and distinct: for some false things bear the semblance of truth. We should always allow some time to elapse, for time discloses the truth. (De Ira, book 2, cap. 22, line 2)*[42]

Abruptly, Gallio silences the crowd and does not permit Paul to begin his defense.

> *Just as Paul was about to speak, Gallio said to them, "If you Jews were making a complaint about some misdemeanor or serious crime, it would be reasonable for me to listen to you. But since it involves questions about words and names and your own law—settle the matter yourselves. I will not be a judge of such things." So he drove them off. (Acts 18:14–16)*

Case dismissed. The supposed injury they are angry about is not something Gallio wants to adjudicate. The crowd turns its wrath on one of their synagogue leaders who seems to have sided with Paul (Acts 18:17; 1 Cor. 1:1). They beat him, but Gallio ignores that. He probably thinks the crowd's anger needs an outlet to let

---

[42] L. Annaeus Seneca, *De Ira* (*On Anger*), tr. Aubrey Stewart, Bohn's Classical Library Edition (London: George Bell and Sons, 1900). Available at en.m.wikisource.org. Some renderings shorten the famous line from Seneca the Younger to "Time discovers truth."

the mob mentality simmer down. Paul walks free. The church in Corinth grows. Had Gallio decided differently, Paul might have had to leave or been imprisoned or even killed.

Unbeknown to him, Gallio does the Christian faith two huge favors: he lets Paul go on his way, and he draws praise from the emperor—for rejuvenating the shrine of Delphi—in a letter that is inscribed on the temple wall in stone.

**Paul's Second Missionary Journey**

*Paul's Mission Field.* Paul the apostle is summoned before the Roman official Gallio in Corinth on this major missionary journey, commonly known as his second one. Most of the cities and regions figuring in Paul's life are shown. Excerpt from *Baker's Concise Bible Atlas* by J. Carl Laney © 1988. Used by permission of Baker Books, a division of Baker Publishing Group.

**CHAPTER 7**

# PROCLAMATION OF THE RESURRECTION IS CLEARLY EARLY

hen do the followers of Jesus begin proclaiming that he rose from the dead? The question is important. If years and years go by and become decades and even centuries before the resurrection narrative takes shape, the protests of the skeptics grow louder. They want to persuade people that the story is a legend, a fiction built up over time. If so, it starts to look like the resurrection account might consist of folklore rather than historical reality.

In this chapter, we will investigate dates and times to deal with these skeptics. At certain points, we will take a dive into mathematics, but the result will be valuable historical evidence for the resurrection.

### Luke Reports the Preaching Begins After a Brief Interlude

The simple answer to the question of when the disciples start proclaiming the resurrection is given in Acts, Luke's sequel to his biography or gospel of Jesus. All four gospels in the NT end shortly after their resurrection accounts. In Matthew and Luke, Jesus commands his disciples near the end to be his witnesses and to spread the message, but from the gospels themselves, we do not know for sure whether they go forth (Mt 28:18; Lk 24:46–48). Acts covers the next thirty years of preaching and outreach on the part of the key evangelists and demonstrates how they fulfill the mission Jesus envisions.

The answer Luke gives to when the disciples first start preaching the resurrection is clear. Luke asserts that Jesus spends more than a month, forty days to be exact, with his disciples after his resurrection (Acts 1:3). As he is about to depart, he instructs them not to hit the road preaching immediately but to wait a few days more.

> On one occasion, while he was eating with them, he gave them this command: "Do not leave Jerusalem, but wait for the gift my Father promised, which you have heard me speak about." (Acts 1:4)

The disciples need the gift to fulfill their mission. They hope the mission will be helping him set up the kingdom of God in their land right then and there (Acts 1:6–7). That time is not yet, Jesus says; the message offering spiritual life and salvation through his death and resurrection must first be spread far and wide.

> "But You will receive power when the Holy Spirit comes on you; and you will be my witnesses in Jerusalem, and in all Judea and Samaria, and to the ends of the earth." (Acts 1:8)

The Spirit of God will indwell them and empower them to be bold and powerful witnesses. For the Spirit to come, they were told earlier, Jesus himself must depart. They are present and watch when he ascends to heaven (Jn 16:7; Acts 1:9). About a week later when they are all together in a house in Jerusalem, the Spirit blows in like a swirling wind and fills the disciples and their entourage according to Luke (Acts 2:1-4). The persons receiving the Spirit probably numbered about 120 (Acts 1:15). It is the Feast of Weeks, or Pentecost, about fifty days after Passover.

Many Jews from diverse countries are visiting the city for the feast. They hear the message of Jesus spoken in their own languages by these native, Aramaic-speaking, Galilean Jews (see chapter 4 for the difference between these languages and the gift of tongues). *What is up with this?* the people wonder. *Are they drunk?*

When Peter steps up to explain how this vocal jam session has happened through what Jesus has done, the preaching of the good news begins in history. Luke records that about three thousand Jews in the packed city respond to Peter's speech with faith in Jesus (Acts 2:41). Unquestionably, Luke depicts the preaching of the resurrection happening quickly, about fifty days after Jesus is crucified.

### Attempts to Stretch the Time for Resurrection Proclamation

Yet certain scholars try to discredit Luke in the hope of stretching the time between when Jesus lives and when he is preached as the risen Lord. This comes from the theory that Jesus does not rise from the dead but that a legend is created later by the disciples or their successors. This theory purports that the gospel writers publish their fiction many years after he dies (see chapter 10). Further, later generations of Christians living in the second and third centuries (the AD 100s and 200s) start imagining Jesus as a divine savior; these later Christians corrupt the already questionable original gospels. It is a travesty because as these critics contend, all Jesus meant to do was teach a higher ethical lifestyle if he existed at all (see prologue).

Luke asserts the preaching of the resurrection occurs within two months of the Jesus events. However, skeptical theories look at when Luke is writing, not when he depicts Peter preaching. This dating method assigns the evidence of resurrection preaching to the date of the writing of the document, not the witness report of Peter's preaching in the document. They count the evidence for the resurrection proclamation as if Luke were the one first preaching the resurrection in his book.

Viewed in this way, the evidence of Peter's preaching at Pentecost is dated to when Luke is writing. Presumably, Luke writes in the AD 80s according to some major dating schemes. Arguably, Luke could be writing in the early AD 60s (see *Background Guide*, resource 2). Here, we will accept the later dating for now given our purpose in this chapter. We assume Jesus dies and is raised in the range of AD 30–31 (see *Background Guide*, resource 3). Given these assumptions, Luke's written evidence that the resurrection was preached publicly is about fifty years later, not fifty days later.

Even at fifty years after the event, that amount of elapsed time is nevertheless an early date for a historical account in that era if judged by ancient standards of historical writing. The most reliable biography of Alexander the Great (d. 323 BC), Arrian's *The Anabasis of Alexander*, is written in the time of Hadrian, at least 440 years later. Less reliable although earlier is a biography from Diodorus of Sicily, who writes about 280 years later. Closer to the time of Jesus, the life of Julius Caesar (d. 44 BC) gets biographical treatment from Suetonius in his *Lives of the Twelve Caesars* more than 150 years later in AD 119, with another account by Plutarch written about the same time. Tiberius (d. AD 37), the emperor during the second half of Jesus's life, waits eighty years before a decent biography is issued in the aforementioned history of the Caesars by Suetonius. At even as many as fifty years after the fact, the written resurrection accounts compare positively to reporting time frames on other, well-accepted ancient figures.

For our present purpose, let us proceed with the theory that dates for the preaching of the resurrection must be based on the written document date itself. Then let us investigate whether there are historical texts besides Acts that proclaim the resurrection and can be dated earlier.

## Hunting for Texts Proclaiming the Resurrection

There are indeed other texts that clearly can be dated earlier. For one, Luke's gospel comes earlier than Acts since he refers to the first book at the outset of his second book (Acts 1:1). How much earlier cannot be determined precisely. If Acts is presently assumed to be dated in the AD 80s, Luke's gospel might be two to ten years earlier, in the AD 70s or early 80s.

Are there any other texts in play? Most scholars agree Luke's gospel incorporates large portions from the gospel of Mark (see *Background Guide*, resource 1), so Mark's gospel must be written before Luke's. That would date Mark to the AD 70s if not earlier. These dates shift the preaching of the resurrection—as evidenced by written texts—from maybe fifty years to forty years after Jesus departs.

Can the dates for the preaching of the resurrection based on dates of written texts be downshifted even further? Yes. We find earlier texts than either Acts or the gospels in the letters of Paul. Paul was not an original disciple of Jesus, but based on the evidence we have,

Interpretive Angle:
Disputes over Paul's Letters

These are the seven letters almost all scholars consider to be from Paul: Galatians, 1 Thessalonians, 1 and 2 Corinthians, Romans, Philemon, and Philippians. Strong arguments for Paul as author or coauthor can be made for the rest, but these six nevertheless are disputed: 2 Thessalonians, Ephesians, Colossians, 1 and 2 Timothy, Titus.

At one point, many teachers thought that Hebrews was written by Paul, but few assert that today. Differences in the book from Paul's established ways include no salutation or author identification; not quoting from the Hebrew OT (Masoretic) but from the Greek OT (Septuagint); and not claiming special revelations but mentioning that he is taught by other apostles (Heb. 2:3). The two leading candidates for the author of Hebrews now are two Bible teachers closely associated with Paul, namely Barnabas and Apollos. (Acts 13:1–4, 18:24) he is the first to write about Jesus in letters (see chapter 6). In the NT, thirteen letters are attributed to Paul. Scholars of course debate whether he actually wrote all of them, but half of them are generally considered beyond dispute as originating from Paul.

Two of these letters that are beyond dispute are critical for our inquiry: 1 Corinthians and Galatians. Along with 1 Thessalonians, they are placed among Paul's earliest letters.[43]

How can these letters of Paul be dated reasonably accurately? As usual in the first century, the letters themselves do not bear dates in the manuscripts, but if we look at 1 Corinthians, we find a number of markers that help us date the letters and Paul's sojourn in Corinth remarkably well.

Before Paul writes the letter, he visits Corinth and plants a church there. Obviously, Paul's preaching the resurrection in person to the Corinthians occurs earlier than his preaching in his letter.

Found in the Ground:
**Erastus Inscription**

Corinth, Greece—Found in 1929, the inscription is carved into a limestone paving stone with letters originally inlaid with metal. Kept in place in pavement at Corinth, northeast of the theater, it can be seen today. It signifies that Erastus, in return for his position (in Latin, the office of *aedilis*), paved this section of road at his own expense.

When Paul writes the letter to the Romans, he resides either in Corinth or in the nearby port town of Cenchrae. Among his companions who send along their greetings is Erastus, whom Paul identifies as Corinth's *"director of public works,"* sometimes translated as "city treasurer." Regardless of the exact title, the inscription supports Paul's assertion that his friend serves in a prominent municipal position. (Acts 19:22; Rom. 16:23; 1 Tim. 4:20)

Index 7.1

This is because in the letter, he reminds them of what he told them during his earlier visit. Which can we date more precisely, his visit

---

[43] See Kenneth Barker, ed., *The NIV Study Bible* (Grand Rapids, MI: Zondervan, 1985), 1819.

there or the time when he wrote the letter? As it turns out, we can date his visit to Corinth most precisely.

In Acts, Luke describes the early days of Paul's visit to Corinth, a less than auspicious start. Corinth lies on the isthmus between the northern and southern peninsula of Greece. As a harbor town, it was prosperous and filled with merchants, sailors, sex trade workers, and other dedicated revelers.

Paul comes to Corinth on his second missionary journey. He goes to the synagogue and preaches Jesus as the Messiah. Many Jews and Greeks respond including a leading official of the city. Yet there is major pushback.

Historical Portal:
## The Roman Exception for the Jews

The high-ranking and highly educated proconsul Gallio would know why the Jewish faith enjoys a carve-out or exception from the usual Roman rules for the worship of the gods. The carve-out harkens back to the war between the two Roman generals, Pompey and Julius Caesar. Pompey with his fleet has Julius bottled up in the Egyptian harbor city of Alexandria. In 45 BC, an army of 3,000 Jewish soldiers (under Hyrcanus) marches south and comes to his rescue by land.* They are motivated to fight against Pompey due to his earlier invasion of Jerusalem in 63 BC. He massacred 12,000 Jews defending the temple grounds. Then Pompey commits a blasphemous violation when he personally enters the temple's inner sanctum (*War* 1.7.6).

The Jewish contingent enables Julius to defeat Pompey. In gratitude, after Julius becomes Caesar, he grants the Jewish faith free exercise in the empire. For the most part, later Roman leaders continue with the tradition partly because the Jews rebel so strongly when their religious principles are violated. For this reason some Romans respectfully refer to the Jews as "porcupines," small but fierce, not prey you want to digest.

*Berel Wein, "Julius Caesar and the Jews," JewishHistory.org, 10 Jan 2011.

Angering people with his preaching, Paul is dragged by a synagogue mob in front of a high Roman official in Corinth (Acts 18:12-17). The mob wants Paul to be judged and punished for disturbing the peace. Ever the detailed historian, Luke names the official who reviews Paul's case, Gallio, a name well established in Roman historical sources.[44]

### Found in the Ground: Gallio or Delphi Inscription

Delphi, Achaia, Greece— Fragments are first found in 1885 and more up until 1910 for a total of nine fragments. A scholarly assessment of the first four fragments was first published in 1905 by Emile Bourget as a thesis at the University of Paris. The inscription recounts a letter from the emperor Claudius commending Gallio as proconsul of Achaia. It dates to the first seven months of AD 52 and confirms the presence of the prominent Roman official Gallio in Corinth in AD 51-52. With cross-reference to Luke's account, the finding confirms that Paul is in Corinth at that time. Verified by both literary and archaeological evidence, this date anchors Paul's chronology. (Acts 18:12)

Index 7.2

### The Roman Proconsul Gallio Leaves a Gift to Historians

Gallio has had some advantages getting to this point in his career. He comes from an equestrian Roman family. Equestrians, similar to knights in medieval times, form the lower order of the two aristocratic Roman classes. The higher order consists of the patricians, from whom senators are elected. Gallio is born in Cordoba, Spain, though his family forebears are probably Roman colonists rather than native Spaniards.

His family is well connected. His father, Seneca the Elder, was a renowned lawyer and educator whose legal texts circulated widely. His younger brother, Seneca the Younger, is a teacher and author of a wide range of

---

[44] Examples of mentions of Gallio in Roman sources: Tacitus, *Annals*, 15.73; Dio Cassius, *History of Rome*, 60.35; Statius, *Silvae*, ii. 7,32.

books many of them dramas or in the genre of self-help or sage advice. Seneca is considered so wise that Claudius appoints him as tutor for his adopted son, creepy Lucius Domitius Ahenobarbus, soon to be known as Emperor Nero (AD 37–68, ruling AD 54–68). Gallio's youngest brother is the father of another Roman writer, the poet Lucan, a boyhood friend of Nero.

Now this is where the archaeological discovery commonly called the Gallio inscription or Delphi inscription comes into play. The Gallio inscription as seen in the chapter prelude is a letter from Emperor Claudius to another official probably in charge of the city of Delphi. It was engraved in stone on the south wall of the renowned Temple of Apollo at Delphi. Enough fragments of the inscription have been recovered to piece together the text. It makes reference to Gallio as the proconsul of Achaia (southern Greece), who has reported that the city needs to be repopulated. The mention of Gallio and the date of the letter are what matter for our investigation. Most scholars date the letter within the first seven months of AD 52 leading to the conclusion that the hearing when

> **Found in the Ground:**
> **Judgment Platform or Bema**
>
> Corinth, Greece—Found in 1935. Made of marble stones, the platform is known as a *bema* in Greek and a *rostrum* in Latin. It still stands in a prominent place in the Roman forum of Corinth. The inscription on the bema dates it to the reign of Augustus or Claudius, between AD 25 and 50. This is likely the spot where Gallio heard Paul's accusers and dismissed the case. It supports the account in Acts that the area could contain an agitated crowd.
>
> An alternative site of the hearing suggested by some scholars is the Julian basilica one block away, the remains of which also have been unearthed. (Acts 18:12–17)
>
> Index 7.3

Paul's case is judged by Gallio occurs between May AD 51 and May AD 52.[45]

From Luke's account in Acts, we learn how Paul is dragged by the synagogue mob to the judgment forum, where Gallio is the presiding magistrate. Because the historical evidence shows us when Gallio was there, it verifies that Paul was in Corinth at this time, AD 51–52. Luke indicates that he stays at least eighteen months and probably a few more in Corinth (Acts 18:1, 11, 18). How exactly Paul's extended stay overlaps with Gallio's term as proconsul remains a disputed issue for scholars. For our purposes, we need not be concerned with the exact overlap, only that the evidence anchors Paul's resurrection message in

---

[45] At this time, the Romans had two main ways of dating documents: the year of a given emperor's reign starting from his taking office, or when that emperor had last received what was called an acclamation, a public celebration of an emperor's achievement, usually a military victory. The letter reads that it is written during the 26th Acclamation of Claudius. Another inscription found at an aqueduct indicates the 27th Acclamation of Claudius is in force by August 1, AD 52 (ending the time span for the 26th Acclamation). Scholars interpolate that a gap in the Delphi letter fragments had carried the year of his reign, which would be his twelfth year starting from his first year that began in January AD 41. Proconsuls customarily served for one year and started in the springtime, usually May 1 (though some scholars assert the annual changeover date was July 1). Using these data points, scholars surmise that the letter is written between January and July AD 52.

Either Gallio had just begun his tenure or was just finishing it. If he had just begun a term running from spring AD 52–53, that assumes a speedy government process; it allows only three months from May to July for the issue of the city's depopulation to arise, to be heard by Gallio, to be decided and then reported to the emperor, and for the emperor to respond. The wheels of Roman bureaucracy tended not to turn that rapidly. For that reason, most scholars presume Gallio serves a term from spring AD 51–52. The letter likely was written before May AD 52. See Klaus Haacker, "Gallio," Freedman, ed., *Anchor Bible Dictionary* (New York, NY: Doubleday, 1992), vol. 2, 901–3. Also see John B. Polhill, *Acts* (Nashville, TN: Broadman & Holman, 1999), 346–47, and Gerhard A. Krodel, *Acts*, Augsburg Commentary on the New Testament (Minneapolis, MN: Augsburg Publishing House, 1986), 98.

Corinth in the period AD 51–52. In that interval, Paul definitely preaches the resurrection to the Corinthians. As a result, the elapsed time for the resurrection announcement is reduced from fifty years since it happened (still assuming Acts is written in the AD 80s) to about just twenty years later. At this point, solid historical evidence places Paul in Corinth inciting opposition to his preaching about Jesus. We have downshifted the proven preaching of the resurrection by about thirty years.

As for Gallio, he misses an opportunity to hear Paul offer the message of salvation through Jesus. About ten years later, he is unfairly accused of being a public enemy by a powerful Roman senator. A while earlier, his brother Seneca and nephew Lucan were condemned for conspiring with rogue senators against Emperor Nero. They were given the noble Roman invitation to "open their veins," that is, to commit suicide, which they do. Gallio had by then reached an even higher position in the government. He was honored with the role of introducing and presiding over Nero's farcical performances, for the emperor performed as a neophyte musician. Nevertheless, Gallio is implicated by his family connections, and he follows them in suffering the same fate of a forced suicide.[46]

### Embedded in the Letter Is the Clue—An Early Creed

Proceeding further in the historical record, is there any other written evidence that the resurrection is preached even sooner than twenty years after the events? There is. It does not bring it quite to the point of fifty days after Passover as Luke reports, but it brings it even closer than twenty years.

The evidence is found in that early letter of Paul to the believers in Corinth. After his case is dismissed by Gallio, Paul stays in Corinth a while building up the fledgling church. Months later, he returns to his base in Antioch, Syria. His home stay is brief. Soon, he begins his third missionary journey traveling again

---

[46] Tacitus, *Annals* 15.73.

through southern Turkey and staying for about three years in Ephesus, near the eastern Aegean coast (today, due to geological changes, the ruins of Ephesus sit well inland). From Ephesus, he writes back to the church in Corinth about AD 55 (Acts 18:11, 18, 23, 19:1–10; 1 Cor. 16:8).

As seen in our prior chapter, the Corinthians have someone teaching them that believers who have died will not be raised from the dead. Paul will answer their doubts with a quiver full of targeted arguments (not our task here, but check chapter 6). However, somewhat miffed, he first takes them back to basics.

> For what I received I passed on to you as of first importance: that Christ died for our sins according to the Scriptures, that he was buried, that he was raised on the third day according to the Scriptures, and that he appeared to Cephas, and then to the Twelve. After that, he appeared to more than five hundred of the brothers and sisters at the same time, most of whom are still living, though some have fallen asleep. Then he appeared to James, then to all the apostles. (1 Corinthians 15:3–7)

Then he adds, "and last of all he appeared to me also, as to one abnormally born" (1 Cor. 15:8). Paul is not so much speaking of birth defects but of a baby born at a much later time than his other older siblings.

Scholars have called attention to how Paul introduces this encapsulation of the resurrection narrative.[47] He writes, "For what I received, I passed on to you as of first importance." He tells them he receives it, so he himself does not craft these lines. His predecessors

---

[47] For this argument, I am indebted to the scholar and professor Gary Habermas. It was first presented to me in the video, Gary Habermas, "The Resurrection Argument That Changed a Generation of Scholars," 9 Nov 2012, at the University of California, Santa Barbara, sponsored by the Veritas Forum, also titled "The Historical Evidence for Jesus' Resurrection That Even Skeptics Believe." See also Gary R. Habermas and Michael R. Licona, *The Case for the Resurrection of Jesus* (Grand Rapids, MI: Kregel, 2004).

in faith put together the evidence. The passage reads like a condensed creed. It distills the faith to a few pointed events in the life of Jesus and lists individuals and groups whom Jesus meets after he is raised. It is easy to see how this simple creed or formula would come in handy to people going out on the preaching circuit. It stabilizes the core message and is easy to remember. It clearly predates Paul's letter and Paul's original visit to Corinth.

Could Paul have meant that he received the condensed creed as a divine revelation to him directly? It is rare for Paul to admit that he receives truth from others. Usually, he is conscious to maintain his authority as an apostle by noting that he has had direct contact with Jesus. If the creed came through a vision, Paul assuredly would indicate it did not arrive through *"any human being"* as he does elsewhere (Gal. 1:15–17, 2:6).

> **Historical Portal:**
> **Galatians Migrate from Gaul**
>
> Early in the third century BC, the Celts originally migrate from Gaul, the north-central area of today's France. They reach the Balkans and then Thrace. A king of Bithynia in northwestern Asia (today's Turkey) invites them to cross over to fortify his side in a power struggle. They are feared warriors and often serve as mercenaries. They establish roots in central Turkey near today's Ankara. The Romans defeat them in 189 BC, and they become a client state. Later, under Pompey in 64 BC, Galatia becomes a Roman province.

The question then becomes, when did Paul receive this early creed? We might be left with that question as a historical mystery except for key data in another early letter of Paul, known as Galatians. First-person accounts, when authors are describing their own lives, are highly valuable data in historical research. Paul's letter to the Galatians qualifies as a primary source. There is no reason to doubt his time frames, and he would be the person best able to calculate his years accurately since he lived them.

## Paul Opens Up His Life to the Galatians with Key Milestones

He writes the letter to churches in Galatia, a central section in today's Turkey.[48] Galatia included the territory of Turkey's current capital, Ankara. In the third century BC, the area had seen a migration of Celtic peoples from Gaul (modern France), hence the name Galatia.[49]

As was often the case, Paul's critics are trying to undercut his authority as an apostle. He wants the Galatians to know that the core of his message comes from his own set of experiences with God; he has not merely copied what the original disciples had to say. He gives his readers a few glimpses into his personal life so they can see how his message has been formed. After his conversion experience in Damascus (see prelude for chapter 6), he heads off on his own only later meeting the leaders in Jerusalem.

> *I did not go up to Jerusalem to see those who were apostles before I was, but I went into Arabia. Later I returned to Damascus. Then after three years, I went up to Jerusalem to get acquainted with Cephas and stayed with him fifteen days. I saw none of the other apostles—only James, the Lord's brother. I assure you before God that what I am writing you is no lie. Then I went to Syria and Cilicia. I was personally unknown to the churches of Judea that are in Christ. They only heard the report: "The man who formerly persecuted us is now preaching the faith he once tried to destroy." And they praised God because of me. (Galatians 1:17-24)*

---

[48] Scholars debate whether Galatians was written from Ephesus about the same time as 1 Corinthians (c. AD 55), or from Corinth after his hearing with Gallio (AD 52), or from Antioch (AD 48) before the Jerusalem council in AD 49-50. I subscribe here to the view that would date Galatians after the council meeting in Jerusalem, which I identify with Paul's description in Gal. 2:1-2.

[49] See "Galatia," wikipedia.org.

Paul explains a second, much later trip to Jerusalem, which had a different purpose.[50]

> *Then after fourteen years, I went up again to Jerusalem, this time with Barnabas. I took Titus along also. I went in response to a revelation and, meeting privately with those esteemed as leaders, I presented to them the gospel that I preach among the Gentiles. I wanted to be sure I was not running and had not been running my race in vain. (Galatians 2:1–2)*

## Two Jerusalem Trips—One Personal, One Business

Paul recounts two of the trips he makes to Jerusalem fourteen years apart. On the first trip, Peter (Paul calls him Cephas, the Aramaic equivalent of "rock") invites him to stay at his house for two weeks in Jerusalem. Paul also meets James the brother of Jesus. Probably due to Paul's past as a persecutor, the visit appears to be secret; this may be why he does not meet many other believers.

He returns to Syria, likely to Antioch, after the Jerusalem visit. Ironically, this is the city where many Jewish Christians fled when persecuted by the Pharisee Saul in Jerusalem. Next, Paul returns to his home province of Cilicia in southeastern Turkey probably to his hometown of Tarsus, a major economic and education center. He remains there about nine years until Barnabas comes calling for him. Barnabas recruits Paul to help him teach the growing numbers of believers in Antioch perhaps at the suggestion of Peter and James, who had met Paul (Acts 11:19–26). Within a few years, the leaders in Antioch ordain Paul and Barnabas to embark on their first missionary journey to the island of Cyprus and southeastern Turkey, the first of Paul's three major missions.

---

[50] According to Acts, there is at least one trip in between these two trips mentioned in Galatians, when Paul goes to Jerusalem with Barnabas on a special mission from Antioch to deliver a monetary gift, and they take John Mark back to Antioch with them (Acts 11:30, 12:25).

On the second trip to Jerusalem that he mentions in Galatians, Paul wants mutually to review beliefs with the core apostles among whom are Peter, James, and John (Gal. 2:2, Acts 15:2–4). The issues involve whether Gentile believers must keep the Law of Moses including being circumcised (see chapter 6). Paul adamantly opposes forcing new believers to keep the Jewish law, and the council favors his view. He wants the Galatians to know that his gospel passed the test of the other apostles and was not missing anything.

Based on the descriptions of the two trips, on which trip is Paul more likely to have received the creedal formula that he passes on to the Corinthians? Evidently on the first trip to Jerusalem rather than on the second. On the first trip, he is a new Christian needing resources and coaching. The two weeks he stays at Peter's house would be the most likely time when he would have received the creed. The fact the creed includes a list that covers appearances to both Peter and James would fit with this visit. On the second trip to Jerusalem, he already is an experienced evangelist due to his teaching in Antioch and his first missionary journey with Barnabas. In reality, he may be going more to be sure that the rest of the apostles are keeping the message straight and not caving in to the circumcisers rather than going to check the validity of his own message. Note his comment on the council result.

> As for those who were held in high esteem—whatever they were makes no difference to me; God does not show favoritism—they added nothing to my message. (Galatians 2:6)

If the other apostles add nothing to his message, this would not be the time Paul receives the condensed creed. It would have been given to him fourteen years earlier on the first trip, when he was a relatively new believer.

## Determining the Year When Paul Clandestinely Visits Peter

Can we determine the approximate year the newly converted Paul stays with Peter in Jerusalem? We can work backward from the anchor date based on the evidence from Paul's first visit to Corinth. From the Gallio hearing and inscription, we know Paul is in Corinth for sure within the one-year range of the spring of AD 51–52 on his second missionary journey. Note that for most dates, it can be helpful to use two-year intervals due to differences in calendars—Jewish, Roman, and our own.

Paul's arrival in Corinth comes after but not long after his second trip to Jerusalem. Some time must elapse for Paul to complete the activities Luke reports that he carries out before he gets to Corinth

> **Bible Sidelight:**
> **John Mark Recovers His Reputation**
>
> The controversial third traveling companion of Barnabas and Paul is John Mark. He left their first missionary journey early, so Paul does not find him reliable when he embarks on his second journey. Later, they reconcile (Col. 4:10; 2 Tim. 4:11; Philem. 1:24).
>
> John Mark is likely the Mark who writes the gospel that bears that name. He is well connected with Peter, who provides much material for his gospel according to tradition. Peter knows his mother Mary, who hosts the disciples in Jerusalem, and he speaks warmly of Mark in a letter (Acts 12:12; 1 Pet. 5:13).

(Acts 15:36–18:1). After the Jerusalem council event, Paul returns to his home base of Antioch and teaches there with his partner Barnabas. The itch strikes Paul to travel and check up on the churches they had planted in their first missionary journey to today's southwestern Turkey.

Barnabas and Paul disagree on a third traveling companion, so they split, and Paul takes a new partner, Silas (Acts 15:36–41). They travel through Syria, Cilicia, Phrygia, and Galatia encouraging the churches planted earlier, and they reach the western coast of

Turkey at Troas (Acts 16:6–8). They sense God leading them to sail to Greece, first to Samothrace, then to Neapolis. Then they travel by land down the coastline of northern Greece, the area called Macedonia (Acts 16:9–10). They conduct personal evangelism or speak in synagogues along the way in Philippi, Thessalonica, and Berea (Acts 16:12–13, 31, 17:1–4, 10).

Antagonizing some synagogue goers with his preaching, Paul becomes a hunted man and must skedaddle on his own to Athens. He preaches near the Acropolis at the Areopagus (see chapter 6). The Athenians with their tendency to intellectualize are not overly responsive; only a few such as Dionysius are willing to commit. So Paul heads to Corinth (Acts 17:18–34, 18:1). Assuming all this activity takes one to two years before he appears to Gallio in Corinth in AD 51–52, his second major trip to Jerusalem (for the council meeting) is likely to have occurred in AD 49–50.

If the second trip is in AD 49–50, Paul's first trip as a new believer occurs fourteen years earlier.[51] Based on this time line, the first trip when Paul receives the creed would occur in AD 35–36.

Before we go further, let us check this conclusion with the time Paul spends in Arabia and the time required for his conversion.

The first trip to Jerusalem takes place after the three years Paul spends in Arabia, which in turn come immediately after his conversion in Damascus. Logically, that three-year period would span either AD 32–35 or AD 33–36. This allows for one to three years to elapse from the estimated dates of the death and resurrection of Jesus, AD 30–31.[52] It allows for two major factors to occur: for Paul to have persecuted Jewish believers as a determined enforcer for the high priest, and then for him to be halted in his tracks and

---

[51] Some scholars interpret the information in Galatians 2:1 to mean that Paul counts the fourteen-year period from the point of his conversion. Along with many others, I interpret Paul's count to begin from the time of his return from his three-year sojourn in Arabia, making it a full seventeen years from his conversion date.

[52] For the calculations behind this time period for the death and resurrection of Jesus, see *Background Guide*, resource 3.

converted on the road to Damascus. At least one year and probably no more than three allow for these two recorded events.

As a result, Paul likely receives the creed in 1 Corinthians 15:1–7 in AD 35–36. This time frame is four to six years after Jesus dies and is reportedly raised from the dead. The breakdown of the range of years works as shown in the following chart. It uses either of the primary options for the year of the crucifixion, either AD 31 or AD 30. If Jesus dies in AD 31 and Paul sees Peter in Jerusalem in AD 35, that allows for a minimum four-year interval between the claimed resurrection event and the documented preaching of the resurrection. If Jesus dies in AD 30 and Paul visits Jerusalem in AD 36, that puts the maximum interval at six years. The interval between the events of the resurrection and the preaching of Jesus as risen from the dead now shrinks to about five years.

Recall that our method here is strictly to base the time for the preaching of the resurrection on dates of the written texts reporting that preaching. As a result, our investigation has reduced the elapsed time between the actual events in Jesus's life to the proven preaching of the resurrection from fifty to about five years.

### *Paul's Chronology Shrinks Elapsed Time for Proclamation*

The data is summarized in the following chart.[53] It shows two closely related timeline options varying by the last year Jesus walks the earth. Some scholars also include the year AD 33 as one candidate for the crucifixion and resurrection. That estimate squeezes Paul's chronology awfully tightly, so here we show the two options that fit better and are generally accepted by most scholars today. (See more on this timeline reasoning in *Background Guide*, resource 3.)

---

[53] One effective source for Paul's chronology is "Apostle Paul's Timeline— Study Resources," blueletterbible.org, *Blue Letter Bible Institute*, retrieved 7 Sept. 2018. See also "Timeline of Paul's Life," Barker, ed., *NIV Study Bible*, 1664–65. In the chart, I have made independent judgments from the data to the extent that this abbreviated timeline is my own best estimate not derived directly from any single source.

## ESTIMATED TIMELINE OF EVENTS IN PAUL'S LIFE (ALL YEARS AD)

| Estimated Year | Key Events in the Life of Paul | References (Acts unless noted) |
|---|---|---|
| 30 or 31 | Jesus Dies/Rises in Jerusalem | Luke 23:1–24:53 |
| | | |
| | The Switch: | |
| 30–32 or 32–33 | Paul Persecutes Believers | 8:1–3; Phil. 3:6 |
| 32 or 33 | Converts on the Damascus Road | 9:1–19 |
| 32–35 or 33–36 | Sojourns in Arabia | Gal. 1:17 |
| 35 or 36 | Stays with Peter in Jerusalem | 9:26–29; Gal. 1:18–20 |
| 35/36–45 | Returns to Tarsus for Years | 9:30 |
| | | |
| | The Missions: | |
| 46–47 | Teaches with Barnabas in Antioch | 11:25–26 |
| 47–48 | Takes Journey One (with Barnabas) | 13:1–14:28 |
| 49 or 50 | Presents at Jerusalem Council | 15:1–30; Gal. 2:1 |
| 50–53 | Takes Journey Two (with Silas, Luke) | 15:40–18:22 |
| 51–52 | Resides in Corinth 18 months plus | 18:1–18 |
| 51–52 | Dismissed by Proconsul Gallio | 18:12–17 |
| 53–57 | Takes Journey Three | 18:23–21:19 |
| 54–56 | Resides in Ephesus two years plus | 19:1–20:1 |
| 55 | Writes 1 Corinthians Letter | 18:1–2,19; 1Cor. 16:19 |
| 56–57 | Travels to Macedonia/Greece | 20:2–5 |
| 57 | Stays in Corinth three months | 20:2 |
| 57 | Writes Romans Letter from Corinth | Rom. 16:1, 23 |
| 57 | Sails back to Judea (with Luke) | 20:6–21:19 |
| | | |
| | The Road to Rome: | |
| 57 | Arrested at Jerusalem Temple Riot | 21:27–36 |
| 57–59 | Incarcerated in Caesarea | 23:23–26:32 |
| 59 | Sails to Rome (with Luke) | 27:1–28:15 |
| 60 | Kept under House Arrest in Rome | 28:16–31 |
| 62 | Likely Released | 2 Tim. 4:16–18 |
| 62–66 | Takes Mission to Spain (possible) | Rom. 15:23–28 |
| 66 or 67 | Rearrested and Martyred by Nero | Eusebius, Chr. Hist. 2.25.5 |

Some scholars take this line of evidence based on the creedal source material even further. The creed that Paul receives probably is not hammered out during his two-week visit to Jerusalem but earlier, maybe a year or more. Paul offers the creed in Greek to the Corinthians, but the original creed was likely written in Aramaic, the language the Jews of Israel spoke in the first century. The language rhythm in the letter suggests Paul does not translate the creed himself but has received it in Greek, so the creed in Aramaic may have been crafted substantially earlier than its translation into Greek. These considerations lead some scholars to estimate that as few as six months elapsed from the time of Jesus's departure from earth to the formation of this creed.[54]

At any rate, reducing the elapsed time of the preaching of the resurrection—as proven by this strict method of dating written texts—from fifty years down to about five years or even fewer has huge ramifications; it means there was no time for a legend about the resurrection to form. With merely five or so years, the idea that a legend based on layers of folklore could accrete in such a short amount of time is absurd.[55]

This evidence embedded in Paul's letter to Corinth adds strong probability to Luke's history that the disciples were preaching the resurrection from the outset. The resurrection account cannot be summarily dismissed as a later invention; it was the core message of the Christian faith from the beginning.

---

[54] Gary Habermas, "The Resurrection Argument."
[55] This exercise in source analysis of the creed in 1 Corinthians has created something of a revolution in the study of Christian origins because it severely undercuts the legend theory. For a legend to develop, it takes two forty-year generations or eighty years at a minimum, according to A.N. Sherwin-White, *Roman Society and Roman Law in the New Testament* (Oxford, UK: Clarendon Press, 1963), 189, cited by Norman L. Geisler, "The Dating of the New Testament," *The Baker Encyclopedia of Christian Apologetics* (Ada, MI: Baker, 2007), bethinking.org., n.p., n.d.

# 7: CONCLUSION

## On the Early Preaching of the Resurrection

The English author and professor C. S. Lewis* wrote that unbelievers were essentially faced with the proposition that Jesus fits one of these three descriptors: a liar, a lunatic or the Lord. Beg your pardon, the skeptics demur. You are leaving out another *L* word, namely *legend.* Many skeptics, not willing to accept any of Lewis's other *L* word options, take refuge in the notion of legend.

But the documented evidence does not afford them that luxury. There was no time for a legend to form. Whether you believe the disciples got it wrong or right, they preached their message of the resurrection of Jesus soon after they claimed they saw him alive. The core message in their preaching or in their succeeding documents of letters and gospels was formulated early and remained consistent. Jesus suffered and died, but then he rose from the dead physically. That was their message. Consequently, if you read what our Jewish prophets foretold, the apostles persistently preached, then the resurrection means Jesus is indeed the Messiah and the Lord not only for Israel but also for the whole world.

*C. S. Lewis, *Mere Christianity* (Glasgow, UK: William Collins, Fontana Books, 1956, first edition 1952), 52–53.

# CHAPTER

# LINE OF EVIDENCE

## SUMMARY

Many tales begin with the indefinite phrases "Once upon a time" or "In a faraway land." A hoax or legend travels better if the storytellers live far from the place where it supposedly happened. Otherwise, locals can deny it ever occurred and call it a crock.

Though some disciples immediately leave to spread the message far and wide, several key disciples base themselves in Jerusalem for twenty years or more after Jesus departs. By continuing to reside where they claim the resurrection occurred, they show they do not believe any locals can produce evidence to contradict their accounts. Their staying put where all events reportedly happened adds greater historical probability that the resurrection occurred just as they asserted.

# PRELUDE

## CHAPTER 8

A bent over figure, an aged man, lumbers up a mountain rising out of three steep valleys. With him is a boy probably in his early teens. He is trailing behind the man and bearing a load on his back. The elevated vista where they are heading is known as Mount Moriah.

Though he lives as a nomad in tents, the man is wealthy. He has many servants, and he owns vast herds of cattle and sheep that multiply like seeds of grass. Producing children has been another matter, a sorrow-laden challenge area for Abraham and his wife, Sarah. For years, in his heart, he has held a promise he was sure he had heard from God that he would be the father of many nations as numerous as the stars.

Decades pass. At one point, he and Sarah desperately devise a plan to help God out with his promise. She lets her husband sleep with her maid to produce a son, a common custom for a barren matriarch. A son results, but he is not the promised one, whose mother must be Sarah (Gen. 16:1-4, 17:16, 19, 21).

So they wait and wait. She passes age ninety, and he passes age one hundred. Then—Mazel tov!—a son of their own finally is born to the elderly couple. They name him Isaac, or *"he laughs."* It may mean his aged father laughs with joy. Or perhaps it is God who chuckles at those who thought he could not manage to keep his promise through elderly people (Gen. 21:1-7; for more laughs from the proud parents, see also Gen. 17:15-22, 18:10-15).

For years, as their son grows up, joy flows through their hearts like a sparkling river.

Yet now, a sorrow beyond tears afflicts the soul of Abraham as he climbs the mountain with his son. Isaac shoulders the wood. He sees the knife his father carries and asks him where the lamb required for offering the sacrifice is. *"God himself will provide the lamb for the burnt offering, my son,"* Abraham achingly utters (Gen. 22:8). Had he heard God rightly? Or was his old mind playing tricks on him? It was unmistakable but really unthinkable. He had heard rightly, but it was wrong. The God who promised him a child, who made him wait a lifetime for a son with Sarah, and who finally kept his promise is now asking him to sacrifice this son upon a stone outcropping on a mountain in Moriah?

With biceps worn lean by sheep shearing and cattle prodding, Abraham cinches up the ropes to bind his son on top of the firewood. He lifts the knife high over the head of his treasured son; his arm is poised to descend when—*"Abraham, Abraham! Do not lay a hand on the boy,"* a voice from heaven calls. There is a rustle in the thicket. A ram is caught by its horns. Abraham captures the ram and sacrifices it on the stone altar instead of his son. Whew. All the way down to the bottom of the mountain where their servants waited, Abraham and Isaac breathe out their adrenaline, their relief, their awe (Gen. 22:1–19).

What was Abraham thinking as he trod up the mountain? The writer of the book of Hebrews explains. *Abraham reasoned that God could even raise the dead, and so in a manner of speaking, he did receive Isaac back from death* (Heb. 11:19).

About eleven hundred years later, a temple is dedicated in about 960 BC atop this same mountain.[56] It is planned by one king

---

[56] The calculation of about eleven hundred years between Abraham's sacrifice and the building of the first temple works as follows. Assuming Abraham is born c. 2160 BC and Isaac c. 2060 BC, their mountain trek occurs c. 2050 BC when Isaac is at least ten. The Jebusite city is not built until c. 1330. David (born c. 1040 BC, crowned king at age thirty, c. 1010 BC) conquers Jerusalem in 1003 BC after reigning seven years in Hebron (1 Chron. 11:4–5). He then reigns thirty-three years from Jerusalem until his death at age seventy in 970 BC. Eleven years later (1 Kings 6:37–38),

238

of Israel, David, and built by his son, Solomon, who succeeds him. It is possible that the rock altar of Abraham formed the floor of the temple's inner sanctum, the holy of holies.[57]

About a thousand years after this first temple is built, there would be a crucifixion, a man dying on a cross just down the mountain from where Isaac reportedly was spared. His disciples preach he is the Messiah descended from Abraham and David. He is crucified yet raised from the dead. He is sacrificed for the sins of all humanity they say. Through him, the promise to Abraham is fulfilled: *"All peoples on earth will be blessed through you"* (Gen. 12:3). The good news about a Messiah who suffered for everyone and then rose from the dead ripples out from Jerusalem to the ends of the earth.

---

Solomon dedicates the completed temple in 960–959 BC, slightly less than eleven hundred years from c. 2050 BC, when Isaac escapes the woodpile. Of course, other calculations are asserted.

[57] See Barker, ed., *NIV Study Bible*, 430. Other scholars locate Mount Moriah near Shechem, where Abraham builds an altar in a separate episode (Gen. 12:6). Moreh is the name of an area near Shechem and may derive from the Amorite tribe. This theory gives credence to the ancient Samaritan claim that the Isaac event took place on Mount Gerizim near Shechem. However, this conflicts with the conversation Jesus has with the woman at the well in which he points out that the Samaritans are on the wrong track with their worship. On the other hand, he says, it won't matter much longer because worship will be in Spirit and truth and not limited to their mountain or the temple mount in Jerusalem (Jn 4:4–26). See Joseph Jacobs and M. Seligsohn, "Moriah," jewishencyclopedia.com, *Jewish Encyclopedia*, 14 Jul 2008, retrieved 14 July 2017.

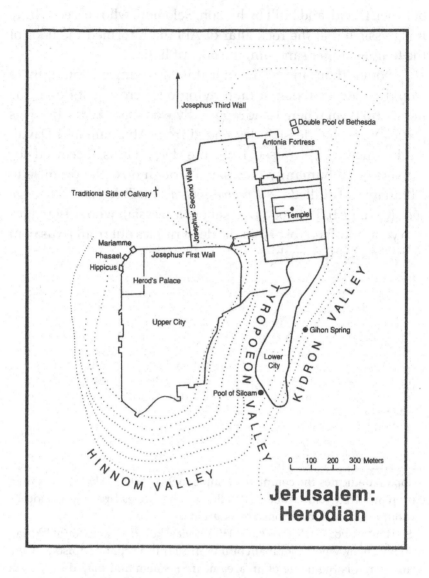

The Jerusalem Jesus Knew. The city's inhabitants remain mostly in the Lower City during King David's time. By the time Jesus arrives, Jerusalem had expanded to the Upper City, and had gained a temple complex massively enlarged by King Herod. Opposite the temple to the east stood the Mount of Olives. The temporary tomb of Jesus was on the west side near the crucifixion at a site denoted here as "Calvary." Excerpt from *Baker's Concise Bible Atlas* by J. Carl Laney © 1988. Used by permission of Baker Books, a division of Baker Publishing Group.

240

## CHAPTER 8

---

# JERUSALEM REMAINS THE EPICENTER OF THE MESSAGE

---

t sounds like Jesus has just about had it with the Jerusalem elites. He calls them out on the temple grounds several days before the first day of the Passover feast, which will bring about his arrest and death.

> *"Woe to you, teachers of the law and Pharisees, you hypocrites! You build tombs for the prophets and decorate the graves of the righteous. And you say, 'If we had lived in the days of our ancestors, we would not have taken part with them in shedding the blood of the prophets.' So you testify against yourselves that you are the descendants of those who murdered the prophets. Go ahead, then, and complete what your ancestors started!"* (Matthew 23:29–32)

Jesus practically dares the leaders to put in motion their plot to kill him.

It was not always this tense for Jesus in Jerusalem. One of the few glimpses of Jesus in his early years is recounted by Luke in his gospel. The family of Jesus journeys from Nazareth to

Jerusalem for the Passover festival when he is twelve. The devout family goes every year. From Nazareth, it is a five-day walk, about sixty-five miles or 105 kilometers. It is not so much a family vacation as a community caravan.

Interpretive Angle:
**Young Jesus Quizzes the Teachers**

Critics challenge this account of Jesus as a preteen as not authentic. Yet it meets a key criterion of historicity, the criterion of embarrassment. It could be interpreted as tarnishing the reputation of Jesus. It looks like he is borderline disobedient to his parents, a grave infraction in that culture. As a result, it would be more improbable to make up this account that might make Jesus look rebellious.

Many villagers from the north travel the road together for safety and company. After the festival ends, the caravan moves out for the return home. His father and mother lose track of where Jesus is, but they figure he is somewhere among their friends or relatives.

After one day, they still cannot find him. They hurry back to Jerusalem and still cannot find him for three more days. Finally, the mystery is solved. He is hanging out with the teachers in the temple courts listening and asking questions (Lk 2:41–46).

*Everyone who heard him was amazed at his understanding and his answers. When his parents saw him, they were astonished. His mother said to him, "Son, why have you treated us like this? Your father and I have been anxiously searching for you." "Why were you searching for me?" he asked. "Didn't you know I had to be in my Father's house?" But they did not understand what he was saying to them. Then he went down to Nazareth with them and was obedient to them. (Luke 2:47–51a)*

As a boy, Jesus is well received at the temple by the teachers. A quick study, he takes advantage of the opportunity to learn from the best teachers in Israel. They marvel at his knowledge and incisive questions. Chances are that he inquires about the predictions in the scriptures concerning the Messiah. Already, his identity as the Messiah may have formed as revealed by his referring to the temple as the house of his Father. It is no accident that this temple seminar is attended by Jesus at age twelve; it is the age of responsibility in Jewish culture.

Now, if we fast-forward about twenty years later, Jesus arranges to ride into Jerusalem on a donkey. He borrows it from a villager living along the road to Jerusalem. He rides out of the village, down the Mount of Olives, through the Kidron Valley, then up to the gates of Jerusalem. It is not a quiet moment. People are streaming into the city for the feast. Jesus is known as a prophet and healer. Some people including children give him a messianic cheer, *"Blessed is he who comes in the name of the Lord."* Some wave palm branches, and others spread coats ahead of the donkey's hooves. Palm branches symbolize victory while spreading coats on the road is a custom to honor a royal figure. Cries of *"Hosanna"* arise, meaning, "Save us." Others shout, *"Blessed is the coming kingdom of our father David!"* (Mk 11:9–10). All these phrases carry messianic overtones.

> Found in the Ground:
> **Trumpeting Inscription**
>
> Jerusalem—Found in 1968 near the south wall of the temple mount. The inscription was a directional sign for priests to find the spot where they were to blow the trumpet to signal the beginning of the Sabbath at sunset and its end at twilight the next day. In Jerusalem, Jesus and his disciples would hear the trumpet sounding from this place. This custom is mentioned by Josephus. (*War* 4.9.12)
>
> Index 8.1

The city is stirred by this one-rider parade, but Jesus senses the party spirit is not shared by the religious power brokers. According to Luke's account, the scene brings Jesus to tears. *As he approached the city he wept over it, and said, "If you, even you, had only known on this day what would bring you peace—but now it is hidden from your eyes" (Luke 19:41–42).*

## Jesus Foresees Judgment Coming Upon Jerusalem

Interpretive Angle:
**Turning the Tables on the Moneychangers**

When Jesus teaches in the temple courts ahead of the Passover feast, he uses the moment to predict judgment on the Jerusalem leaders (Mk 12:1–12; Lk 20:9–19). His clearing of the moneychangers is seen by some scholars as a reform effort, but due to his quotations from the prophets, he appears to be not reforming but pronouncing judgment on the temple system. (Mk 11:15–17; Isa. 56:7; Jer. 7:11)

In his last week, Jesus senses that not only is his own fate on the line but also that of the city with its leaders on the verge of rejecting him as Messiah. When Jesus returns the next day and begins upsetting the tables of the temple-sanctioned moneychangers, he infuriates the high priests. They conspire to find an opportune time to capture him when the festival crowds, who esteem him for his healings and his teachings, are not around. The stakes are high as seen in the tense discussions Jesus has with the leaders at the temple complex the week before he dies (see these chapters: Mk 11–12; Mt 22–23; Lk 20). According to Matthew's account, he grieves earnestly, tenderly, even maternally over the people of the city, for what might have been.

> *"Jerusalem, Jerusalem, you who kill the prophets and stone those sent to you, how often I have longed to gather your children together, as a hen gathers her chicks under her wings, and you were not willing." (Matthew 23:37)*

Then he predicts judgment will come upon Jerusalem. *"Look, your house is left to you desolate"* (Mt 23:38). Almost certainly, Jesus is alluding to the words Solomon recounted as spoken by the Lord when he appeared to him upon the completion of the first temple. The Lord warns Solomon that if he or his descendants worship other gods, the temple will be rejected.

> *"This temple will become a heap of rubble. All who pass by will be appalled and will scoff and say, 'Why has the Lord done such a thing to this land and to this temple?' People will answer, 'Because they have forsaken the Lord their God, who brought their ancestors out of Egypt, and have embraced other gods, worshiping and serving them—that is why the Lord brought all this disaster on them.'" (1 Kings 9:8–9)*

Based on that allusion, Jesus has Jerusalem's judgment in mind. Perhaps trying to change the subject to ease the tension, several unidentified disciples point out how beautiful the temple buildings look. Jesus is not impressed.

> *"Do you see all these buildings?" replied Jesus. "Not one stone here will be left on another; every one will be thrown down." (Mark 13:2)*

Found in the Ground:
**Western Wall**

Jerusalem—The wall is on the southwestern side of the temple mount. It is the only remaining structure from the second temple, the temple renovated by Herod the Great as opposed to the first temple built by Solomon. It is not a wall of the temple or any building that stood on the temple complex. It is a set of large stones functioning as a retaining wall Herod built to enlarge greatly the esplanade or plaza to create a wide and flat space on the temple mount. After 1967, the wall became a prayer and pilgrimage site for reverent Jewish believers. The site supports the gospel accounts of the expansive area on the temple mount where crowds could gather to hear Jesus teach and later to see the disciples preach and sometimes get arrested (Mk 11:27, 12:35, 41; Acts 2:46, 3:11–4:4; 4:1–4). The stones stacked on top of one another do not negate Jesus's prediction that no stone would remain left upon another. That historically accurate prediction applied to buildings on the site, not to the retaining walls. (Mk 13:1–2; Mt 24:1–2; Lk 21:5–6)

Index 8.2

These somewhat offhand words of Jesus distinctly remembered by the disciples proved true. When the Romans invade Jerusalem after a lengthy siege, the temple and the surrounding buildings are destroyed in AD 70. Indeed, not one stone of any building is left on another. When the heat of the fire sends inlaid gold from upper surfaces running down between stones, the Roman soldiers turn over each stone of the buildings to dig out the gold. However, the huge stones forming retaining walls to hold up the earthen platform of the temple complex remain to this day. One of these retaining walls is known in present-day Israel as the Western Wall; it is renowned as a sacred space for prayer.

Jesus tells his disciples that the city of Jerusalem is dangerous and treacherous. They kill the prophets here. They are about to reject Jesus. They face certain judgment. Why then after Jesus departs the earth do the disciples remain in Jerusalem?

For twenty years, while some disciples have left on international missions, the core leaders continue to base themselves in the city. We know they stay because Peter, John, and James the brother of Jesus all still reside there when an urgent conference is called. The heated issue is whether Gentile converts must keep the Law of Moses and particularly the tradition of circumcision. It turns out they do not, as the council waives the requirement.

## Importance of Leaders' Long-Term Jerusalem Residence

We will explore shortly the reasons the leaders stay, but the fact that they stay for two decades or more in Jerusalem is another line of evidence for the reality of Jesus's resurrection.

Their residing in Jerusalem means the message about Jesus is preached very near the places where the events reportedly happened. If the story is false, preaching the message in the same locality where the events take place creates an ongoing vulnerability; local witnesses can contradict it. If the authorities wish to suppress the movement, all they need do is point to the sealed grave or produce the bones of the

Found in the Ground:
**Arch of Titus South Panel Relief**

Rome—An arch has stood on Palatine Hill for nearly two millennia, erected in AD 82. The south relief panel on stone depicts the Roman general Titus Vespasian destroying Jerusalem in AD 70. It shows telltale symbols of victory over the Jews with spoils of war including a menorah, trumpets, fire pans used for catching ashes from the temple altar, and the table of showbread. The arch was constructed to honor the victories of Titus by his younger brother, Emperor Domitian. The design serves as a template for other arches in history, among them the Arc de Triomphe in Paris. The panel relief celebrates the success of the Roman siege and confirms Jesus's predictions about the devastating destruction of the city and people of Jerusalem. (Lk 19:41–44, 21:5–6, 20–24; Mk 13:2)

Index 8.3

deceased to make such patently false beliefs peter out. These conditions are why legends and fairy tales are often set in lands far, far away from where they are retold.

On the other hand, if the story is true, preaching in the vicinity can allow it to be confirmed; local witnesses can back it up. The places like the crucifixion site and the burial tomb can be checked objectively. The witnesses who testify to seeing Jesus after his death can be checked by skeptics for their level of cognition and general mental health.

### Jesus Bids His Followers Stay in Jerusalem Short-Term

At the time, the disciples were not thinking how they could provide us with the helpful historical fact of their long-term Jerusalem address to increase the historical probability of the resurrection narrative for us. Instead, they probably were thinking strategically about their mission based on how Jesus had instructed them.

Initially, he tells them to remain in Jerusalem until they receive power from the Holy Spirit coming upon them, as promised.

> *"Do not leave Jerusalem, but wait for the gift my Father promised, which you have heard me speak about."* (Acts 1:4b)

His disciples are hoping this would be the moment when he would *"restore the kingdom to Israel."* He does not deny the existence of that plan but does not commit to a certain time. He has something else he wants them to do first.

> He said to them: *"It is not for you to know the times or dates the Father has set by his own authority. But you will receive power when the Holy Spirit comes on you; and you will be my witnesses in Jerusalem, and in all Judea and Samaria, and to the ends of the earth."* (Acts 1:7–8)

Jesus instructs his disciples to stay in Jerusalem for the giving of the Spirit, which happened at the Feast of Weeks (or Pentecost) about fifty days after Passover. On the day the Spirit comes, after the preaching of Peter, thousands of Jews embrace the good news and are gathered into the Jesus community in Jerusalem (see chapter 4). Once this promise is fulfilled, the apostles' task becomes to witness to the resurrection and the message of forgiveness through faith in him starting in Jerusalem.

Peter and John fearlessly carry the message of Jesus before the high priests and the state council, or Sanhedrin in the heart of Jerusalem. They make other trips beyond the city. They head out to Samaria to follow up on Philip's prior mission to that region, which Jesus specifically mentioned as a priority (Acts 1:8). Peter is recorded visiting Joppa (now part of today's Tel Aviv) then Caesarea, and he probably helps start the thriving church in Antioch, Syria. It is a well-traveled destination a good distance away of 225 miles or 360 kilometers from Jerusalem (Acts 10:5, 23–24, 11:22, Gal. 2:11–13).

After that, the apostles could go anywhere with the good news. Jesus said to stay weeks in Jerusalem, not necessarily for decades. There were clear reasons to leave Jerusalem right away.

---

Found in the Ground:
**Temple Sundial**

Jerusalem—Found in 1972. A limestone sundial is left behind by the Romans in the rubble after the destruction of the temple in AD 70. The sundial face is calibrated to tell the time and seasons from the vantage point of Jerusalem. Engraved on the reverse side is a seven-branched menorah. It was used by priests to perform rituals at scheduled times. The finding supports the destruction of the temple area as predicted by Jesus. (Lk 19:41–44)

Index 8.4

## There Is Serious Danger of Persecution in Jerusalem

In Jerusalem, the apostles are vulnerable to the whims of the central religious and secular Jewish and Roman occupying authorities. Peter and John are arrested and jailed more than once. James the brother of John is executed as a martyr by a Herodian king ten to twelve years after Jesus leaves. Peter narrowly escapes execution by the same hand (Acts 12:2). James the brother of Jesus, known in tradition as James the Just, continues to lead the home church for thirty years until the early 60s. He maintains the respect of Pharisees and Sadducees with his meticulous keeping of Jewish ethical and ceremonial law. Yet during a choppy transition between Roman governors when a brief vacancy ensues, a rogue high priest executes James for supposedly violating the Jewish law; it amounts to judicial murder. When the people protest, the newly installed Roman governor dismisses the abusive high priest (see chapter 5).

## Evidence of Sustained Financial Distress in Jerusalem

Besides the constant threat of persecution, the Jerusalem church suffers from economic pressure. That would give them another reason to leave the city. It is not completely clear why believers are so poor in Jerusalem though some explanations make sense. First, the glory days of Herod the Great, when Israel is a trading center and financial powerhouse, do not continue. Seamless trade is impeded after the country is divided between his ruling descendants in outlying regions and direct Roman control of Judea.

Second, Roman records show several empire-wide famines under Claudius during his reign as emperor from 41–54.[58] Third,

---

[58] At least four famines occur during the reign of Claudius (AD 41–54). The first afflicts Rome in AD 41–42 during his first year as ruler. The second in AD 45 in his fourth year affects Judea, likely the one Luke records (Acts 11:28). The third famine troubles Greece in AD 50. The fourth again harms Rome in AD 52. See wordsfitlyspoken.org, *The Gospel Guardian*,

there was a trend for widows and the elderly to retire to Jerusalem. This way, these seniors could feel closer to God and be buried near the temple. As a result, the church probably felt an obligation to assist them should they run out of means. Yet too many retirees may have overburdened the community.

Fourth, believers living in Jerusalem may have faced employment discrimination for their alternative faith in Jesus as the Messiah. Paul on his journeys and in his letters counsels the new churches in Gentile countries to lend a hand financially to the poor and needy in Jerusalem. Since the Gentiles received spiritual blessings through the Jews, Paul says they can show their gratitude to God by giving his original people material blessings (2 Cor. 8:3–5, 13–15, 9:1–3, 12–15; Rom. 15:25–27).

Given the financial stress and constant threat of persecutions, living conditions in Jerusalem are less than ideal. Why might the leading disciples remain for so long? To answer the question, we will look first at how their staying in Jerusalem helped them fulfill their evangelistic mission. Then we will consider how their staying may have been due in part to a fear of missing out on a big deal, the return of Jesus to earth, which they expected sooner rather than later. They actually did not know when he would return, but they did know it would be to Jerusalem due to the Messiah's connection to the esteemed King David.

About a thousand years after David when the disciples come on the scene, they consciously make reference to David and the promises made to him. It will be worth briefly reviewing how David made the city of Jerusalem so central to the faith of Israel. This way, we will know some of the thinking and assumptions that were in the minds of the leading disciples as they based the critical mass of their leadership in that city for at least the first two decades of their outreach.

---

Dec. 1, 1955, vol. 7 no. 30, 2–3a. Attesting to these famines are the Roman writers Suetonius in *Claudius* 18.2, Tacitus in *Annals* 12.43, and Dio Cassius in *History* 40.11, from William H. Shea, "Famine," Freedman, ed., *Anchor Bible Dictionary*, vol. 2, 772.

## The Most Efficient Way to Evangelize Their Own Ethnicity

Remaining in Jerusalem makes sense when we consider that the disciples at first primarily focus on reaching their fellow Jews. Three times per year, most Jewish males who could afford the time off were expected to travel to Jerusalem (Ex. 23:14–17; Deut. 16:16–17) for three distinct feasts: in the spring, the Passover or the Feast of Unleavened Bread (barley harvest, Ex. 34:18; Lev. 23:5–7, recounting the liberation from Egypt); the Feast of Weeks fifty days later in early summer (wheat harvest, Ex. 34:22; Lev. 23:16–17, recounting the giving of the law); and the Feast of Booths (of Tabernacles or Ingathering) in late summer or early fall (olive and grape harvest, Ex. 34:22; Lev. 23:33–43, recounting mobile-home living in the wilderness on the way to the Promised Land).

With this cyclical influx, the apostles do not need to go to the Jewish people living in enclaves all around the Mediterranean; the Jewish people come to them three times per year, and that presents constant opportunities for evangelism. It also means the church serves as a training station. Preachers can learn the ropes in Jerusalem and then go out to the Jewish communities in other lands.

In the first two decades of the church, Paul is the outlier focused on the Gentile world. However, his practice in pagan cities is to start preaching first in the synagogues if they will hear him and only then moving out to reach the assorted pagans in town (see chapter 6).

For an extended time, Peter, John, and James felt called to their own Jewish people (Gal. 2:7–10). They leave the pagans to Paul. Later, all but James move out from Jerusalem to live among the Gentiles as the pagans respond more readily to the preaching of the good news. Christian tradition globally repositions John in Ephesus near the west coast of Turkey and

Peter in Rome but not for at least twenty years from the time Jesus departs earth.[59]

## They Want Kingdom to Come Sooner Rather Than Later

Another possible reason the disciples may have stayed for a long term in Jerusalem could be their expectation that Jesus might return quickly. At the very moment when Jesus tells his disciples to be his witnesses, they are wondering if this will be the time when he restores the kingdom to Israel. They expect him to take political power and rule from the throne of his ancestor and the great king of Israel, David (see chapter 9). Many OT prophets predicted the Messiah, a descendant of David, would rule the earth from David's throne in Jerusalem.[60]

The disciples were told by Jesus of the need for the evangelistic mission first, but all the same, they would like to reign with him sooner rather than later (Acts 1:6, 3:21). They do not want to miss the event of Jesus's return in power if it is going to happen soon. Not only the original disciples see Jesus returning soon, but along with them, Paul seems to think Jesus will return in his lifetime (1 Thess. 4:16–17). To be sure, it is advantageous for their mission that the early apostles were under the impression Jesus might return soon because that gave them a compelling sense of urgency to evangelize. But Jesus himself never committed to a specific time (Mt 24:36).

The disciples do not know when Jesus will return, but they do know where.

---

[59] The contention that Peter and John remain based in Jerusalem for the first twenty years is based on dating the departure of Jesus to around AD 30–31 and the Jerusalem council in Acts 15 to around AD 49–50.

[60] The OT provides strong grounding for the belief that the Messiah from David's line would rule the nations. Among the references: 2 Sam. 7:16–29; Ps. 45:6–7, 89:3–4, 132:11–12; Isa. 9:7; Jer. 33:17–26; Ezek. 37:24–28; Dan. 2:44, 7:14, 7:27; Mic. 4:7; Zech. 14:9. See chapter 9.

### God Is Not Finished with the Mount of Olives Yet

At his ascension, the disciples are told he will return to the same spot whence he left. That spot Luke locates on the Mount of Olives in Jerusalem across the valley from the temple on the east side (Acts 1:9–12).

This was a place Jesus definitely enjoyed. From the Mount of Olives, one of his favorite spots, he could look west over the Kidron Valley and see the temple and the place of burnt offering over the low eastern wall. In this garden, Jesus spends his last night intensively praying while his drowsy disciples go in and out of consciousness.

Then he is arrested in that place under the torchlights of temple guards. Earlier that evening, he had told his disciples they all would fall away in the heat of the night. But that was then. Now, Jesus is back from the dead alive and well among them. The resurrection has burst open the entrance into a whole new direction in life for all of them.

Right after Jesus ascends from the Mount of Olives into a cloud, the disciples are told Jesus will come back in the same way they saw him go (Acts 1:11). Centuries earlier the prophet Zechariah, son of Berechiah and grandson of Iddo, foresaw that the Messiah will stand victoriously on the Mount of Olives after he returns and defeats all enemies amassed against Israel.

When he does arrive at the mount, things on earth will start shifting right away according to the prophet. The feet of the Messiah will stand on the mountain before an earthquake splits it in two with the split running east to west. This geological change will create new river flows. Armies of many nations will surround Jerusalem and capture half of it, but the Lord will fight against the nations and strike them with plague, panic, and civil war in their ranks. Jerusalem will be wealthy from the war reparations, secure, and never again destroyed. Survivors from the defeated nations will worship God at annual feasts in Jerusalem (Zech. 14:1–11).

Their Messiah, now their king, will rule from Jerusalem and

fulfill the prophecies that he would come in power with authority over all nations.

> *The Lord will be king over the whole earth. On that day*
> *there will be one Lord, and his name the only name.*
> *(Zechariah 14:9)*

The disciples know enough of these prophecies to expect Jesus to return to Jerusalem, nowhere else. In their day, the city already had been the spiritual center of Israel for the prior thousand years. Yet in Israelite history, Jerusalem's position at the center of religious and government life was not always the case. The one who made it happen is the OT figure most associated with the city and the Messiah. That would be David.

---

Found in the Ground:
**Inscription on the Reign of David**

Tel Dan, Israel—Found in 1993 in northern Israel near the base of Mount Hermon is a stone stele dated to the ninth century BC. On the stele, an Aramaean king recounts how he defeats in battle two southern neighbors, which he identifies as "the king of Israel" and the "king of the House of David." This is the first archaeological evidence discovered that affirms the existence of King David, a major figure in the OT writings. It shows that a century after David's death, he continues to be recognized as a significant enemy of the Arameans. The finding confirms that King David was an actual historical figure, not a fictional creation of the OT writers or editors. (2 Sam. 8:6; 1 Chron. 18:6; Acts 2:22–36, 13:34–37)

Index 8.5

---

Historical Portal:
## Jerusalem Awaits David's Conquest

The city was occupied by a Canaanite tribe, the Jebusites, at least three hundred years earlier than David's conquest, so it is not surprising the name of the city derives from Canaanite terminology. It is generally accepted that the city was known as Urusalim with *uru* meaning city and *salim* commonly meaning peace. Scholars trace the meaning of salim to a Canaanite god variously known as shalim, shalem, salem, or salim all based on the Semitic consonantal root S-L-M. This supposed god controlled dusk and the evening star (the planet Venus) as the completion of the day with a sunset or evening star encompasses a sense of peace.

## David Captures Jerusalem and Makes It the Capital City

David is thirty when he becomes king. At first, he bases himself in the town of Hebron in southern Israel. Then he decides to conquer the small outpost of a tribe of Jebusites already called Jerusalem.

Moses never makes it to Jerusalem or even west of the Jordan River. His successor, Joshua, conquers Jericho, the fortress town on the west bank of the Jordan. Jericho lies to the east of Jerusalem, eighteen miles or twenty-nine kilometers down a steep, winding, hazardous road.

On his way to conquering vast regions in the land of Canaan to be settled by the twelve tribes of Israel, Joshua never attempts to take Jerusalem. Now, it affords David a neutral site for his capital as it sits between the lands of the ten tribes to the north and the two tribes to the south.

David probably also wants the city for the same reason Joshua does not try to conquer it—it has highly defensible geography. To the west was the Tyropoeon Valley, to the east the Kidron Valley, and to the south the Hinnom Valley. Only the north was open and vulnerable, but it faced up the mountain known as Mount Moriah. As for the mode of conquest, a valiant few from David's

Bible Sidelight:
The Ark of the Covenant

When out and about, the ark is covered with skins and blue cloth and the box is not to be seen or touched. It is carried by priests, who shoulder long poles, or staves, that slip through rings on four corners of the ark. The poles remain inserted at all times. The ark symbolizes the presence and glory of God. It marches out to battle ahead of the Israelite fighting force, staying ahead of the soldiers by at least 2,600 feet or 800 meters. When the ark finally is lodged in the holy of holies in the newly erected temple, the temple is filled with a cloud signaling the presence of the Lord God. (1 Kings 8:10–11; 2 Chron. 5:13–14)

forces led by the warrior Joab locate and climb through a tunnel built to access an underground spring. David's commandos surprise the overconfident Jebusites and conquer from within (2 Sam. 5:6–10; 1 Chron. 11:4–9).

### David Wants the Ark Back for a Future Worship Center

David moves his government base from Hebron to Jerusalem. He wants to centralize worship and government in the city. He needs to relocate the ark of the covenant. The ark is a box made of acacia wood (wood that does not rot) about the size of a sailor's treasure chest. Two angels of gold (cherubim) are sculpted on the top cover of the chest, their wings forming a mercy seat. It is in this spot in OT times where God agrees to intersect with humanity. Its stature as the locus for divine contact gives the ark its immeasurable value. For the previous nearly twenty years, the ark has sat quietly in a home in a village.

Two years after he bases himself in Jerusalem, David secures the ark. After several false starts, he brings the ark to Jerusalem, surrounds it with its own tent, and makes sacrifices before it (2 Sam. 6:17–18). Many of the psalms likely are written around this time. The glory of the Lord returns, with music and dancing. David himself strips down and leads the uproarious celebration.[61]

David sets the stage for central worship of God in Jerusalem. He conquers the city that Joshua's generation had not. He senses the location for the future temple at a threshing floor higher up the mountain from the city.[62] He buys the floor and the surrounding land from the Jebusite farmer who owns it. That stone becomes the floor of the holy of holies in the temple that David plans and his son Solomon builds according to some scholars. Some also identify that same stone as the altar on which an aggrieved Abraham nearly sacrifices his son.

The first temple is finished by Solomon, David's son, about 960 BC. It is destroyed by the armies of Babylon in 586 BC. The temple mount remains in ruins until a new power arises, the Persians. The Persian king Cyrus gives permission in 538 BC to rebuild the temple as predicted in Isaiah (44:28, 45:1, 13) and recorded in Ezra (1:1–8, 3:7–8, 4:1–5, 5:11–17, 6:1–15).

The construction continues from 537 BC until it is completed in 516 BC. The reconstructed temple is a disappointment to those who knew the splendor of the first temple (Ezra 3:12).

About five hundred years later, Herod the Great starts a major renovation of the temple and the mountain on which it sits. It is flattened and expanded using retaining walls, vaults, and fill dirt to create a sweeping esplanade. It forms an irregular trapezoidal shape. The area is usually estimated to total about 150,000 square

---

[61] Much to her regret, David's first wife Michal, daughter of King Saul, scoffs at his dancing bare chested in public and despises her husband's demonstrations of joy at the ark arriving at Jerusalem (2 Sam 6:14–16, 20–23).

[62] The threshing floor of Araunah, a Jebusite farmer, clearly lies on the mountain that becomes the temple mount. There is some dispute on whether the rock to which Abraham brought Isaac is on the same mountain (see footnote in prelude). Even when scholars hold that both rocks are on the mountain, scholars can disagree on whether the threshing floor and the stone altar are necessarily the same rock. Here, I take the view that both are on the temple mount leaving the question open whether they are one and the same rock.

meters (1.6 million square feet or thirty-seven acres), but some prefer the telltale figure 144,000 square meters (in either case about twenty-seven American football fields).[63] The buildings on the esplanade are destroyed by the Romans after a fierce four-year war in AD 70.

### Occupied Tomb of David to Empty Tomb of Jesus

Almost precisely one thousand years after David dies, Peter delivers a rousing message to a Jewish crowd in Jerusalem.[64] He calls David as his witness to the resurrection of Jesus. He cites as his reference Psalm 16.

*Therefore my heart is glad and my tongue rejoices; my body also will rest secure, because you will not abandon me*

Found in the Ground:
**Rock of Abraham**

Jerusalem—A large rock is kept in an Islamic shrine known as the Dome of the Rock. The dome is built on the foundations of an octagon-shaped church from the era of Constantine (fourth century). The building is not a mosque but a shrine. The rock is positioned at the highest point on the hill known as Mount Moriah. This point is believed to be where Abraham prepared to sacrifice his son Isaac (Gen. 22:1–14). It also is believed to be the location for the threshing floor of Araunah, the Jebusite who allowed David to buy the land and build an altar to the Lord (2 Sam. 24:18–25). The rock may have been the floor for the sacred room known as the holy of holies in the first temple of Solomon and in the rebuilt second temple.

Index 8.6

---

[63] Dimensions for the temple esplanade: north side, 313 m/1020 ft; east side, 470 m/1530 ft; south side, 280 m/910 ft; west side, 485 m/1578 ft. See "Temple Mount," n.a., n.d., jewishvirtuallibrary.org, Encyclopedia Judaica, Gale Group, 2008, *American–Israel Cooperative Enterprise*, retrieved 5 Dec 2018.

[64] David dies in the year 970 BC, while Peter speaks on Pentecost in AD 30–31, just about exactly 1,000 years apart.

*to the realm of the dead, nor will you let your faithful/*
*holy one see decay.*
*(Psalm 16:9–10)*

Peter argues that David is not talking about himself but a descendant of his who will be the Messiah.

*"Fellow Israelites, I can tell you confidently that the patriarch David died and was buried, and his tomb is here to this day. But he was a prophet and knew that God had promised him on oath that he would place one of his descendants on his throne. Seeing what was to come, he spoke of the resurrection of the Messiah, that he was not abandoned to the realm of the dead, nor did his body see decay. God has raised this Jesus to life, and we are all witnesses of it."*
*(Acts 2:29–32)*

Peter makes an incontrovertible point. David cannot be talking about himself because his tomb with his bones is just down the street. David died long before Peter preaches, his body decayed, and his bones are there. On the other hand, the tomb of Jesus is empty. If the people

Historical Portal:
**Mount Zion Defined**

Before the ravine is filled in with landfill in later ages, the Tyropoeon Valley (also known as the valley of the cheesemakers) separates two mountains, Mount Moriah to the east (2,520 feet or 768 meters), where the temple is built, from Mount Zion to the west (2,510 feet or 765 meters), where a royal palace and citadel are built. The term Mount Zion has multiple meanings in the OT. Early on, it refers to the Jebusite city that David conquers and renames the City of David. After Solomon builds the temple farther up the hill, the name Mount Zion often refers to the temple mount (usually the case in the Psalms, and in Isaiah 60:14). Josephus, writing at the end of the first century, and others even later refer to Mount Zion as the western hill, across from the temple mount on the eastern hill of Moriah. These are the customary referents today.

doubt Peter, they can go check the tomb for themselves. He uses the occupied tomb of David to point out the contrast with the empty tomb of Jesus.

Peter demonstrates the great advantage of preaching the message in the location where it all happened. The assertion can be validated by visits to the sites and by questioning local witnesses. The disciples operate with full confidence in the city as if they have nothing to fear from anyone who wants to undertake a close investigation of the startling claims they make about their Messiah.

# 8: CONCLUSION

### On the Disciples Staying Long Term in Jerusalem

Jerusalem remains the epicenter of the shocking resurrection message for two to three decades after Jesus dies on the cross. The staying power of the Jerusalem church brings us to an important historical conclusion. This historical factor of the message going out near to where the actual events occurred permits easy verification—or invalidation—that these events happened.

None of the obvious ways to negate the message worked. The movement stayed strong right where it began—in the midst of powerful opposition. From a historical viewpoint, the sustained presence of believers in Jerusalem makes it less likely that the Jesus narrative can be dismissed as mere folklore or legend. The cultural and religious authorities in the vicinity of the actual events would have done everything possible to contradict and soundly disprove the claims. Without being effectively countered, the word of the risen Messiah, descendant of David and offspring of Abraham, spread from Jerusalem to the rest of the Mediterranean world, and to nations far beyond.

# CHAPTER

# LINE OF EVIDENCE

## SUMMARY

Many prophets in the Old Testament predict a Messiah who will come in power as a king. He will rebuild the temple, defeat Israel's enemies, and will rule all the nations from Jerusalem.

Jesus does not achieve this punch list. However, another strata of prophecies, not as prominent or obvious but still present in the OT, predict a suffering Messiah who rises from the dead. Historically, there is no retrojection of these prophecies. Manuscript discoveries confirm they are written hundreds of years before Jesus walks the earth. Many of these prophecies Jesus remarkably fulfills. In the NT documents, the disciples claim he will return a second time to fulfill the rest of them.

Jesus is recorded after the resurrection telling his followers that it is written in OT prophecies that the Messiah will suffer and rise again. But the passages that quote him asserting this do not cite any specific OT references that he may have used. Can we detect these references to prophecies that describe the journey of Jesus in his death and resurrection? If so, the series of ancient Hebrew prophecies astoundingly fulfilled by Jesus from 1,500 to 500 years after they are predicted adds additional credibility to the reality of the resurrection.

# PRELUDE

## CHAPTER 9

She must have watched intently from her seat in the synagogue in Nazareth on the Sabbath as Jesus stands up to read. It is the only recorded time he returns to his hometown after leaving for his itinerant ministry. He is handed a scroll of the prophet Isaiah.

*Unrolling it, he found the place where it is written: "The Spirit of the Lord is on me, because he has anointed me to proclaim good news to the poor. He has sent me to proclaim freedom for the prisoners and recovery of sight for the blind, to set the oppressed free, to proclaim the year of the Lord's favor." Then he rolled up the scroll, gave it back to the attendant and sat down. The eyes of everyone in the synagogue were fastened on him. He began by saying to them, "Today this Scripture is fulfilled in your hearing." (Luke 4:17b–21)*

Mary must have wondered what reaction her hometown neighbors would have to her son. The secret is out. He is claiming to be the Anointed One prophesied in the Hebrew scriptures. The people of her village seem to be hanging on his every word.

Then—Oh no!—a sudden change. Something Jesus says about prophets having no acceptance in their hometown stirs up the listeners. They seem to want him to do the healings in Nazareth that he did down on the lakeshore in Capernaum. In response, he mentions examples of prophets sent to non-Jews when their Jewish brethren reject them. Their murmuring turns to fierce anger, and they drive her son out of the synagogue to a ridge on the outskirts of town where they are about to throw him off a cliff (Lk 4:24–29).

He outmaneuvers the mob. He escapes. Yet the volatile incident likely leaves his mother's heart aching and fitfully concerned over what the future holds.

Thirty or so years earlier, she surely remembers his dedication at the temple. The old man held and blessed her baby, yet he said that her son would upset the status quo and that a sword would pierce her own soul too. Then again, did not the angel announce to her on that breathtaking day in Nazareth as a girl in her teens that she would bear a son whose kingdom would never end? (Lk 1:26–38, 2:25–35.)

### CHAPTER 9

---

# GOSPEL ACCOUNTS CORRELATE WITH MESSIANIC PROPHECIES

---

Two travelers are walking on the road from Jerusalem to a village called Emmaus, about seven miles or eleven kilometers away. Their faces are downcast as they sort through a heavy topic. A man strides up to them and asks what they are discussing. A prophet recently was crucified by the authorities, say the two travelers. They are somewhat surprised the stranger does not know anything about recent events in the city. They had been counting on this executed prophet *"to redeem Israel,"* to unshackle the country from their Roman occupiers. That morning, a few women they know went to the tomb to further embalm the body, but it was gone. Nobody knows where it is, but the women saw a *"vision of angels."* They said this prophet is alive, but he is nowhere to be found. Up to that point, the stranger listened, but then he could feign ignorance no longer.

> *He said to them, "How foolish you are, and how slow to believe all that the prophets have spoken! Did not the Messiah have to suffer these things and then enter his glory?" And beginning with Moses and all the Prophets,*

*he explained to them what was said in all the Scriptures*
*concerning himself. (Luke 24:25–27)*

As the sun is about to set and they have reached their village,
the two travelers invite the well-read stranger to stay with them.
He appears to hesitate before he agrees. They sit down. He prays
and breaks bread. Then they have their aha moment and finally
recognize who he is—Jesus, the prophet whose death they were
mourning. He disappears from their midst.

*They asked each other, "Were not our hearts burning*
*within us while he talked with us on the road and opened*
*the Scriptures to us?" (Luke 24:32)*

After this shock, they cannot just sit down to digest a calm
dinner. They get back on the road again. They retrace their steps the
seven miles or eleven kilometers to Jerusalem despite the onset of
nightfall. (For more on the travelers' identities, see chapter 1.) They
arrive at the meeting place of the disciples and report that Jesus
is alive. The gathered disciples are not entirely surprised. Earlier
that day, they have heard the same thing from Peter, but they have
not seen Jesus for themselves. While the travelers are telling what
happened to them, Jesus appears. He denies he is a ghost; he invites
them to touch him and he eats a piece of broiled fish.

*He said to them, "This is what I told you while I was*
*still with you: Everything must be fulfilled that is*
*written about me in the Law of Moses, the Prophets*
*and the Psalms." Then he opened their minds so they*
*could understand the Scriptures. He told them, "This*
*is what is written: The Messiah will suffer and rise*
*from the dead on the third day, and repentance for the*
*forgiveness of sins will be preached in his name to all*
*nations, beginning at Jerusalem." (Luke 24:44–47)*

## Tracking Prophecies of a Suffering and Rising Messiah

In each of these two extended appearance accounts, Jesus is adamant that it is written in their Hebrew scriptures that the Messiah will suffer then rise again. Yet in neither account does the writer, Luke, include specific OT passages that Jesus cites.

Likewise, in Matthew's account of the abrupt arrest at night on the Mount of Olives, Jesus twice gives his reason for submitting: that the prophetic scriptures would be fulfilled. But no mention is made of which prophecies Jesus may have had in mind (Mt 26:53–56).[65] Looking at it from an author's angle, a series of citations could slow down the story. Still, it would be valuable to know which specific OT passages Jesus references. If there are ancient prophecies predicting a suffering Messiah who dies yet returns to life, the journey of Jesus correlates with them. These correlations or fulfillments raise the probability that Jesus actually was raised from the dead in history.

## Messianic Prophecies the Gospels See Fulfilled

Certain prophecies of the Messiah were expected more prominently than were others by first-century Jews according to the NT. The gospel writers highlight some of these and directly comment on their fulfillment in Jesus.

*The Messiah must be a descendant of David.* (Isa. 11:10; Jer. 23:5–6, 30:8–9, 33:14–16; Ezek. 34:23–24, 37:24–26; Hos. 3:4–5)

Mark quotes Jesus affirming this OT prophecy that the Messiah descends from David (Mk 12:35–37; also Mt 22:41–46; Lk 20:41–44). Matthew and Luke indicate this fulfillment with their detailed genealogies (Mt 1:1–17; Lk 3:23–38).

---

[65] Other moments where the apostles are said to prove from the OT Jesus is the Messiah also do not cite any specific references. These include Paul in Damascus (Acts 9:22), Paul in Thessalonica (Acts 17:3), and Apollos in Corinth (Acts 18:28).

*The Messiah must be born in David's hometown, the village of Bethlehem.* (1 Sam 17:12; Mic. 5:2)

Matthew and Luke dramatize and locate Jesus's birth in Bethlehem (Mt 2:1; Lk 2:11–16) though he is raised in Nazareth, Galilee (Mt 2:23; Lk 2:39). John reports people wonder how Jesus can be the Messiah if he comes from Galilee, not Bethlehem (Jn 7:42).

*The Messiah must be preceded by a messenger.* (Isa. 40:3–5; Mal. 3:1, 4:5)

This forerunner was thought to be Elijah, who would return to earth after never dying but being taken up alive in a chariot of fire amid a whirlwind (2 Kings 2:11–12). All four gospel writers identify the prophecy's fulfillment in John the Baptist (Mt 3:3; Mk 1:3; Lk 1:17, 3:3–4; Jn 1:21–23; with the first three gospels also quoting Jesus directly on the subject in Mt 11:13–14; Mk 9:11–13; Lk 7:24–27).

*The Messiah must remain forever.* (2 Sam. 7:15–20; Isa. 9:7; Ezek. 37:25; Dan. 7:14, 27; Mic. 4:7; Ps. 89:3–4, 110:4)

Peter preaches that the resurrection shows Jesus remains forever. By being raised, he fulfills Psalm 16:10 that he will not undergo decay (Acts 2:30–31). John notes people questioning how Jesus can be *"lifted up"* or killed by crucifixion and still be the Messiah who remains forever (Jn 12:27–36).

The gospel writers point out other fulfilled messianic prophecies in the course of their accounts. Matthew specializes in fulfillments in a birth narrative: Jesus is born of a virgin mother (Mt 1:22–23 fulfilling Isa. 7:14); he escapes a terrible slaughter of two-year-olds and under (Mt 2:16–18 fulfilling Jer. 31:15); and he returns after fleeing as a refugee to Egypt (Mt 2:14–15 fulfilling Hos. 11:1).

John focuses on fulfillments in a death narrative: Jesus is hated without cause (Jn 15:24–25 fulfilling Ps. 35:19, 69:4, 109:3); gamblers vie for his garment (Jn 19:24 fulfilling Ps. 22:18); he drinks vinegar and gall (Jn 19:28–29 fulfilling Ps. 69:21); none of Jesus's bones are broken when breaking the legs of crucified persons was the usual way to expedite their deaths (Jn 19:32–36 fulfilling Ps. 34:20; also, Ex. 12:46; Num. 9:12); and his side is pierced (Jn 19:34, 37 fulfilling Zech. 12:10).

All these prophecies, the gospel writers point out, are fulfilled already in Jesus. For them, he meets the major qualifications for the Messiah as well as these more detailed fulfillments. In fact, one modern list cites 365 prophecies of the Messiah that Jesus already has fulfilled.[66]

### No Easy Task to Fulfill Both Types of Prophecies of the Messiah

Yet there is another set of messianic prophecies that Jesus does not fulfill in his first-century sojourn on the earth. These expectations also derive from the OT prophets. They continue to be the criteria for the Messiah that many practicing Jews use today. Here are seven major ones.

*The Messiah will gather Jews back to the land of Israel, apparently in phases.* (Initial phase: Isa. 11:11–12; Ezek. 20:33–38, 36:22–38; Zeph. 2:1–2; Later phase: Deut. 4:29–31, 30:1–10; Isa. 27:12–13; 43:5–7; Jer. 16:14–15, 31:7–10; Ezek. 11:14–21; Amos 9:13–15; Zech. 10:8–12)

*The Messiah will rebuild the temple.* (Ezek. 37:26–28, Isa. 2:2)

---

[66] One intriguing list of prophecies unlike many does not follow the order of events in the life of Jesus but rather follows the order of appearance of the prophecies starting with Genesis. "365 Messianic Prophecies," 14 Jun 2016, jewsforjesus.org, *Jews for Jesus*, retrieved 12 Jul 2016. See also "100 Prophecies Fulfilled by Jesus," (Peabody, MA: Rose, 2001), and at hendricksonrose.com. Another shorter list of forty-four comes in a clear matrix format in Mary Fairchild, "Prophecies Fulfilled by Jesus," thoughtco.com, 29 Mar 2017.

*The Messiah will rule from Jerusalem as the king of earth.* (Zech. 14:9; Isa. 2:2, 11:10, 32:1, Dan. 7:13)

*The Messiah will spread the knowledge of God worldwide.* (Isa. 2:3, 11:9)

*The Messiah will establish an era of justice and world peace;* he will eliminate injustice, oppression, and war. (Isa. 2:4, 11:1–5, 60:17–20)

*The Messiah will reorder creation.* Predatory animals no longer will seek out their former prey, human labor will be justly rewarded, and weeping will be no more. (Isa. 11:6–9, 65:17–25)

*There will be no end to the just government of the Messiah.* (Isa. 9:7; Dan. 2:44, 4:3, 7:14)

How do Jesus and his disciples explain these unfulfilled prophecies? Not surprisingly, Jewish tradition asserts that because he did not fulfill these obvious messianic prophecies, he cannot possibly be the Messiah.

Back on the road to Emmaus, Jesus asks his fellow travelers, *"Did not the Messiah have to suffer these things and then enter his glory?"* (Lk 24:26). The Messiah travels a path of suffering, but it does not end there. He is raised up not just from the dead but to be exalted and to rule *("his glory")*. Suffering was the first sequence in a two-stage event Jesus predicted.

In a private sit-down with his inner circle of Peter, James, and John plus Andrew, Jesus reveals that he will come back but in another mode. From their perch on the Mount of Olives overlooking the temple and its esplanade, Jesus delineates events leading up to his return. The next time, he will come not as a vulnerable baby born into the family of a humble village craftsman but in great power and glory with angels at his command (Mk 13:3–27). Later after Jesus departs, the leading disciple, Peter, grasps this two-stage mission for the Messiah. In his first coming, he suffers for all.

*"Now, fellow Israelites, I know that you acted in ignorance, as did your leaders. But this is how God fulfilled what he had foretold through all the prophets, saying that his Messiah would suffer." (Acts 3:17–18)*

In his later coming, the Messiah raises Israel to worldwide prominence just as the prophets predicted.

*"Heaven must receive him until the time comes for God to restore everything, as he promised long ago through his holy prophets." (Acts 3:21)*

The phrase *"to restore everything"* means that Israel will be the center of the world because God will rule from Jerusalem through his Messiah, fulfilling the seven OT prophecies listed above (and many more). In other words, the promises are still valid. There is a delay between the two stages of the messianic mission, but the same Messiah is set to accomplish both. (Other writings underscore this essential NT assertion of the wait between messianic inbreakings: Heb. 9:28; 1 Pet. 1:3–5, 2 Pet. 3:8–10; James 5:7; Jude 1:21; 1 Thess. 1:10, 4:13–5:2; 1 Cor. 1:7, 4:5, 15:23; Rom. 8:23–25; Titus 2:13.)

The human preference for the powerful Messiah over the suffering Messiah explains why Jesus in early appearances after he rises pointedly insists that the prophets say the Messiah will suffer. Most everyone had overlooked the predictions of suffering. Not seeing the suffering also meant that most everyone did not see what Jesus saw, that the prophets also predict the Messiah rises from the dead. Jesus tells his followers that the prophets predicted his death and resurrection, but the gospel writers do not include a list of OT citations Jesus must have taught his disciples. So this is what we will search out here, specific OT prophecies that point to a suffering or a rising Messiah with primary attention to the contexts that feature both.

## Two Methods Turn Us into Messianic Prophecy Sleuths

This investigation employs two main modes of inquiry in this chapter. First, we check back through the narratives for times when Jesus is quoting or alluding to OT scripture or when he is taking deliberate action to fulfill a prophecy intentionally. This approach helps us spot passages that are highly likely to have made his internalized list of prophecies that require the Messiah to suffer and rise again. That is our focus for part 1.

Next, in part 2, we look at some of the early speeches of the disciples as recorded in Acts.[67] Recall that the disciples' time window for briefings on these prophetic scriptures was not limited to that first Sunday of Jesus's initial appearances. The disciples also spend a stretch of forty days with him before his ascension. They must have absorbed much of his OT teaching over that time. Definitely, they could better recognize these predictions now that they had gained a retrospective view of the scriptures based on the resurrection events. So this is our second method of detection. By scanning the scripture sections they use to convince their hearers that Jesus is the Messiah, we can trace back to more OT prophecies that Jesus likely identified as being written about him when he taught them to his disciples.

Critics may charge that the disciples, the NT writers, and Jesus himself may have twisted the OT meanings to force-fit them to NT events. What they miss is the interpretive mode that the NT assumes: that OT passages may contain multiple layers. They can apply both to an original OT context and predict and apply to events far into the future. The earlier event may or may not directly foreshadow the later event. The reality that the original passage applies to along with the fact that it might find a fulfillment in an intervening circumstance does not eliminate the chance that it may apply to an even later event. There can

---

[67] The speeches in Acts are excerpts that capture the main points but are not likely to have been word-for-word transcripts. For a compelling case for their overall reliability, see F. F. Bruce, *Speeches*. See full reference in chapter 4 and more discussion in *Background Guide*, resource 1.

be construed an initial fulfillment and a full fulfillment. This is the way the disciples thought about and mulled over prophecy, probably taking their cue from Jesus himself.

# ⑨: PART ONE

## JESUS REFERS TO PROPHECIES IN WORDS AND ACTIONS

Using our first method, we now survey recorded teachings and actions of Jesus himself before his death to discover the OT prophecies he likely brought to the attention of the disciples after he was raised.

### The Double Meaning in the Term Lifted Up

The gospel of John depicts Jesus making pointed use of the term *lifted up* to foretell his suffering on the cross.

> *Just as Moses lifted up the snake in the wilderness, so the Son of Man must be lifted up, that everyone who believes may have eternal life in him. (John 3:14–15)*

Jesus makes reference to an incident that would be well known to his audience of Jewish people. After a solid military victory for the Israelites in the wilderness, supplies run low and the people virulently complain. They *"spoke against"* God and Moses wishing they could go back to Egypt. Venomous snakes enter the camp, bite people, and cause many fatalities. The people confess their sins and ask Moses to intercede.

Following the Lord's instructions, Moses sculpts a snake out of bronze and attaches it to a pole (likely in the form of a *T* or a cross). The record concludes, *"Then when anyone was bitten by a snake and looked at the bronze snake, they lived"* (Num. 21:6–9). Jesus compares his being lifted up on a cross to Moses lifting up the snake. As people could simply look at the bronze snake and live, people may simply believe in his work on the cross and have eternal life. Later, at a festival in Jerusalem, Jesus employs the same phrase.

> "Now is the time for judgment on this world; now the prince of this world will be driven out. And I, when I am lifted up from the earth, will draw all people to myself."
> (John 12:31–32)

In the contexts where John shows Jesus using it, the term *lifted up* refers to the horrific fate of being crucified. The crowd is dumbfounded by the idea that the Messiah could be lifted up when tradition says the Messiah remains forever (Jn 12:34). Yet the word has another meaning in Greek, "to be exalted." This second passage in John highlights the second meaning while continuing to contain the first meaning. Most people are not drawn to one who is lifted up in crucifixion (they recoil with revulsion), but when one is exalted, people are drawn to a triumphal figure. John, often on the lookout for a deeper insight, clearly intends the term to bear this dual meaning.

However, we must keep in mind that Jesus would have spoken Aramaic, not Greek. The wordplay belongs to John's reflection. Even so, it remains likely that Jesus made the original connection between his mission and the incident in the Hebrew scriptures where the upraised snake saves lives in the wilderness, just as he is about to do in his cross and resurrection. This incident of Moses's bronze artistry likely makes Jesus's list of OT references that depict his mission.

### The Big Fish Story About the Man Who Did Not Get Away

Another OT passage featuring a suffering and rising Messiah comes in the episode when the Pharisees demand a sign from Jesus (see also chapter 3). They will not believe in him as the Messiah unless on demand he shows them a sign of power.

They expect something more than a mere healing or exorcism, something closer to the level of the parting of the Red Sea. For starters, maybe he could tip the Roman regional capital Caesarea Maritima into the Mediterranean, which just might impress them. Otherwise, without a sign of great magnitude, they refuse to believe. Their resistant and manipulative attitude accounts for the indignation in Jesus's reply.

> He answered, "A wicked and adulterous generation asks for a sign! But none will be given it except the sign of the prophet Jonah. For as Jonah was three days and three nights in the belly of a huge fish, so the Son of Man will be three days and three nights in the heart of the earth." (Matthew 12:39–40)

Here, Jesus is identifying with Jonah's suffering; he predicts he will face similar suffering. He will not suffer inside a fish but in a grave for a similar length of time.[68] This time limit implies that Jesus like Jonah will emerge from the confinement alive. Cryptic though it is, this reference by Jesus to the account in the book of the prophet Jonah seems to play a big part in his thinking about his mission. It stands as the primary source in the OT for Jesus's repeated prediction that he will endure a three-day duration in the grave. (The one other OT source for a three-day duration, in Hosea 6:2, refers to the healing and regathering of a sinful and not yet fully repentant Israel as a nation rather than referring to an individual being raised.) The ocean adventure of the prophet Jonah almost certainly makes the list of OT references Jesus applied to himself.

---

[68] Note some scholars argue Jonah died in the fish and was raised from the dead before (or in the messy process of) being vomited forth on the beach. See Brant Pitre, *The Case for Jesus* (New York, NY: Image, 2016), 186–88.

### It Behooves Us to See the Symbolism in the Donkey Ride

Jesus winds down his ministry in Galilee and decamps for Jerusalem. He grows increasingly conscious of fulfilling a destiny he derives from the prophets. On this epic trip, he repeatedly reveals the fateful details of his upcoming suffering to the disciples, as we have seen (see chapter 3).

Once he is near Jerusalem, he has a well-laid plan. In Bethany, about two miles or three kilometers outside the city, he knows where a young donkey is kept and that it will be available to him to ride into Jerusalem. He sends two of his trusted disciples to fetch it (Mk 11:1–7). John recounts the prophecy-fulfilling ride this way.

> *Jesus found a young donkey and sat on it, as it is written: "Do not be afraid, Daughter Zion; see, your king is coming, seated on a donkey's colt." (John 12:14–15)*

Jesus intentionally takes action to fulfill this prophecy from Zechariah 9:9 (rendered in paraphrase in the gospel of John). This was a symbolic act that your average politicking Sadducee or Pharisee could not miss.

It is worth a quick look at kings and mules to understand the significance of Jesus's deliberate action. At King David's behest near the end of his life, his son Solomon mounted a mule on his way to be anointed king (1 Kings 1:33, 38, 44). This practice became a tradition for Israelite kings. Riding a mule rather than a warhorse was a way of showing that the king accepts his role as a servant and humbles himself under God. Given that context, it is clear what Jesus is doing. Essentially, Jesus is offering himself to the nation and their leaders as their rightful king.

At the same parade, people wave palm branches, a signal that they believe Jesus will lead them to victory as a nation over their enemies. They lay their cloaks on the ground before him, a way of honoring the path of a king (2 Kings 9:13). It is not a small, compartmentalized event. *"The whole city was stirred,"* Matthew reports (Mt 21:10). Was Jesus expecting a positive embrace from the Jewish leaders? Unlikely. Was he moving events forward and essentially triggering what he predicted would happen to him? Much more likely.

The adulation of Jesus continues when he dismounts and walks into the temple courts. Children shout, *"Hosanna to the Son of David!"* The word *hosanna* means "save us now." It is a welcoming call for the Messiah to come. The chief priests and temple teachers are infuriated.

> Bible Sidelight:
> **Praise on the Parade Route**
>
> While still on the parade route to the temple, Jesus endures a hostile reaction in this case from Pharisees. They watch the people and object to their calling Jesus a king and blessing him as such. They ask Jesus to shush his followers. He refuses. He responds using a phrase from the prophet Habakkuk (Hab. 2:11). *"I tell you,"* he replied, *"if they keep quiet the stones will cry out"* (Lk 19:40). The stones of a house are considered as knowing truth-tellers because they metaphorically see what really happens. Jesus is saying the people are accurate in their assessment, that he is a king. Even if they kept mum, the stones still would know and shout the truth.

*"Do you hear what these children are saying?"* they asked him. *"Yes,"* replied Jesus, *"have you never read, 'From the lips of children and infants you, Lord, have called forth your praise?'"* (Matthew 21:16)

No mincing of words there. Jesus comfortably receives praise as he appears publicly welcoming royal treatment. He quotes Psalm 8:2, another OT reference indicating that he sees himself as Lord and worthy of praise. Undeniably, his plan for this epic entry into Jerusalem on a donkey derives from the prophecy of Zechariah. Then later that week at night in the Garden of Gethsemane, Jesus again draws on Zechariah.

## Zechariah's Prophecies Are Much on Jesus's Mind

On the Mount of Olives, Jesus warns his disciples they do not have the courage they imagine. In the heat of the night, they will run.

> Then Jesus told them, "This very night you will all fall away on account of me, for it is written: 'I will strike the shepherd, and the sheep of the flock will be scattered.' But after I have risen, I will go ahead of you into Galilee." (Matthew 26:31–32)

Peter of course protests the prediction by Jesus that they all will fall away. Maybe them but not me, he declares. His chutzpah does not last long, and his denials nearly destroy him (see prelude for chapter 4). The prophecy Jesus refers to also comes from the prophet Zechariah (Zech. 13:7). As we noted above, Jesus drew on the book of Zechariah for his symbolic and kingly entry into Jerusalem mounted on a young donkey (Zech. 9:9). Now, this other passage from Zechariah predicts the shepherd will suffer, he will be struck, and his flock will be scattered.

Jesus identifies himself as that shepherd. It is clear that he knows his Zechariah well. No surprise. Right around this reference is a further indication of a suffering Messiah who lives again. The Messiah speaks in the first person about the day when he returns and the renewing effect that his pouring out of a *"spirit of grace and supplication"* will have on the inhabitants of Jerusalem.

> "They will look on me, the one they have pierced, and they will mourn for him as one mourns for an only child, and grieve bitterly for him as one grieves for a firstborn son." (Zechariah 12:10b)

Going further, Zechariah predicts a day is coming when the Lord will stand with his feet on the Mount of Olives. Geological changes will occur, rivers of cleansing will run from the city, he will defeat the armies of the nations arrayed against Israel, he will be king over the whole earth, and Jerusalem will be secure. Here we have another passage that would almost certainly make the list of Jesus. Zechariah pictures a Messiah figure suffering yet living again. He will be mourned over by those who consented to his death. Yet he will return to defeat their enemies, revive their fortunes, and rule from Jerusalem (Zech. 14:1-11).

## A Violent Parable Exposes the Plotters

Jesus spends his last week before his death teaching in the temple courts. He commutes into the city from the bedroom community of Bethany (Mk 11:11-12, 15, 19-20, 27, 14:3). His temple teachings include multiple allusions to the Messiah's sufferings while his enemies lurk nearby. Jesus captivates the people milling around the temple esplanade while the chief priests and teachers of the law patrol within earshot and butt in whenever they want to ask him trick questions (Mk 11:28, 12:13-15, 12:18, 28). At one point, Jesus launches into a thinly disguised parable known as the parable of the tenants. The first three gospels all cover this episode (Mk 12:1-12; Mt 21:33-46; Lk 20:9-19). Jesus sets the scene in a vineyard. The owner rents it out to tenants who will pay rent with a share of their harvest. When he sends his servants to collect his fruit from the harvest, the tenants beat or kill them. Tired of this, the owner sends his son assuming they will respect him. Instead, they kill him too. What will the owner do? He will come and kill the tenants and give the rights to bear fruit in the vineyard to others. The violence in the parable is unnerving. Luke records that the regular people in the crowd, not the elite priests, react to it with *"God forbid!"* (Lk 20:16). Jesus then delivers his punchline taken from Psalm 118:22.

> *"Haven't you read this passage of Scripture: 'The stone the builders rejected has become the cornerstone; the Lord has done this, and it is marvelous in our eyes?'"*
> *(Mark 12:10-11)*

Mark recounts the response from the rulers.

> *Then the chief priests, the teachers of the law and the elders looked for a way to arrest him because they knew he had spoken the parable against them; so they left him and went away. (Mark 12:12)*

The parable of the tenants is a story of the rejection of the son of the vineyard owner as well as of the owner. Jesus connects this rejection with the stone rejected by builders in the prophetic psalm. In the parable, the body count is high and there is no hint of the servants or the son rising from the dead. But in the reference to the stone, there is. The stone is rejected, but it becomes something else. Not any old stone in any old building but the cornerstone, the stone that sets up all the dimensions for what the Lord is building next. Psalm 118:22–23 assuredly makes Jesus's list of messianic prophecies. This notion will be reinforced when shortly we look at the way that the apostles apply this same psalm in part 2.

### Sham Trial Forces Priests to Face Prophecies

We go back to the garden on the Mount of Olives, where the rulers have figured out a way to arrest Jesus without stirring up the crowds. At night, Jesus is taken by force from his encampment, downhill through the Kidron Valley, and into the city to the house of the high priest. At this rushed, illegal night trial before the priests, Jesus listens to the accusing witnesses but remains silent.[69] Finally when he is forced to speak, he quotes scripture predicting his ascension.

> *The high priest said to him, "I charge you under oath by the living God: Tell us if you are the Messiah, the Son of*

---

[69] See Karen Ruth Myers, "Jewish Trials," in Jolene Nolte, ed., *Jesus, Rediscover His Final Days on Earth* (Yorba Linda, CA: Engaged Media, 2016), 56–59.

God." "You have said so," Jesus replied. "But I say to all
of you: From now on you will see the Son of Man sitting
at the right hand of the Mighty One and coming on the
clouds of heaven." (Matthew 26:63b-64)

Jesus combines two passages. First, he employs a verse the gospels have seen him use before at the temple grounds to puzzle the Pharisees, Psalm 110:1 (Mt 22:44; Lk 20:41-44). The irony is this: the Messiah is a descendant of David, yet David as psalmist nevertheless calls him his Lord, who sits at God's right hand (see more on this brainteaser in Peter's Pentecost speech coming up in part 2).

The second reference Jesus uses is a prophecy of Daniel that describes a figure ascending to the right hand of God returning from earth through the clouds to heaven. Daniel describes his night vision this way.

> Historical Portal:
> ## Illegal Night Trial
>
> The illegality of the trial of Jesus under Jewish law at the time resulted from several violations. No trials were allowed at night, nor were trials permitted during feasts. Votes for the death penalty were to be taken individually among the Sanhedrin members, not by group consensus. Further, when the verdict entailed the death penalty, an interim of one day was required before the condemned person could be executed. The hierarchy clearly was in a hurry to dispose of Jesus.

*In my vision at night I looked, and there before me was
one like a son of man, coming on the clouds of heaven.
He approached the Ancient of Days and was led into his
presence. He was given authority, glory and sovereign
power; all nations and peoples of every language
worshiped him. His dominion is an everlasting dominion*

*that will not pass away, and his kingdom is one that will never be destroyed. (Daniel 7:13–14)*

Bible Sidelight:
**Comings and Goings from Heaven**

It is worth pointing out the similarity of the image Daniel conveys of a figure going into heaven to the image John describes in Revelation of a figure returning to earth from heaven.

*"Look, he is coming with the clouds,"*
*And "every eye will see him,*
*even those who pierced him";*
*and all peoples on earth "will*
*mourn because of him." So shall it*
*be! Amen. (Revelation 1:7)*

John's image in Revelation merges the prophecies of Daniel (7:13) and Zechariah (12:10).

By referring to this vision, Jesus ignites the fiery hostility of the high priest and his cohorts. They know exactly his shocking meaning. Jesus, a mere man, at most a self-styled prophet from the hinterlands, is claiming he is entitled to be in the presence of God and to be given sovereign authority.

*Then the high priest tore his clothes and said, "He has spoken blasphemy! Why do we need any more witnesses? Look, now you have heard the blasphemy. What do you think?" "He is worthy of death," they answered. (Matthew 26:65–66)*

The Romans will condemn Jesus as a political rebel, a delusional Jewish man who would be king. The priestly leaders have a different accusation. They charge him with blasphemy, a spiritual crime; it deserves capital punishment in their culture usually by stoning. Blasphemy in their eyes is a mere human making himself equal to God, claiming a unique relationship with God, or speaking falsely against God (see also chapter 5).

If Jesus were not in a special relationship with God, he would rightly fall under the charge of blasphemy. Not so if he is speaking the actual truth about his identity. He is forcing them to make the decision for themselves whether he is that authority figure in Daniel. They do not believe him. Nevertheless, he tells them that eventually, either at their deaths or at his second coming, they will see him as the ruler he truly is.

Clearly, Jesus read the book of Daniel and sees key things written about himself. He sees in this passage an alive and ascended Messiah in human form. It is highly likely that he saw as well a suffering Messiah in another related vision of Daniel. Two chapters later, Daniel receives an end-time calendar in a vision. The vision indicates that the Messiah will be *"cut off"* or in some translations *"put to death"* prior to the destruction of the city of Jerusalem (Dan. 9:26). This destruction by the Romans occurs in history in AD 70, about forty years after the departure of Jesus. Here, just two chapters in Daniel beyond the passage Jesus cites to the high priests at his trial, he would find the prophet also writing about the death he will face as a suffering Messiah. These passages in Daniel are highly likely to have been among those that Jesus taught to his disciples after his resurrection.

### On the Cross, Jesus Voices His Anguish in a Psalm

Scripture remains on Jesus's mind even amid the course of his agony on the cross. He is heard by onlookers to utter several phrases. It was not easy to speak because it was not easy to breathe. For all its blood and gore, crucifixion was a slow death meant to suffocate its victim. Once the victim ran out of strength to push off his nailed feet and lift his nailed (or sometimes rope-tied) arms to raise his lungs to breathe, he would expire. Scholars debate the authenticity of some of the on-the-cross phrases recorded in the gospels, but this phrase has few critics.[70] Both Mark and Matthew record it including the original Aramaic.

> *And at three in the afternoon Jesus cried out in a loud voice, "Eloi, Eloi, lema sabachthani?" (which means "My God, my God, why have you forsaken me?").*
> *(Mark 15:34)*

While the gospel writer renders the phrase in Aramaic and Greek, the original line was written in Hebrew in Psalm 22. This direct quote by Jesus points our investigation to that passage. Is Jesus simply expressing himself emotionally through the words of the psalmist, or is there more in that psalm that would put it on the list of prophecies of a suffering Messiah?

It is a psalm of David that on one level describes his experience of rejection. But Hebrew scriptures can operate on multiple levels especially when it comes to poetry. Composed nearly a thousand years before the crucifixion, a remarkable set of verses in this psalm appear to describe the experience of Jesus on the cross.

> *But I am a worm and not a man,*
> *scorned by everyone, despised by the people.*
> *All who see me mock me; they hurl insults, shaking their heads.*
> *"He trusts in the Lord," they say, "let the Lord rescue him. Let him deliver him, since he delights in him."*
> *(Psalm 22:6–8)*

The physical feelings the psalmist describes bear an uncanny resemblance to what is suffered by a victim of crucifixion.

---

[70] Critics tend to trust items that run counter to the perceived agenda of the writer. They call it the criteria of embarrassment. It clearly looks bad for the argument that Jesus is the Son of God if he is questioning God the Father and feeling abandoned by him as he suffers on the cross. For more on these historical criteria, see addition 3.

*I am poured out like water,*
*and all my bones are out of joint.*
*My heart has turned to wax;*
*it has melted within me.*
*My mouth is dried up like a potsherd,*
*and my tongue sticks to the roof of my mouth;*
*you lay me in the dust of death.*
*Dogs surround me,*
*a pack of villains encircles me;*
*They pierce my hands and my feet.*[71]
*All my bones are on display;*
*people stare and gloat over me.*
*They divide my clothes among them*
*and cast lots for my garment. (Psalm 22:14–18)*

The psalm describes in detail the pain of unjust suffering. The details correlate closely with the way the gospels record both the emotional and physical pains of Jesus. It begins in the first verse with the cry of despair that Jesus echoes on the cross. Yet the psalm offers a strong ray of hope.

*For he has not despised or scorned*
*the suffering of the afflicted one;*
*he has not hidden his face from him*
*but has listened to his cry for help. (Psalm 22:24)*

It is important to recognize that being listened to in the Jewish mind-set implies action. It means being rescued from the distress by the one who hears. That is the pivotal moment of triumph in the circumstance. Further on in the psalm, David rejoices that all the nations will bow down and be ruled by the Lord (Ps. 22:27–31).

---

[71] A textual issue exists on the word translated as *"pierce"* (Ps. 22:16). It may refer more to the idea of a lion tearing hands and feet rather than piercing with nails. Yet the very reference to hands and feet being bloodied correlates with the crucifixion.

This journey in the psalm from devastation and death to life and dominion gives it strong messianic overtones in its subtext.

This psalm likely would have made it onto Jesus's list of material written about him. For the disciples, this reference might have been difficult to locate in advance of the crucifixion, but afterward, it would all make sense.

### Over Dinner Jesus Alludes to a Prophecy Most Profound

One of the most intentional acts of Jesus in his final week was the arrangement he made to eat a meal with his disciples at the outset of Passover week.

At the start of the meal, similar to the custom for all Jewish hosts, Jesus takes bread, gives thanks in prayer, breaks it, and gives it to the disciples. He invests the broken bread with new meaning when he tells them, *"This is my body."* Three gospels record it that way with Luke adding, *"given for you"* (Mk 14:22; Mt 26:26; Lk 22:19). At the end of the meal, the custom is for the host to take a cup of wine and pass it around to his guests. But before Jesus does this, he tells them, *"This is my blood of the covenant"* which is *"poured out for many,"* according to Mark (Mk 14:24) and Matthew (Mt 26:28). Luke's version words it, *"This cup is the new covenant in my blood, which is poured out for you"* (Lk 22:20).

When Jesus uses the words *"poured out"* underscored in two versions *"for many,"* it immediately resonates with the words of the final verse in a monumental passage in the OT, Isaiah 53.[72]

*Therefore I will give him a portion among the great,*
*and he will divide the spoils with the strong, because he*
*poured out his life unto death, and was numbered with*

---

[72] Richard Bauckham calls this term *"for many"* a "key catchphrase" that alludes to the "enigmatic narrative" of the servant of the Lord in Isaiah 52:13–53:12. His discussion of the allusion by Jesus at the Last Supper to the servant in Isaiah is considerably illuminating. His work originally pointed me toward these revealing connections. See Richard Bauckham, *Jesus: A Very Short Introduction* (Oxford, UK: Oxford University Press, 2011), 101–2.

*the transgressors. For he bore the sin of many, and made
intercession for the transgressors. (Isaiah 53:12)*

Adding *"for many"* reinforces the connection Jesus is making
between the upcoming Passover festival celebrating the liberation
of Israel from Egypt commemorated in the sacrificed lambs and
the ultimate bearing of sin by the servant figure in Isaiah. His
message that his death draws near should come as no surprise
to the disciples. Jesus repeatedly had told them on their journey
from Galilee that he would die in Jerusalem (see chapter 3). One
can wonder as well whether any of the disciples would have
remembered how early on, when they were at first following John
the Baptist, the rugged prophet had pointed out Jesus as *"The
Lamb of God who takes away the sin of the world"* (Jn 1:29).

Now, as Jesus senses the time has come, he is not just
predicting he will die; he is initiating them into the meaning of
his imminent death. It will not be the death of a rejected prophet,
a failed rebel, or a false messiah. It is the death described in
Isaiah, a death voluntarily submitted to on behalf of others, a
death prefigured by the death of the Passover lambs about 1,200
to 1,500 years earlier in the Exodus account. It is a death reenacted
by the animal sacrifices in the tabernacle of Moses and in the
Jerusalem temple, for Isaiah 53:10 describes a sacrificial guilt
offering. It is a death where the servant absorbs the sin and the
punishment deserved by others so that they may not die but live
in a relationship with God.

Yet it is a death where the servant does not remain dead.
Instead, he will see *"the light of life and be satisfied."* He is raised
up and exalted in triumph, and he has offspring who benefit
from his spiritual victory (Isa. 53:10–12). The concept of *"offspring"*
may harken back to the covenant with Abraham, where he is
promised, *"And through your offspring all nations on earth will be
blessed"* (Gen. 22:18). Jesus transforms everyday bread and wine
into symbols of his sacrificial death for all humanity. From then
on, these common, earthly actions of taking bread and wine
become vital to Christian worship and continue to this day.

290 | Resurrection S H O C K

On their way out to the Mount of Olives after the Last Supper, Jesus again quotes from Isaiah 53. The line he uses comes in the same verse (53:12) and immediately follows the line—"*he poured out his life unto death*"—that he had alluded to around the table.

> "*It is written: 'And he was numbered with the transgressors'; and I tell you that this must be fulfilled in me. Yes, what is written about me is reaching its fulfillment.*" (Luke 22:37)

By searching out that searing poetic chapter in Isaiah, his disciples and we ourselves can see what he saw: a suffering Messiah who atones for the sins of the entire human race and then returns to life.

Near the end of the upcoming part 2, we delve further into the meaning of Isaiah 53. It comes in the account of a roving evangelist who must have heard how Jesus applied this passage to himself and was therefore ready when the moment demanded to pass on the insight to others.

From this part 1 investigation of the words and actions of Jesus himself, we have deduced so far a set of prophecies that he likely taught his disciples were written about him—specifically the ones about his suffering and his rising from the dead. These include the following (chapters): the writings of Moses in Genesis (12, 22) and Numbers (21); the prophets Isaiah (53), Daniel (7, 9), Zechariah (9, 12-14); and the Psalms (22, 118).

In part 2, we follow the clues in the apostles' preaching to find more OT prophecies that predict a suffering and rising Messiah.

# ¶: PART TWO

## PROPHECIES DETECTED IN THE APOSTLES' PREACHING

A crowd forms in the streets after hearing Peter and his fellow Galileans speak of God's wonders in languages known around the Mediterranean world (Acts 2:7–11). Most of the people in the crowd were Jews coming to the temple to worship at the Feast of Weeks. It is the wheat harvest festival, or Pentecost, coming about fifty days after Passover.

### *Writings in the Psalms Explain that Jesus Is the Messiah*

First, Peter explains that the outbursts of praise in various languages fulfill the prophecy of Joel (Joel 2:28–32). Next, he directly accuses the people of being complicit in Jesus's death along with the Romans, who actually carried out the execution. Yet that is not the end of the story of Jesus, Peter says.

> *"But God raised him from the dead, freeing him from the agony of death, because it was impossible for death to keep its hold on him." (Acts 2:24)*

Where does Peter get his assertion that it is impossible for Jesus to stay dead? Normally, we assume it is the other way around; it is impossible for a person to be raised from the dead, but Peter says the opposite is the case with Jesus. He finds the evidence for this impossibility in the psalms of David. He quotes Psalm 16:10 (note the translated version below is the one reported in Acts).

> *"'Therefore my heart is glad and my tongue rejoices; my body also will rest in hope, because you will not abandon me to the realm of the dead, you will not let your holy one see decay.'" (Acts 2:26–27)*

In explaining the prophecy, Peter acknowledges that some may think the author, David, is talking about himself as the psalmist often does. But in this case, he cannot be referring to himself declares Peter because David's body decayed. The tomb where he was buried a thousand years before is right there in Jerusalem. So if the subject is not David, who is it? Peter says David has an inside track on the answer.

> *"Seeing what was to come, he spoke of the resurrection of the Messiah, that he was not abandoned to the realm of the dead, nor did his body see decay. God has raised this Jesus to life, and we are all witnesses of it."* (Acts 2:31–32)

Peter concludes that the suffering and rising to life of Jesus is foretold by the prophet and king, David, in one of the core materials of Jewish scripture, the book of Psalms.[73]

Peter further asserts that Jesus not only has been raised to life but also has been exalted to the right hand of God. Where does he get this stuff? He presents as evidence Psalm 110:1, attributed to David.

> *"The Lord said to my Lord: 'Sit at my right hand until I make your enemies a footstool for your feet.'"* (Acts 2:34–35)

Obviously, David did not ascend to heaven Peter contends because his tomb is right here in our midst. So it cannot be David as the psalmist speaking about himself. Rather, David again speaks of the Messiah Jesus. In this case, Jesus has fulfilled the prophecy that he would ascend to the right hand of God, a position of spiritual and universal rule.

Peter has this interpretation on good authority. We need not

---

[73] Later, preaching in the synagogue of Pisidian Antioch, Paul will use this reference (Ps. 16:10) to convince his listeners that Jesus is the Davidic Messiah and the source for forgiveness of sins (Acts 13:34–38).

speculate on whether this prophetic word was on Jesus's list. It had to be. The gospel narratives show Jesus alluding to this passage himself. In three gospels, Jesus uses this verse to anchor a discussion. Actually, he turns it into a riddle (Mt 22:41-46; Mk 12:35-37; Lk 20:41-44). He engages with the rulers, teachers, and Pharisees in the temple complex during the week before his death. He asks them whose son is the Messiah. The Son of David, they reply. So Jesus queries them. If David speaking *"by the Spirit"* in the psalm, calls the Messiah *"my Lord,"* how can he be his son? Behind this question is a cultural taboo: a progenitor/ancestor never customarily refers to his progeny/descendant with the honorific title of *"Lord."* Jesus does not attempt to give them the solution; he just leaves their heads spinning.

In this moment after the resurrection and ascension, Peter shows how Jesus fulfills this second psalm-based prophecy of David. He puts it in simple terms. The very descendant of David they were complicit in crucifying is now the one in heavenly authority (as Lord) and the one who (as the Messiah) brought forgiveness of sins (Acts 2:36). People are *"cut to the heart"* by this message. Reportedly, three thousand Jewish listeners believe and are baptized (Acts 2:37-41).

### Writings from Moses Foresee the Messiah

A while later, Peter holds the rapt attention of another crowd after healing a well-known disabled man at the temple gate (see chapter 4). Peter tells the crowd, *"You disowned the Holy and Righteous One"* but *"God raised him from the dead"* (Acts 3:14-15). Next, Peter contends that Jesus already has fulfilled a famous prophecy of Moses.

> *"For Moses said, 'The Lord your God will raise up for you a prophet like me from among your own people; you must listen to everything he tells you. Anyone who does not listen to him will be completely cut off from among his people.'" (Acts 3:22-23)*

Moses prophesies that God would raise up *"a prophet like me"* (Deut. 18:15, 18–19). Scholars debate at length what is meant by *"like me."* It is enough for our purposes to catalog prophetic passages that Jesus likely told the disciples were written about him. Here we see Peter asserting that Jesus fulfills the prophecy of Moses. We do not absolutely need to unpack all that is meant by *"a prophet like me,"* but we can guess.

> **Bible Sidelight:**
> **New Life in a New Covenant**
>
> In using the term *"new covenant,"* Jesus also echoes the majestic prediction of Jeremiah 31:31–34. In the new covenant, all will have the law written on their hearts, all will know the Lord personally, and all will have their sins forgiven permanently. For more NT explanations on the blessings of living in the new covenant, see Heb. 8:1–10:18; 2 Cor. 2:12–4:18.

In his moment of martyrdom, Stephen also directly refers to this prophecy of Moses that God will send a prophet like himself (Acts 7:37). Probably the meaning of this term is that the prophet will be one who not only speaks but who also mediates a covenant that forms a new people. Moses mediated a covenant on Mount Sinai, when the law was given. Like Moses, Jesus is a prophet and a covenant founder. Unlike Moses, he is the blood sacrifice that seals the new covenant.

As we saw in part 1 at his last meal with the disciples before the cross, Jesus explained to them that he would be making a new covenant, yet it would be made only *"in my blood"* (Lk 22:20). Unlike Moses, he atones personally for the sins of others. (Yet Moses unknowingly depicts Jesus's sacrificial death in the Passover event and tabernacle sacrifices, Ex. 12:1–28; Lev. 1–7.) Then, while Moses gives the Law as the way to right standing with God in the old covenant, Jesus gives the Spirit, writing the Law on people's hearts, in the new covenant. Peter continues down the line of OT prophets.

*"Indeed, beginning with Samuel, all the prophets who have spoken have foretold these days." (Acts 3:24)*

In 2 Samuel, the prophet Nathan prophesies that the covenant God makes with David will put one of his descendants on his throne forever (2 Sam. 7:17). David feels humbled and unworthy but nevertheless believes and is thrilled (2 Sam. 7:29). Peter notes how David knew this promise and looked ahead to its fulfillment (Acts 2:30). This key turning point in the OT likely made the list of Jesus's prophecies written about him because he readily endorses the view of his contemporaries that the Messiah must come from David's lineage (Mk 12:35–37).

Peter then traces back further to spotlight a promise that predates David and even Moses, which Jesus also fulfills.

*"And you are heirs of the prophets and of the covenant God made with your fathers. He said to Abraham, 'Through your offspring all peoples on earth will be blessed.' When God raised up his servant, he sent him first to you to bless you by turning each of you from your wicked ways." (Acts 3:25–26)*

Peter takes them all the way back to their original common ancestor, Abraham (see prelude for chapter 8). He identifies Jesus as the offspring of Abraham through whom all nations and ethnicities will be *"blessed"* or made prosperous and spiritually whole (Gen. 22:18). In part 1, we saw this Genesis passage alluded to in the Isaiah 53 prophecy; now, in Peter's preaching, this Abrahamic prediction is applied directly to Jesus.

At this point in the episode, the captain of the temple guard arrests Peter and John. They are jailed overnight and interrogated by the high priests the next day (see chapter 4). Even in our brief excerpt of Peter's message, we have seen him reveal passages Jesus likely applied to himself, from *"the prophet like me"* that Moses foresaw to *"the offspring"* that would bless many nations promised to Abraham.

Bible Sidelight:
The Genesis Prophecy Filmgoers Do Not Forget

There is no evidence in Acts that Peter specifically cites another
passage earlier in the book of Genesis (Gen. 3:15). It records God
speaking to the evil one who appears as a serpent: *"And I will put
enmity between you and the woman and between your offspring and
hers; He will crush your head, and you will strike his heel."* The passage
pictures a drama of the evil serpent biting the heel, which can be fatal
but will not be. The bite is counteracted by the offspring of the woman.
He ostensibly stomps his foot on the head of the serpent to smash
it with a fatal blow. Believers have seen in this metaphor the death
of Jesus (the heel bite) and his resurrection (the head crushing) that
conquers the evil one who wields the power of death over humanity.

While there is no direct NT preaching from this passage,
allusions are detectable in the apostles' writings (Rom. 16:20;
Heb. 2:14; Jn 8:44; 1 Jn 3:8; Rev. 12:17). Incidentally, this scene
taken from Genesis profoundly figures in Mel Gibson's epic
2004 film on Jesus's suffering, *The Passion of the Christ.*

## Writings from the Prophets Reveal a Rejected Messiah

The next day, in the face of the chief priests and elders
(probably the entire Sanhedrin council), Peter ups the ante with
more prophetic evidence for Jesus as the Messiah. They want to
know the power behind the healing of the paralyzed man at the
temple gate the day before.

> *"Then know this, you and all the people of Israel: It is
> by the name of Jesus Christ of Nazareth, whom you
> crucified but whom God raised from the dead, that this
> man stands before you healed. Jesus is 'the stone you
> builders rejected, which has become the cornerstone.'"*
> *(Acts 4:10–11)*

This is the same OT scripture that Jesus skewered these rulers with in the temple plaza two months earlier when he told the parable of the tenants about them. Peter probably was on hand at that moment and absorbed the way Jesus implied that this prophecy of the rejected stone in Psalm 118:22 was actually about him. Now, Peter can validate that Jesus being raised and exalted fulfills this prophecy. Jesus becomes the cornerstone of a new construct, a spiritual one formed of people, not of building materials. In a later letter, Peter waxes eloquent on this metaphor. He frames the key verse in Psalm 118 with two verses from Isaiah—both about a stone—to show two different responses to that stone.

> *As you come to him, the living Stone—rejected by humans but chosen by God and precious to him—you also, like living stones, are being built into a spiritual house to be a holy priesthood, offering spiritual sacrifices acceptable to God through Jesus Christ. For in Scripture it says: "See, I lay a stone in Zion, a chosen and precious cornerstone, and the one who trusts in him will never be put to shame." Now to you who believe, this stone is precious. But to those who do not believe, "The stone the builders rejected has become the cornerstone," and, "A stone that causes people to stumble and a rock that makes them fall." (1 Peter 2:4–8a)*

Peter (probably quoting from the Greek translation of the OT, the Septuagint, c. 200s BC) refers to the *"precious cornerstone"* in Isaiah 28:16. That reference assures a positive outcome for believers who accept and do not reject the cornerstone, Jesus. Then Peter refers to Isaiah 8:14 describing a stumbling stone (also meaning Jesus) that brings disaster on unbelievers.

In Luke and in most manuscripts of Matthew (though not in Mark), Jesus warns the temple priests about rejecting him with an even starker translation of Isaiah 8:14–15.

*Everyone who falls on that stone will be broken to pieces;*
*anyone on whom it falls will be crushed. (Luke 20:18)*

If you happen across that stone and stumble over it, you will be broken to pieces. Even if you do not stumble over it, it will fall from a height on you and you still will be crushed. The starker version in the gospel accounts makes your fate clear should you reject the cornerstone.

Peter is not the only later apostle who riffs on the prophetic metaphor of Jesus being for some a cornerstone and for others a stumbling stone. Paul in several places comforts believers, who receive Jesus as their cornerstone (Rom. 9:33, 10:11; Eph. 2:20–22 from Isa. 28:16). Elsewhere, he bewails unbelievers who make Jesus their stone of stumbling (1 Cor. 1:23; Rom. 9:32–33 from Isa. 8:14).[74] Paul does not directly cite Psalm 118:22 as Jesus and Peter do. Nevertheless, the two Isaiah passages Paul and Peter mention (Isa. 8:14, 28:16) are so closely related that they also along with Psalm 118:22 are likely to have made it onto the list of prophecies that Jesus explained to his disciples as predicting his suffering and rising.

### A Hitchhiking Evangelist Knows the Prophecies of Isaiah

It is likely that more than just the original group of disciples were listening at the sessions after the resurrection when Jesus taught the OT passages written about him. Some additional insiders could listen starting that Sunday evening after Jesus made his first appearances. Afterward, more believers could hear him during the forty days before he ascended.

---

[74] In Romans 9:33, Paul merges both Isaiah passages and sandwiches the rock causing people to fall (from Isaiah 8:14) between two phrases from Isaiah 28:16: one about the laying of the stone in Zion and one about the believer never being put to shame. In a way, it shows how powerfully embedded in his mind is the reality of Jesus as the stone dividing believers and unbelievers.

Beyond the eleven original disciples, there were women followers (see chapter 1) along with other men. Among these men were seven who were known to the disciples and would be appointed to attend to practical matters of the community. These tasks were needed once the preaching started drawing thousands of believers (Acts 6:5). One of these highly regarded men was Stephen (featured in chapter 5), and another was Philip. Philip would be known as the evangelist or the deacon as opposed to Philip the disciple or apostle, who was one of the twelve. (It is possible that this Philip and Stephen were among the seventy-two people Jesus sent out in pairs on his major Galilean outreach in Lk 10:1.)

The team of seven deacons first focus on resolving a cultural grievance by providing equal support for both Aramaic-speaking and Greek-speaking widows from low-income households (Acts 6:1–7).

When persecution breaks out and believers scatter, Philip heads to the land many Jews customarily shun—the mixed-race area of Samaria. This region is despised for its syncretistic, bad religion (Acts 8:4–8). The response to the Jesus message is so strong that Philip connects the Samaritans with Peter and John and need not base himself there. Philip next approaches his most famous evangelistic encounter, with a foreigner

Bible Sidelight:
The Daughters of
Philip the Deacon

Philip was known for evangelism and by the way he raised four highly spiritual and articulate daughters who prophesied (Acts 21:9). The bishop and historian Eusebius, who lived in the same coastal area of Caesarea (though three hundred years later), reported that they were "great lights" or "mighty luminaries," leaders in their churches and participants with their father in evangelism. Not being married probably allowed them to travel more and devote themselves to faith communities. See the report in *Church History*, 3.31.3–5 though beware that Eusebius, like several early Christian writers, mistakenly conflates Luke's two Philips, the disciple and the evangelist.

from Africa (covered in detail shortly below). Then he will go to the coastal town of today's Ashdod, Israel, and will eventually settle farther north along the coast in the Roman headquarters city of Caesarea Maritima, where he will host Paul and Luke on their way to Jerusalem about twenty years later (Acts 21:8-9). In the meantime, he raises a famous family of four daughters who are spiritually strong and speak forcefully. Philip's track record shows he is adaptable and highly inclusive and connects with people multiculturally—valuable qualities for an evangelist.[75]

In his most famous episode, he heads south from Jerusalem down a desert road that leads to Gaza. Apparently fleet-footed, Philip catches up with a chariot rolling down the road. He hears the passenger in the chariot reading aloud from the prophet Isaiah. It turns out that the man is the senior treasury official in the Ethiopian government.[76] The job is elite with one major downside: to work so closely

> **Historical Portal:**
> **Uniqueness of Eunuchs**
>
> A eunuch is a castrated male. He retains his male member, but his testicles are deleted; no procreation is possible. Eunuchs in royal households were highly valued in the ancient Near East. They could be trusted to guard harems of kings, or to work closely as servants or advisors to queens.

---

[75] The Philip who evangelizes in Samaria along the road to Gaza and eventually in Caesarea is identified by most scholars as one of the seven deacons, not one of the twelve original disciples. Luke cites both Philips in Acts (1:13, 6:5). After Stephen's murder, a persecution breaks out. Luke notes, *"All except the apostles were scattered throughout Judea and Samaria."* The term *the apostles* would seem to refer to the original eleven disciples (plus the added appointee), which would not include Philip, the deacon. Luke then narrates the adventures of this Philip as an example of those who were scattered but *"preached the word wherever they went"* (Acts 8:4-8).
[76] In that era, Ethiopia likely refers to the Upper Nile Region from the first cataract at Aswan to the area of today's Khartoum, Sudan, a region also known as Nubia or Kush. See Barker, ed., *NIV Study Bible*, 1659.

with the ruling queen, one must be a eunuch. The official is returning from Jerusalem, where he worshiped the God of Israel. He is reading Isaiah 53, the same passage Jesus referred to at the Last Supper when he told his disciples his life would be *"poured out for many"* and later that he would be *"numbered with the transgressors"* (Mk 14:24; Lk 22:37).

This section of scripture (Isa. 52:13–53:12), known as a servant song, stands like a translucent, jewel-like alpine peak rising higher than the mountain range of other prophetic heights in the OT books. In its pathos, rhythm of images, and emotional intensity, it ranks as one of the most deeply profound poems in the Bible and all literature. (I suggest reading it all at once if you can right now before proceeding further because the passage in its full length is so moving.)

Meanwhile, we return to the dusty road. Jogging up to the Ethiopian official's chariot, Philip asks the man if he understands what he is reading aloud.

*"How can I," he said, "unless someone explains it to me?" So he invited Philip to come up and sit with him. This is the passage of Scripture the eunuch was reading: "He was led like a sheep to the slaughter, and as a lamb before its shearer is silent, so he did not open his mouth. In his humiliation he was deprived of justice. Who can speak of his descendants? For his life was taken from the earth." The eunuch asked Philip, "Tell me, please, who is the prophet talking about, himself or someone else?" Then Philip began with that very passage of Scripture and told him the good news about Jesus. (Acts 8:31–35)*

The official, clearly an inquisitive and precise thinker, starts with the question of who in the poem is the subject or protagonist. As a eunuch, he may be intrigued that the subject of the prophecy has no physical descendants due to a life shortened by unjust execution. His new hitchhiker friend Philip is unfazed by the question for it is likely that he heard Jesus expound this passage over those forty days of appearances. While the chariot bumps along, Philip probably takes the official through the rest of the chapter making connections between the prophecy and the life of Jesus.

### Strong Correlations Between Jesus and Isaiah's Servant

The connections we can see between the servant in the Isaiah prophecy and the life of Jesus are profound. There is no chance that these Isaiah prophecies are retrojected, or made up later after Jesus lives. Nearly an entire manuscript of Isaiah was discovered along with parts of many other OT books in clay jars in caves near the Dead Sea initially in 1946. These document copies are indisputably dated at least a century before Jesus is born (though the prophetic texts in their originals date back at least four hundred years earlier with some texts originating a thousand or more years before Jesus).

Found in the Ground:
## Isaiah Scroll from the Cave Near the Dead Sea

Qumran, West Bank—The scroll is one of the collection known as the Dead Sea Scrolls. Scrolls are first located in 1946 in clay jars at Qumran, now part of the West Bank and overseen by Israel. The site is a mile or 1.6 kilometers from the northwestern shore of the Dead Sea. The Isaiah scroll length is twenty-four feet or about eight meters long on parchment. It is nearly a complete copy of the book of Isaiah. It was found in the initial cave along with six other manuscripts.

From 1946 to 1956, parts of every OT book were found except for Esther among more than 1,000 manuscripts in twelve caves. The scrolls are dated to between 300 BC and AD 100. The finding catapulted the earliest Hebrew-language manuscripts of the OT books back by more than 1,000 years, from the Masoretic text c. the tenth century AD to the Dead Sea Scrolls c. the second century BC. Surprisingly, few differences emerged between the texts beyond minor grammatical changes due to studious, meticulous copying over the generations. The astounding scroll confirms that the dramatic Isaiah prophecies are written at least five hundred to seven hundred years before the ministry of Jesus. (Isa. 9:2, 7, 11:1–10, 52:13–53:12)

Index 9.1

As is common in poetry, the poem spirals around the subject looking at his suffering from different angles rather than in chronological sequence.[77] Let us match the correlations in this servant song section (Isa. 52:13–53:12) with the reports of fulfillments in the NT documents about five hundred to seven

---

[77] The poetic and prophetic nature of the passage understandably invites alternative interpretations. In the *Background Guide*, resource 4, I contrast this classic Christian interpretation with different rabbinic interpretations of the servant in Isaiah.

hundred years later (depending on the view one has about when Isaiah is written).[78]

> 52:13: *he will be raised and lifted up and highly exalted.* He will triumph in the end and God will exalt him (Acts 1:9-11, 3:13-15).

> 52:14: *his appearance was so disfigured.* He will undergo severe physical suffering (Mt 26:67, 27:2; Mk 15:17-20; Jn 19:1-3).

> 52:15: *he will sprinkle many nations.* His offer to make people spiritually clean and connected to God will go out to all ethnicities (Mt 28:19, Acts 1:8).

> 53:1: *who has believed our message.* Many people in Israel as well as outside will reject the message though some accept it (Jn 12:37-46, Mt 13:10-12).

> 53:2: *tender shoot.* A branch or shoot is a frequent image of the promised Messiah (Isa. 4:2, 11:1-5, 10; Job 14:7; Jer. 23:5-6, 33:15-16; Zech. 6:12-13). A new shoot may grow out of a stump or ground that looks all but dead (Mt 1:5-6; Lk 3:32; Rev. 5:5).

> 53:2: *no beauty or majesty.* This figure has humble origins; Jesus came from a low-income craftsman's

---

[78] Not vital for our study, a debate continues over sections of Isaiah. The book frequently is divided into three sections, chapters 1-39 written in the 700s BC, chapters 40-55 written during the exile in Babylon from 586-515 BC, and then chapters 56-66 written after the exile. Commonly, the exile is considered concluded historically (though not necessarily theologically) by the Persian King Cyrus in 538 BC. He gives Jewish people the right to return to their land but not all do so right away (Isa. 44:24-45:6, 13; Ezra 1:1-4). Other viewpoints consider the exile concluded physically once the second temple is completed in 516 BC, almost exactly seventy years after the exile began.

family in a backward hill town of Nazareth (Lk 2:23–24; Mk 6:3).

---

Found in the Ground:
**Modest House in Nazareth**

Nazareth, Israel—Found in 2009 is a house with two rooms and a courtyard with a water cistern hewn from rock. No adorning mosaics or frescoes are present. In surrounding areas, evidence shows work activity in vineyards, terraced farming, stone masonry, and grape and olive presses all reflecting scenes captured in the teachings of Jesus. The finding confirms that Nazareth was populated during the time of Jesus, contradicting prior claims that the village was deserted during Jesus's time in the first century. (Mk 1:9; Mt 21:11; Lk 2:4, 39, 4:16; Jn 1:45–46, 18:5–7, 19:19; Acts 2:22, 3:6, 4:10, 10:38, 22:8, 26:9)

Index 9.2

---

53:3: *despised and rejected.* Jesus offers himself as king on his entry into Jerusalem on a donkey, but later that week is betrayed and arrested (Mk 14:43). At the priestly trial, he is accused of blasphemy (Mk 14:60–64). At the Roman hearing, he is charged with sedition (Mk 15:12–13). On the cross, he hears the mockers (Mk 15:31–32; Mt 27:41–44; Lk 23:35–39).

53:3: *one from whom people hide their faces.* A Roman whip of leather and cut-stone tips tore through his back (Mk 15:15; Jn 19:1). A crown of large, sharp-edged thorns and repeated fist blows bloodied his face (Mk 15:17–19; Jn 19:2–3).

53:4: *we considered him punished by God.* In that culture, blasphemy against God in claiming to be a divine figure has to be punished (Mk 14:60–64). Though he is hung on a Roman cross, his death on a tree in the Jewish mind-set symbolizes him coming under God's curse (Deut. 21:22–23; Gal. 3:13; Mk 15:29–32).

53:5: *he was pierced through.* As a victim of crucifixion, Jesus has each wrist torn through by an iron nail and probably both feet by a third nail (Lk 23:33). His side is pierced after he succumbs to death (Jn 19:34–37).

53:6: *we all like sheep have gone astray.* Jesus says he would voluntarily lay down his life like a shepherd for the sheep (Mk 6:34, 14:27, Mt. 15:24, Jn 10:15; 1 Pet. 2:25).

53:7: *he did not open his mouth.* At the trial before the priests, he says nothing in his defense to reply to the false witnesses. He speaks only when the judge, the high priest, demands he answer whether or not he is the Messiah (Mk 14:55–64: Mt 26:63–66). He is silent before Herod Antipas (Lk 23:8–9). He amazes the Roman governor Pilate by not answering the accusations of the priests (Mk 15:1–5).

53:8: *by oppression and judgment he is taken away.* Jesus was arrested and taken to an illegal Sanhedrin night trial and then a second trial by the Roman governor (Mk 14:43–50, 65, 15:1–15; Mt 27:11–26; Lk 23:18–25; Jn 18:29–19:16).

53:9: *cut off from the land of the living.* Jesus is executed and dies. He breathes his last (Mk 15:37). A Roman spear punctures his side, and blood and water pour out indicating he has expired (Jn 19:33–34).

53:9: *with the rich in his death.* A wealthy member of the Sanhedrin, Joseph of Arimathea, steps up to bury the body in his own tomb (Mk 15:42–47; Mt 27:57–61; Lk 23:50–56; Jn 19:38–42).

53:10: *the Lord makes his life an offering for sin.* In place of an animal at the tabernacle or temple, Jesus serves as the final sacrifice for the sins of all humanity, fulfilling the promise of forgiveness foreshadowed by the sacrificial system given to Moses (Jn 1:29; 1 Jn 4:10; Acts 20:28; 1 Pet. 1:18–19; Heb. 2:17, 9:12, 14, 28, 10:4, 13:12; Rom. 3:25–26, 5:9; Eph. 1:7).

53:10: *he will see his offspring and prolong his days.* Jesus makes multiple appearances to his disciples over forty days and then ascends to heaven (Lk 24:1–53; Jn 14:2–3, 20:11–21:25; Acts 1:1–3).

53:11: *after he has suffered, he will see the light of life and be satisfied.* Jesus would not remain dead in the tomb according to the multiple witnesses (Jn 20:14–18, 21:1; Mt 28:9–10, 16–20; Lk 24:17–49; Acts 1:1–9, 2:24; 1 Cor. 15:5–8).

53:12: *a portion among the great.* This is military language for being granted exalted status as a result of a great victory (Acts 2:33–36; Rom. 8:34; Phil. 2:9–11). His status as commander has been established in heaven and will be revealed at the second coming when armies accompany him (Rev. 1:5, 19:14).

53:12: *because he poured out his life unto death, and was numbered with the transgressors.* Jesus agreed to die for the sins of others, enduring the shame of dying the humiliating death of a criminal or insurrectionist (Mk 14:24, 15:27; Mt 26:28, 27:38; Lk 22:20, 23:32).

53:12: *for he bore the sin of many, and made intercession for the transgressors.* By absorbing the sins of others, standing between them and their fate of eternal separation from God, he is able to rescue them into a new covenant and bring them into an eternally restored relationship with God (Mt 20:28; Lk 22:37; Acts 2:38–39; Jn 3:16–17; 1 Jn 2:1; 1 Pet. 2:24, 3:18; Heb. 12:9; Rom. 8:34).

### A Chariot Rest Stop Starts a Transformed Destiny

Now going back to the chariot ride, it is reasonable to presume that Philip took the Ethiopian official beyond the passage he already was reading in Isaiah 53:7–8 through verse 9 describing the burial of Jesus, and then on to verse 10.

> *Yet it was the Lord's will to crush him and cause him to suffer, and though the Lord makes his life an offering for sin, he will see his offspring and prolong his days, and the will of the Lord will prosper in his hand. (Isaiah 53:10)*

The official likely hears the reference to Jesus as a sacrificial offering taking away the sins of others. Something surges inside him.

> *As they traveled along the road, they came to some water and the eunuch said, "Look here is water. What can stand in the way of my being baptized?" And he gave orders to stop the chariot. Then both Philip and the eunuch went down into the water and Philip baptized him. (Acts 8:36–38)*

As the palace official just had seen animals being sacrificed in front of the temple at the burning altar, the notion of Jesus as the sacrifice for his sake would likely have made a deep impression on him. That may be the reason he immediately insists on being baptized then and there. He orders his chariot to a halt beside a waterway. With Philip, he climbs down and takes the plunge. Soaked to his skin, the Ethiopian official emerges from the water as a man assured that his sins are forgiven and that his life is eternal now that he trusts in the suffering and rising Servant Messiah, who fulfilled the stirring words of the prophet Isaiah.

# 9: CONCLUSION

### On Jesus Fulfilling Messianic Prophecies

With the travelers on the road to Emmaus and then with the disciples later that Sunday evening, the risen Jesus takes pains to show that his journey as the suffering and rising Messiah was predicted long before by many prophets. He says it was predicted in Moses (the Torah or first five OT books), in the Prophets, and in the Psalms. In these accounts, Jesus does not give exact citations, but we successfully detect the OT prophecies in two ways: from the words and actions of Jesus in the gospel narratives and from the preaching of the apostles after Jesus departs as recorded in Acts and reflected in their collected NT letters.

*Moses.* In the books of Moses, the Messiah is predicted in the promise to Abraham that through his descendant all nations will be blessed. Through the lens of the gospel of John, we see how Moses lifting up a bronze serpent in the wilderness prefigures an atoning savior who is crucified yet exalted. Later, Moses predicts the sending of *"a prophet like me"* who will mediate a new covenant for a new people. Only unbeknown to Moses, this mediator will seal the covenant in his own blood as the human embodiment of the Passover lamb or temple sacrifice. The evangelists Stephen and Peter also cite the prophet like Moses and the promises to Abraham.

*Prophets.* As for the prophets, Jonah's experience of spending three days inside an ocean creature before being spit up on the shore alive represents the burial and return that Jesus senses he will undergo. Drawing on the prophet Zechariah, Jesus fulfills predictions of a king coming to his people on a donkey and a shepherd being struck and his sheep scattering. Yet Zechariah goes on to predict a Messiah returning to restore his people, who first mourn over *"the one they have pierced."* In the prophet Daniel, the Messiah is *"cut off"* or executed. Yet Daniel also sees a Messiah figure arriving in heaven in glory. When Jesus implies at his trial that he is this figure, it gets him in a heap of trouble with the priests—because it is code they know identifying a divine being.

The extended poem or servant song (from Isaiah 52:13–53:12) describes a Messiah who suffers for the sins of others then regains life and takes joy in the many who are saved. Over dinner with his disciples, Jesus explains the meaning of his death by alluding to this prophecy. He says his blood, like a cup of wine, will be *"poured out for many."* The evangelist Philip explains this Isaiah prophecy in his road-trip conversation with the Ethiopian official. The decisive executive opts for immediate roadside baptism.

*Psalms.* Regarding the Psalms, Jesus teaches at the temple grounds from Psalm 110 about the Messiah sitting at God's right hand and cites it again at his trial before the priests. Peter quotes this psalm extensively in his initial street preaching on Pentecost along with Psalm 16. He pinpoints how the *"anointed"* or *"holy one"* shall not *"see decay."*

Not long before he is arrested, Jesus tells the parable of the tenants using the rejected stone in Psalm 118:22 as his punchline. In their letters, Peter and Paul apply the symbol of Jesus as a stone from Isaiah 8:14, 28:16. For believers, Jesus is a foundation stone of blessing but for unbelievers a stumbling stone of disaster. On the cross, Jesus shouts in anguish expressing his feelings of abandonment through the words of Psalm 22. It is a poem preternaturally describing suffering in terms correlating with a crucifixion victim. Yet the victim's cry is heard (Ps. 22:24), implying he will live again.

In hindsight, after the cross and resurrection, these prophecies come into focus. They make sense when applied to Jesus. The disciples certainly thought so and became convinced. It is reasonable to conclude that Jesus almost certainly directed his disciples to these passages that elucidate a suffering and rising Messiah. These fulfillments, coming five hundred to fifteen hundred years after the prophecies were given, increase the probability of the historical reality of the resurrection.

# CHAPTER

CHAPTER

10

## CHAPTER 10

---

# ALTERNATIVE THEORIES
# DENYING THE RESURRECTION

---

espite the evidence cited in the previous chapters, many scholars and skeptics do not believe Jesus was physically raised from the dead. Over the centuries, a number of alternative theories have been proposed. Here, I assess ten of the most common. Most involve accepting some of the evidence in the NT narratives while dismissing other portions. Some of the succeeding theories add highly imaginative material. In fact, two theories are anticipated and mentioned in the original gospel narratives: the one about the disciples stealing the body (Mt 27:64), and the one about the risen Jesus being a ghost (Lk 24:39).

This chapter first describes each of the ten theories in simple, straightforward terms. Next, additional beliefs the theory requires are itemized. Then, evidence against the theory is listed, most of it drawn from the lines of evidence in the preceding chapters.

All the alternative theories deny that Jesus rose from the dead physically. The first two deny that Jesus died on the cross; they contend that he survived. The rest agree he died but say his body was disposed of in one way or another. Only one theory asserts that the disciples intentionally created a hoax. The others in different ways contend that their minds were confused and simply got it wrong about the resurrection.

By denying the resurrection of Jesus, these theories directly contradict Jesus's predictions of his destiny (see chapter 3). They also rule out Jesus's eligibility to be considered as the servant figure prophesied in Isaiah 53 (see chapter 9, and for more discussion of rabbinic interpretations, see *Background Guide*, resource 4). As we have seen, that figure suffers and dies only to be raised to life. His death atones or substitutes for others by taking the death penalty for their sins upon himself.

Both in the Isaiah passage and in traditional NT interpretation, the resurrection verifies that the substitutionary work of Jesus was enough to absorb the sins of all humanity (Rom. 1:2-4; 1 Pet. 1:3-4, 2:24, 3:18; Heb. 2:9; Jn 3:16-17, 11:25-26). Without that verification, with Jesus remaining dead, there is no guarantee sins are covered and salvation can result as Paul informs the Corinthians.

> For if the dead are not raised, then Christ has not been raised either. And if Christ has not been raised, your faith is futile; you are still in your sins. Then those also who have fallen asleep in Christ are lost. If only for this life we have hope in Christ, we are of all people most to be pitied. (1 Corinthians 15:16–19)

In the event of his death without his resurrection, the attempt on the part of Jesus to save others fails. Because skeptics deny that he has been raised back to life physically, any concept that Jesus's death atones for others is eliminated by these theories. That is the reason the stakes are justifiably so high.

Each of these ten alternative theories are considered and evaluated.

1. Swoon-Coma Theory
2. Fake-Death Theory
3. Disciples-Stole-the-Body Theory
4. Others-Stole-the-Body Theory
5. Wrong-Tomb Theory
6. Mass-Grave Theory
7. Group-Hallucination Theory
8. Borrowed-Myth Theory
9. Spiritual-Resurrection Theory
10. Legend-Grows Theory

Today, skeptics do not adhere to the alternative theories in equal proportion. The last two on the list seem to be the most commonly held today. These are the main theories, but other ones crop up periodically or these familiar ones get recycled in new forms.

For those who want more detail than this section offers, I recommend these books.

- William Lane Craig, *Assessing the New Testament Evidence for the Historicity of the Resurrection of Jesus* (Lewiston, ID: Edwin Mellen Press, 1989).
- William Lane Craig, *Reasonable Faith* (Wheaton, IL: Crossway Books, 2008).
- Gary R. Habermas and Michael R. Licona, *The Case for the Resurrection of Jesus* (Grand Rapids, MI: Kregel, 2004).

Due to its structure presenting each theory in specific categories, this chapter is oriented less for reading straight through and more for use as a reference guide to locate handy responses to the alternative theories as you may encounter them in your own study or in conversations. For each alternative theory, there are three brief sections: a summary of the *main assertion* of the theory; the *beliefs* the theory requires, including premises often hidden that need to be spelled out to truly assess it; and then, the *historical evidence against* the theory. Much of the evidence you will recognize since it is already laid out in the previous nine chapters. Here, it is applied to specific alternative theories in an easy format for quick reference. There is by necessity a certain degree of repetition in the evidence asserted against the theories since a single piece of evidence can counteract more than one theory. A brief summary of the main areas where each theory falters concludes the chapter.

*theory* 1 : **The Swoon-Coma Theory**

*Assertion of the Theory*

Jesus narrowly escapes death by "blacking out" on the cross. He falls into a coma, possibly drug-induced. That condition is caused by the potion he drinks while on the cross when it is offered to him by a Roman guard.[79]

Jesus is taken down from the cross unconscious but alive. Joseph of Arimathea brings him to his own tomb apparently unaware that Jesus is not dead. The stone is rolled over the entrance to the tomb.

Sometime over the next day or two (or three), Jesus revives in the cool tomb. The spices and myrrh wrapped in the linen cloths around his body help resuscitate him. He is able to push the stone away from the door. Or he pounds on the stone until the guards hear him, they open it, and he slips out of their grasp.

A variant on the theme asserts that neither Jesus nor the two criminals crucified on either side of him actually end up dead, truly a case of Roman military malpractice. One of the criminals is a doctor, a character out of Acts named Simon Magus. He trails Jesus to the tomb and administers medicine that revives the comatose Jesus.

At any rate, the theory says the survivor Jesus finds his disciples. He is severely injured but living, bloodied but unbowed. The disciples and Jesus think he has been raised from the dead though he merely experiences a swoon in the tomb. There is no intention to deceive, just a huge, monumental, mutual misunderstanding.

---

[79] All four gospels include the incident on the cross when wine vinegar is offered to Jesus: Mk 15:36; Mt 27:48; Lk 23:36; Jn 19:29–30.

### The Swoon-Coma Theory Requires These Beliefs

- The Romans do not know how to crucify effectively.
- The Romans do not check or cannot tell if a victim is truly dead.
- Jesus possesses incredible stamina. He endures a brutal whipping, a long haul carrying a crossbeam on his shoulder, and hours of crucifixion without expiring.
- The disciples interpret a still bloodied and injured figure as having been raised from the dead.

### Evidence Against the Swoon-Coma Theory

*Known Expertise.* The Romans know exactly how to crucify their victims. For them, it is a key deterrent punishment, one major way they keep order in their empire. After they put down the slave revolt spearheaded by Spartacus in 71 BC, the Romans crucify six thousand rebel slaves. They plant their crosses like telephone poles at intervals along the Appian Way, a distance of 120 miles or 193 kilometers from Capua to Rome.[80] Recounting the siege of Jerusalem forty years after Jesus departs (AD 70), Josephus records a period when five hundred Jews were crucified each day.[81]

*Blood Loss.* Jesus is unlikely to have survived the ordeal laid out in the gospel accounts. He suffers a severe whipping, probably thirty-nine lashes from a whip of leather strips with sharp stones on the ends to slash the skin making the cuts deeper (Mk 15:15; Mt 27:26; Jn 19:1). The crown of thorns causes deep cuts in the head (Mk 15:17; Jn 19:2). He takes blows to the face that likely open cuts (Mk 15:19; Mt 27:30; Jn 19:3). He was unable to carry his heavy wooden crossbeam through the city to the execution site;

---

[80] For an original source on the Spartacus revolt and crucifixions, see Appian, *Civil Wars*, 1.120, at livius.org, Jona Lendering, ed., 30 May 2016.
[81] Josephus records the massive Jerusalem crucifixions of rebel Jews (*War* 5.11.1).

he needed help from a muscular onlooker who is enlisted to help him (Mk 15:21; Mt 27:32; Lk 23:26).[82]

*Pulse Check.* The gospels specifically record the Romans ensuring that Jesus is dead. Pilate delays granting the request of Joseph of Arimathea until he receives confirmation from the centurion on duty that Jesus has in fact expired (Mk 15:44–45). In the rush to take down the bodies from the crosses before sundown as required by Jewish law, the Roman soldiers break the legs of the two criminals to terminate their lives. When they are unable to push up from their legs, their lungs cannot lift up to breathe, so they suffocate. The soldiers check Jesus and see that he is dead already with no need to break his legs.

A soldier thrusts a spear into his side. It is nowhere recorded which side, but probably the left. The fact that water and blood pour out indicates the pericardial sac lining the heart is pierced. The collapse of Jesus on the way (Mk 15:21–22) and his thirst on the cross (Jn 19:28) are signs that his blood volume and pressure were very low, a condition known as hypovolemic shock. To compensate, the heart beats faster, which leads to fluid pooling in the sack around the heart and in the lungs.

Because of the way he suffers the loss of so much blood before being nailed to the cross, some experts speculate that Jesus most likely does not die of suffocation like most crucifixion victims but of congestive heart failure.[83]

---

[82] As with the cameo appearance of Joseph of Arimathea, another cameo occurs on the part of Simon of Cyrene, whom the Romans pressed into service to carry the crossbeam when Jesus falters on the way to the crucifixion site. Cyrene was in the eastern part of today's Libya. Many Jews were forced to settle there c. 300 BC by the ruler Ptolemy I, a boyhood friend and trusted general of Alexander the Great. The Greek colony comprised a reported 100,000 Jews. In ethnicity, Simon may have been North African, Jewish, or both. It is likely he was a Jewish worshiper as he was in town for the Passover festival. It also is likely that he embraced Christian beliefs. He is identified in Mk 15:21 as *"the father of Alexander and Rufus,"* who are known to tradition as Christian missionaries (Rom. 16:13).
[83] See "Why did blood and water come out of Jesus' side when He was pierced?" n.a., gotquestions.org, *Got Questions Ministries*, n.d.

*Not Inspiring.* A severely injured Jesus who is limping, bloodied, and in need of major recovery and medical care is not likely to inspire the disciples to categorize him as raised from the dead. They might view him as a stoic survivor rather than the triumphant Messiah. They would not likely carry a message of stoic stamina to the ends of the earth at the risk of their lives.

*theory* 2: **The Fake-Death Theory**

*Assertion of the Theory*

Jesus himself hatches a precise and carefully laid plan to fake his own crucifixion and resurrection. He expertly plans his entry into Jerusalem on a donkey ostensibly to fulfill a messianic prophecy (Zech. 9:9). Now he is in too deep. He must fulfill other prophecies. He will bamboozle his own disciples into believing he is the Messiah.

He sequesters money from the disciples' limited treasury. He bribes the centurion in charge of his crucifixion to take him within an inch of his life but to stop the madness while he still breathes. Likewise, he bribes Joseph of Arimathea to transport his body to the tomb. Guards at the tomb are bribed to roll away the stone at a designated time. He appears to his disciples as if he rose from the dead and is able to show them his scars from his sufferings.

A variant of this theory involves Jesus finding the suffering was more than he anticipated and he is about to die. Not wanting to disappoint his disciples or invalidate his own prediction of resurrection, he has a backup plan. A body double who resembles him (highly imagined in some versions to be his unknown twin brother) steps out to appear to the disciples. Privately, the real Jesus quietly dies and is taken by Joseph of Arimathea to a common grave.

*The Fake-Death Theory Requires These Beliefs*

- Jesus has no trust in God to raise and deliver him but must take things into his own hands.
- Jesus possesses such low character as to deceive his disciples into preaching a false message.

- Jesus has the gall to create a conspiracy through skimming funds and bribery.

## Evidence Against the Fake-Death Theory

*Trust in God.* The words Jesus speaks on the cross show he is trusting God, not taking things into his own hands. As he senses his life slipping away, he cries out, *"My God, My God, why have you forsaken me?"* (Mk 15:34). This cry reveals he was expecting God the Father either to rescue him or at least to be present in spirit to comfort him. Yet Jesus seems shocked to feel that spirit now is terribly distant or withdrawn. Jesus quotes Psalm 22:1, rendered by Mark in both Greek and in the original Aramaic language that Jesus spoke. A hero Messiah figure of the gospel accounts described as feeling abandoned by God the Father meets the historical criterion of embarrassment, supporting its validity (see addition 3).

*Character of Jesus.* Nothing in the reliable annals of Jesus depicts a character flaw that would lead him to intentionally deceive his disciples. This would mean his enemies, the ruling priests, are right about him when they level the charge against him that he is a *"deceiver"* (Mt 27:63). The theory imagines Jesus expropriating funds from the treasury, but he delegated treasury management to Judas (Jn 12:6). Judas would have known and likely objected if Jesus was skimming funds for future bribes. Moreover, engaging in bribery of Roman guards at the cross and tomb and then asking them to lie directly conflicts with Jesus's teaching (Mt 5:19–20). Essentially, this theory requires Jesus to lie, steal, and bribe others to disobey their superiors. This depiction of a hypocritical teacher turned conspiracy plotter conflicts with the multiply attested portraits in the gospels of Jesus as a righteous man.

*Critical Accomplice.* It is doubtful Joseph of Arimathea would agree to be an accomplice. As a rich man, he would not be vulnerable to a bribe. As a timid, secret follower of Jesus, he likely would not have the courage to conspire (Mt 27:57; Jn 19:38).

*Jerusalem Base.* A core team of disciples remains in Jerusalem for decades preaching the message of Jesus's death and resurrection (see chapter 8). If there was a conspiracy, it is highly likely a conspirator would break sooner or later and come forth to contradict the disciples' version of events. Local witnesses outside the conspiracy could also debunk the claim that Jesus was raised by guiding people to his tomb at least for a year until his bones were boxed up.

*Secular Historians.* The first-century Jewish historian Josephus and the early second-century Roman historian Tacitus brook no dissent that Jesus was summarily executed and died at the hands of the Romans under the Roman governor Pontius Pilate.[84]

---

[84] For reports of Pontius Pilate presiding over the trial and execution of Jesus, see Josephus, *Antiquities of the Jews* 18.3.3, and Tacitus, *Annals* 15.44. Both excerpts are quoted in the prologue. Neither writer shows signs of working from Christian sources for their comments on Jesus. Both had Roman sources, with Josephus in addition drawing from Jewish sources. See Lawrence Mykytiuk, *Did Jesus Exist?* (cited in prologue).

## theory 3: The Disciples-Stole-The-Body Theory

### Assertion of the Theory

The disciples are not mere country rustics from the northern outer limits of Israel as the gospels make them appear to be. They are wily, manipulative, and muscular. Clearly, they are disappointed and put to grief by Jesus's death and failure to restore Israel to political greatness as they expected of their Messiah. However, they are not about to lose their status with the crowds, who also hoped in him. They quickly work through their grief and come to their senses.

They are strong men used to outdoor labor. If they can push boats into the sea and pull them back onshore, they can heave-ho a rolling stone blocking the tomb doorway. In the dead of night, they creep into the tomb zone. They knock out the guards as if they had clubbed big fish they had caught in their nets back at the lake. They roll away the stone and carry off the corpse of Jesus. They dig a grave in a lonely place out of sight. It is never found. They proceed to wait a few weeks. Then once crowds descend on Jerusalem for the next festival, the Feast of Weeks (or Pentecost), they start preaching that Jesus has been raised from the dead.

### The Disciples-Stole-the-Body Theory Requires These Beliefs

- The disciples are brave and have the audacity to figure out how to roll away the stone blocking the tomb entrance.
- They are ingenious and devious con artists who plan and carry out an epic hoax.
- They can enlist skeptical outsiders to join them in their conspiracy.
- All accounts of Jesus's appearances are invented and never occur.

## Evidence Against the Disciples-Stole-the-Body Theory

*Not in Character.* The disciples are depicted in the gospels on their better days as slow to learn and doubtful and on their worse days as bumbling and cowardly. True, they grow bold and assertive after the resurrection (Acts 2). But this theory requires they change into brave geniuses in order to fabricate the resurrection message though they know that the leader in whom they invested so much is dead and gone.

*Hiding in Fear.* It was embarrassing to be sure that the disciples feared for their lives and stayed hidden after Jesus's arrest and trial. In contrast, brave women in their entourage stayed late at the crucifixion site, witnessed the burial, and headed back out to the tomb early on the first day of the week.

Some critics say the men should have been waiting at the tomb for the rising of Jesus if Jesus had told them he would rise after three days. Because they fail to show up, the theory goes, Jesus never told them and never rose. That means the disciples stole the body and made up the whole resurrection story. This subtheory obviously dismisses the much more probable reasons the disciples did not show up at the tomb on schedule: they did not understand Jesus's prediction, or did not believe it, or they were too scared of being crucified themselves to act on any thread of belief that their abused and dead rabbi would rise.

*Out-of-Towners.* The disciples come from the agrarian region of Galilee in northern Israel. They do not know their way around Jerusalem in detail. That makes it harder for them to plan a getaway from the tomb and stash the body where it cannot be found.

*Multiple Appearance Accounts.* If the disciples steal the body, the body never rises, and all postresurrection accounts of Jesus appearing to the disciples are nullified. The appearance accounts are numerous, mostly taking place in groups of at least two or more and at one point five hundred. They occur in Jerusalem and in Galilee to women and men. The variety, the time elapsed, and some of the more detailed accounts of appearances make them hard to dismiss categorically (see chapter 2).

*Hard-to-Convince Prior Hostile Unbelievers.* It is unlikely the disciples could pull the wool over the eyes of previous unbelievers and by themselves convince James the brother of Jesus to convert and later Paul, who was a fierce opponent of Jerusalem believers. Accounts show that for them to believe, it took Jesus appearing to James individually and speaking in a vision to Paul (1 Cor. 15:7-8, Acts 9:3-9; see chapters 2 and 6).

*Culturally Self-Sabotaging.* In their Jewish social and religious context, the disciples face sneering ridicule over preaching a suffering Messiah instead of the expected military liberator. They incite persecution against themselves by championing their heresy. They also risk the religious consequence of a destiny in the afterlife where they are condemned by God for blasphemy, for intentionally misrepresenting that Jesus is Messiah and Lord. There is little self-interest to motivate the disciples to create a hoax in a cultural situation with these pressures against them.[85]

*Jerusalem Base.* The wider a conspiracy, the harder it is to keep it a secret as time goes on. A core team of disciples remains in Jerusalem for several decades (see chapter 8). To quell the movement, the rulers or priests would likely break one or more conspirators to divulge the plot. There is no reliable evidence that any disciple ever broke rank, confessed to a fraud, and led them to the hidden location of the body.

*Not Rational.* It is absurd to assume that the disciples would invest the rest of their lives in a hoax and eventually die the death of martyrs for what they knew was a lie.

---

[85] See the discussion in David Limbaugh, *Jesus on Trial* (Wash., DC: Regnery Publishing, 2014), 282-83. A lawyer by trade, Limbaugh logically and succinctly captures a set of insights he credits largely to the research of Gary Habermas.

*theory* 4: **The Others-Stole-the-Body Theory**

## Assertion of the Theory

With a heavy stone blocking the tomb entrance and a guard posted outside, it is not easy to snatch the body of Jesus. At a minimum, it would take an organized group. The Jews do not place valuables with their dead, so grave robbers are unlikely suspects. However, other groups in Jerusalem could have stolen the body.

Maybe the people who stole it are the Pharisees, who believe in the resurrection of the dead. They might want to get back at their rivals, the ruling Sadducees, who were the main perpetrators of Jesus's execution. Maybe the chief priests steal the body before the disciples can retrieve it, as the priests clearly fear they might (Mt 27:63–66). Perhaps they dump the body in a mass grave. When to their horror they realize their action only encourages the deception of the resurrection, they somehow cannot locate the body.

Maybe the tomb gardener steals the body. Maybe a contingent of retired or current Roman soldiers take the body hoping to be paid by either the disciples or by the high priests for its safe return. Maybe the one who took the body was the supposed real father of Jesus, a Roman soldier who had struck up an affair with Mary. Maybe the angels spirit the body away directly to heaven. The list goes on with varying degrees of imagination.

## The Others-Stole-the-Body Theory Requires These Beliefs

- The Roman guards at the tomb were not up to the job.
- All accounts of Jesus's appearances after the resurrection are invented and did not occur.
- Whoever stole the body never produced it for any purpose.

*Evidence Against the Others-Stole-the-Body Theory*

*Lack of Motive.* On the council (the Sanhedrin) that agrees to execute Jesus were Pharisees and Sadducees. Not all Pharisees agree with the verdict including Joseph of Arimathea and Nicodemus (Lk 23:51; Jn 7:5–51), but others are envious of Jesus's status with the people (Mk 15:10). The Sadducees fear an uprising led by Jesus that would cause the Romans to further oppress their nation; they have no motive for wanting people to think that Jesus is alive. The Roman soldiers might have had a motive to make money, but they would do so at the risk of their lives and honor since they were violating an official Roman seal on the tomb and crossing a posted guard (Mt 27:66). As for the disciples, they had little money to offer soldiers as bribes even if they had wanted to especially after their treasurer killed himself (Mt 27:5; Acts 1:18–19).

*Mary's Character.* The agonizing search for a motive takes some scholars back to the late second-century AD Greek philosopher Celsus, likely based in Alexandria, Egypt. According to the Christian writer Origen, Celsus asserted that Mary of Nazareth had an affair with a Roman soldier named Pantera, which produced the baby Jesus. If this soldier had lived thirty or so more years, he might have wanted to nab the body of his supposed son from the tomb. This Celsus theory is propagated in the Talmud (c. AD 300), where Jesus is referred to as "Yeshu ben (son of) Pantera."[86] Pantera (or sometimes spelled "Panthera") was a common Roman name. It may have been chosen as a pun on the Greek name for virgin, "parthenos." (The Parthenon temple in Athens is named after the goddess Athena Parthenos.) Conveniently, a gravestone of a Roman soldier named Pantera was found in Germany in 1859. Further, the stone says he hailed from Sidon in today's Lebanon, not far from Galilee. Of course this leads to massive speculations. But there are problems. One

---

[86] Craig Evans, *Fabricating Jesus* (Downers Grove, IL: InterVarsity Press, 2006), 217–219, 268. Evans notes one prototypical example from the Talmud is found in Tosefta *Hullin* 2.22–24.

problem is the dates and biology do not match up. Some scholars trace the soldier's birth to 10–12 BC, too soon to be the biological father of Jesus in 4–6 BC. Another problem is its logical conflict with other historical data. Matthew's gospel account reports that Joseph suspected Mary of cheating due to the pregnancy during their betrothal. At that point, he planned to end the marriage, although quietly, so that Mary would not be shamed publicly (Mt 1:18–19). Had this charge of scandal been true, he likely would have followed his plan. In cases of cheating or even in the terrible case of rape, betrothals in that culture likely would have been abruptly broken off (Deut. 22:13, 24:1). In contrast, Joseph and Mary stay together (Lk 2:41, 48). They produce more children, including Jesus's four brothers and at least two sisters (Mt 12:46, 13:55–56; Jn 2:12, 7:3, 5; Acts 1:14; 1 Cor. 9:5). Jesus's brother James in particular receives much additional historical verification from Paul in Gal. 1:19, from Luke in Acts 12:17, 15:13, and from Josephus in *Antiquities* 20.9.1. Understood in this way, the very existence of the siblings of Jesus discredits the Pantera theory.

To be sure, Celsus hated Christians and cannot be considered an objective source. Also, the Pantera narrative is not corroborated by texts outside later rabbinic commentary. Perhaps most appallingly, it directly contradicts the gospel accounts of the noble character of Mary (Mt 1:20, 25; Lk 1:27, 29–30, 38, 2:19, 22, 39; Acts 1:14).

*Linen Strips.* A detail multiply attested by independent sources mentions that there were strips of linen lying in the tomb where the body of Jesus had lain (Lk 24:12; Jn 20:5–6). In that era, Jewish burial practice called for these linen strips to be wrapped around the body similar to an Egyptian mummy. Those stealing a wrapped body would be unlikely to take the time to unwrap it strip by strip. The wrapped body would be much easier to carry away.

*Multiple Appearance Accounts.* If the body is stolen, Jesus does not rise as asserted and all accounts of Jesus appearing to the disciples are nullified. The accounts are numerous, mostly taking place in groups of at least two or more and at one point five hundred in Jerusalem and Galilee. This makes them hard to dismiss categorically (see chapter 2).

*Transformation of Disciples.* When appearances by Jesus are ruled out by the theory, the disciples cannot be inspired by the return of their leader. They are bewildered by the disappearance of the body (Lk 24:12; Jn 20:9, 13). It is unlikely that they would vigorously preach the resurrection—as we know from history they did—if they did not experience a risen Jesus (see chapters 4-5).

*Jerusalem Base.* As we have seen, some key disciples remain in Jerusalem for the next several decades (see chapter 8). To shut down the movement, all the Roman or Jewish authorities need do is produce the body or even just the bones of Jesus. They could procure the body from the group that steals it. No such action is ever taken implying the body could not be retrieved.

# theory 5 : The Wrong-Tomb Theory

## Assertion of the Theory

The women who go to the tomb early on the first day of the week are emotionally overwhelmed and mentally confused. They go to the first open tomb they can find rather than the sealed tomb where the body of Jesus actually lay.

A young man loitering among the tombs tells them that there is no dead body in the open tomb. In great fear, they flee. With a sudden flash of insight, they mistakenly conclude Jesus must have risen from the dead. That is the news they bring to the disciples. They direct the disciples to go check out the same open and empty but wrong tomb.

## The Wrong-Tomb Theory Requires These Beliefs

- Several of the women do not leave the crucifixion site and trail behind as Joseph of Arimathea transports the body of Jesus to the tomb as the gospels attest.
- If the women do trail behind, they are forgetful, easily confused, or do not have a good sense of direction—arguably a sexist interpretation.
- Joseph of Arimathea, a Pharisee and leader on the ruling council, would not bring to the disciples' attention that his tomb continued to hold the corpse of Jesus.

## Evidence Against the Wrong-Tomb Theory

*New Tomb.* The tomb was freshly cut out of rock. No one ever had been laid there. In color and texture and without any weathering, the tomb likely stood out from the other tombs worn by seasons of winter rains and summer sun. Stone cuttings likely were scattered around as well making it easier to find a new tomb.

*Strong Motivation.* Culturally, women of that time usually took the lead in lamenting the dead and preparing the body with linen wrappings and scented ointments and spices. Despite their overarching sorrow, they would likely be alert enough to track the path to the tomb to fulfill their duties (Lk 23:55).

*Observers Named.* The gospels specifically identify the women (Mary Magdalene and Mary mother of James the disciple) who follow the transport of the body to the tomb. They observe how the men rush the preparation feverishly trying to beat the clock to have the tomb closed up by sundown (Mk 15:47; Mt 27:61; also see chapter 1).

*Linen Strips.* A detail multiply attested by independent sources mentions that there were strips of linen lying in the tomb where the body of Jesus had lain. The women observing the wrapping likely would know if the strips matched what they saw the men using (Lk 24:12; Jn 19:40, 20:5).

*Jerusalem Base.* The disciples make Jerusalem their base and preach the resurrection publicly within about seven weeks of the crucifixion. To disprove the deception, all the priests or Romans need to do is take people to the right tomb; they know where it is (Mt 27:65-66). There, they would find the corpse of Jesus decomposing for a year. Later, as the disciples keep preaching from Jerusalem, their opponents could go find the bone box (or ossuary) of Jesus. No record exists of the priests or Romans tracing back to locate the body or bones of Jesus.

*theory* 6 : **The Mass-Grave Theory**

*Assertion of the Theory*

The Romans customarily did not treat the bodies of crucified individuals well. Usually, they left them on the cross to writhe in agony for several days until they could not lift their lungs to breathe and therefore suffocated. Even after they expired, their dead bodies could be left upright and exposed to be pecked at by scavenging birds. Eventually, the disfigured bodies were thrown into mass graves or pits. Sometimes, dogs were allowed to roam the pits and eat the carcasses.

To avoid the risk of inciting the Jews to rebellion, the Romans agreed to abide by the Jewish insistence that executed bodies be taken down and buried before sundown. Often, the crucified victims were still alive and pushing themselves up to breathe for many hours. To respect the Jewish custom, the Romans broke the legs of their victims with clubs, inducing quick suffocation. This was especially important the day Jesus died since the annual Passover celebration began that evening at twilight (following the time frame given in Jn 18:28, 19:13–14). The two crucified on either side of Jesus suffer this fate of broken legs and sudden suffocation at the soldiers' hands. When they come to Jesus, they determine he is dead.

As for the burial, Jesus is treated no differently than the common criminals according to this theory; all three are tossed into a pit. Because he is buried in a mass grave, no one knows where his corpse lands. Unfortunately, his followers can pretend that he rose from the dead and no one can produce the body to prove he did not.

*The Mass-Grave Theory Requires These Beliefs*

- The Romans toss all crucified persons into mass graves.
- Jesus does not have followers with enough status and courage to intervene with the Romans to honor him with a decent burial.
- Jews classified all of those crucified under Roman law but not Mosaic law as "hung on a pole" and therefore accursed by God and unworthy of honorable burial (Deut. 21:23).
- Not only all gospel accounts of appearances but also all tomb site accounts are falsely contrived including the role of Joseph of Arimathea.

*Evidence Against the Mass-Grave Theory*

*Crucified Man Entombed.* Notably, a first-century individual by the name of Yehohanan, son of Hagkol, was crucified and placed in a tomb. His bone box or ossuary includes his anklebone with a 4.5 inch or 11.5 centimeter iron nail thrust through it.[87] Normally, iron nails were pried out and recycled for the next crucifixion, but this one could not be extracted. Scholars have detected olive wood fragments on the nail indicating the nail hit a knot in the beam and bent. The artifact proves a crucified man could be buried with honor in a tomb and not consigned to a mass grave (see *Background Guide*, Found in the Ground 1.2, and shorter description in chapter 1).[88]

*Religious Laws Are Different.* The Jews reserved a separate,

---

[87] Joe Zias and Eliezer Sekeles, "The Crucified Man from Giv'at ha-Mitvar: A Reappraisal," *Israel Exploration Journal* vol. 35 (1985), 26. Also see "Jehohanan," wikipedia.org.

[88] Jodi Magness, "What Did Jesus' Tomb Look Like?" in Hershel Shanks and Ellen White, eds., *Jesus & Archaeology* (Wash., DC: Biblical Archaeology Society, 2016), 87. Magness describes how strongly the incredible discovery of Yehohanan's anklebone, with bent nail and olive wood particles, in the affluent tomb section of Jerusalem, underscores the biblical account of the honorable burial of Jesus.

nondescript cemetery for violators who were stoned to death according to religious law. Jesus was condemned under Roman law, so to the Jews, it was permissible for him to be buried honorably in a tomb. The curse applies to those executed (or literally hung on a tree or pole in Deut. 21:23) as a result of violating Mosaic law, not pagan Roman law.

*High-Status Followers.* The accounts of Joseph of Arimathea (Mk 15:43–46), Nicodemus (Jn 19:38–42), and Joanna (Lk 8:3, 24:10) show the message of Jesus reached the upper echelon in Jewish society (see chapter 1). They had the power to bury Jesus properly if they could muster the courage.

*Women First.* The account of the women being the first to discover the tomb is both multiply attested and embarrassing to the disciples resulting in strong historical probability. It is unlikely to have been invented. Therefore, it helps counter the sweeping assumption of a non-tomb, mass-grave burial for Jesus based solely on the fact that he was crucified (see chapter 1 and addition 3).

*Unexpected Hero.* Joseph of Arimathea cuts a heroic figure in the crucifixion accounts. His role is multiply attested (in all four gospels) and is embarrassing to the disciples;[89] these factors strengthen the historicity of the burial account. The disciples go into hiding too frightened to bury Jesus with honor. Yet here is a man stepping in for them who has attributes like many of their opponents: he is rich, a Pharisee, and a member of the Sanhedrin that sentences Jesus to death. He is not someone you would at all expect the gospel writers to hail as a hero.

---

[89] All four gospels name and describe the actions of Joseph of Arimathea (Mk 15:43–46; Mt 27:57–60; Lk 23:50–54; Jn 19:38–42). While Luke and Matthew follow Mark's account, John and Mark provide two distinct independent sources. Luke and Matthew access sources other than Mark for their appearance accounts and for some details on the burial accounts (tomb guards in Mt 27:62–66, Peter's run to the tomb in Lk 24:12; see chapter 2).

## theory 7: The Group-Hallucination Theory

### Assertion of the Theory

After the disciples process how Jesus is arrested, tried, convicted, and crucified, they simply lose their minds. They become so overwrought with grief, guilt, and disenchantment that they start imagining different endings to the Jesus story. Funny thing is, they all imagine the same things in their individual minds. Jesus appears to them in bodily form back from the dead. He walks, speaks, breaks bread, eats fish, invites them to touch him, and teaches prophetic scriptures about himself. These hallucinations occur individually but also astoundingly in pairs, in small groups, and in one large crowd of more than five hundred.

### The Group-Hallucination Theory Requires These Beliefs

- Group hallucinations are possible despite the fact that little scientific evidence confirms even single occurrences.
- Group hallucinations can be repeated and extended multiple times over more than a month when few if any precedents of this magnitude are established in the annals of psychology.
- Outsiders of a given group will hallucinate the same thing as the insiders do.
- All appearance accounts are figments of the disciples' imaginations.
- No authorities ever counter the hallucination-prone preachers by opening the tomb in Jerusalem to display the corpse or his bone box.

## Evidence Against the Group-Hallucination Theory

*Outsider/Hostile Converts.* It is doubtful that James the brother of Jesus, a skeptical outsider before Jesus dies, would hallucinate right along with the disciples (Jn 7:5). Yet he receives an individual appearance, converts, and leads the movement's base in Jerusalem for about thirty years.[90] This same immunity to group hallucination applies in the case of Paul even more because he was so publicly and violently hostile to believers in Jesus (1 Cor. 15:7; Acts 15:13, 21:18–19).

*Extended Time.* A group hallucination, while rarely confirmed, is slightly more probable if it occurs at a single point in time. The accounts claim the hallucinations or appearances occur over a period of forty days (Acts 1:3).

*Diverse Groups.* A group hallucination is more probable if it occurs to the same type of people in one location. The NT records claim appearances occur at different places to a wide spectrum of persons—women and men, insiders and outsiders, and individuals and larger groups in Galilee and Jerusalem (see chapter 2).

*Commanding Figure.* The figure people are jointly hallucinating about adamantly teaches them scripture passages about himself. Then he commissions them to tell the world his message (Mt 28:18–20). It is unlikely that they all hear the same words in their individual imaginations without their hearing an actual speaker who calls them to joint and difficult action (Lk 24:45–48).

*Jerusalem Base.* A core team of disciples stays in Jerusalem as the base of the movement. If there were group hallucinations that go on for more than a month and involve women and men, insiders and outsiders, the silliness can easily be stopped. The only thing that needs to be done by the priests or Romans to make the movement evaporate is to show people the occupied tomb of Jesus. The tomb is just outside the walls of the city where the message is being forcefully preached. Apparently, this simple counteraction is never undertaken and easily explainable on the grounds that the tomb was in reality empty.

---

[90] For the reference to James, see Josephus, *Antiquities* 20.9.1 and chapter 5.

## theory *8* : The Borrowed-Myth Theory

### Assertion of the Theory

The concept that Jesus died and was raised from the dead originates with the dying and rising gods of ancient Near Eastern agricultural fertility myths. The gods' journeys are tied to the agrarian cycle of planting and sprouting. These ancient civilizations relied on grain, usually wheat or barley, to sustain life. As a result, they sought to honor any gods they imagined were involved in making crops happen. Early sages observe how a seed is planted as if it dies and is buried. Given enough water, the seed germinates unseen and produces a stalk and then a head of grain.

To explain the pushing up of the grain from the ground below, they envision a god of the underworld. Versions of the myth vary by culture over how the god dies. Usually it is by murder (by a devious brother or demonic thugs for instance). The Egyptian version puts Osiris full time in the underworld after he is buried by his loyal wife, Isis, who collects the parts of his murdered and mutilated body.

The Babylonian version derived from prior Sumerian/ Akkadian cultures assigns the god Tammuz/Dumuzid to split time in the underworld with his consort Ishtar/Inanna.[91] In some versions and notably with Osiris, the underworld god of fertility becomes the god of the afterlife. As humans usually are buried in the ground, the underground agricultural god also represents the natural human hope for eternal life. He becomes the judge of

---

[91] The onset of summer heat often leading to drought conditions was the time when the transition would occur between underworld shifts for Tammuz and Ishtar. Associated with this transition was the religious tradition of a funeral of sorts for Tammuz complete with weeping. In the OT, this ritual conducted by some syncretistic people of Judah at the temple precinct is emphatically condemned (Ezek. 8:14–15).

the dead and determines who lives on in bliss or in torment in the spirit world.

The Greeks and Romans absorbed these ancient myths while often altering the plots and names of the gods (among them Mithras, Dionysus, Adonis, Attis, and Serapis). According to this theory, the Jews of Galilee and later Gentile Christians mourned and reflected on the death of Jesus to the point that they borrowed and applied these myths of dying and rising gods to Jesus. Using their vivid imaginations, they depicted him as another in the long line of pagan heroes rising from dead.

## The Borrowed-Myth Theory Requires These Beliefs

- Jews from the rustic confines of Galilee in the AD 20s and 30s were educated in Sumerian/Babylonian, Egyptian, and Greco-Roman myths.
- Devout monotheists like most first-century Jews would embrace multi-god, idol-filled pagan myths or their Greco-Roman derivations.
- The narrative of the resurrection of Jesus was a legend that forms over time by borrowing from ancient lore and rituals.

## Evidence Against the Borrowed-Myth Theory

*Historical, Not Mythical.* The resurrection narrative ties the life and death of Jesus to specific times, places, and persons in history that are validated by normal historical methods. Myths float outside history.

*Judaism Resists Paganism.* The narrative of Jesus is grounded in Judaism, not paganism. He is descended from human patriarchs such as Abraham and David. He debates Jewish issues in the synagogues and the temple complex in Jerusalem. The issue that gets Jesus in trouble with the ruling priests is the notion that he is blaspheming. He claims that he is sent by and specially connected with the Creator God of the OT. Existentially, Israel in its OT scriptures is warned repeatedly not to copy the practices of pagan nations (Deut. 18:9–13; Ezek. 11:12).

*Conflict in Details.* In contrast to the Osiris myth, no evidence is given that Jesus has a sister-wife who collects his severed body parts. The gospels report no bone is broken and his body is not dismembered but laid in a tomb. In contrast to Mithras, Jesus does not sacrifice a bull but rather offers himself as the sacrifice.[92]

*Sources Are Late.* Many sources for the myths postdate the NT writings in their Greco-Roman adaptations (in the second and fourth centuries) and borrow the other way around, from NT accounts.

*Early Christian Comparisons Are Misinterpreted.* Early Christian writers sometimes themselves identified parallels between pagan myths and Jesus. Their intent was to show how the narrative of Jesus was not so strange and threatening that Christian beliefs should be ostracized or made illegal. They did not concede that the Christian story was based on or a continuation of pagan myths.[93]

*Real, Not Symbolic.* In the myths, the dying and rising of a god is a metaphor for the physical reality of planting and sprouting. The NT report of a human corpse coming back to life on earth is not a metaphor for agricultural cycles but is considered an actual historical event carrying as well its own spiritual meaning.

---

[92] Some scholars have noted that the dying and rising myths fall into two categories that do not closely correlate with the journey of Jesus. One group of myths portray the hero disappearing and then returning while alive on earth and never having actually died. The other group of myths envisions the hero dying and never returning to earth but rather operating from the underworld in a new spirit-world existence. Jesus actually dies, returns to earth in bodily form, and ascends to heaven promising however to return to earth to set things right. Jonathan Z. Smith, "Dying and Rising Gods," with Mircea Eliade and Charles J. Adams, *The Encyclopedia of Religion*, vol. 4 (New York, NY: Macmillan, 1987), 522, cited in James M. Rochford, "Was Christianity Copied from Pagan Myths?" evidenceunseen. com, 19 Sep 2015.

[93] See writings of Tertullian, Clement of Alexandria, and Justin Martyr.

*Once for All.* The Jesus event is not an annual repetition of dying and rising to generate cycles of nature but rather an event occurring once and for all and never to be repeated. *"It is finished,"* Jesus says on the cross as he is quoted in the gospel of John (Jn 19:30).

*Spiritual Power.* The death of Jesus atones for the sins of all humanity who receive him, and his resurrection validates that his sacrifice is enough and that it succeeds. The pagan gods do not atone for sins of others; they are too busy dealing with their own predicaments. In the case of Mithras, he may be said to mediate, but not between God and humanity but rather between good and evil gods.[94]

*Span of Control.* Jesus's kingship is not limited to the underworld but spans all heaven and earth (Mt 28:18).

---

[94] Particularly with the figure of Mithras, the comparisons with Jesus are heavily exaggerated. No texts survive of the Mithras cult in its original Persian or Roman versions. The paintings and murals without captions that survive leave interpretations about this Persian pastoral god wide open to skeptical scholarly embroidery. J. Warner Wallace, "Is Jesus Simply a Retelling of the Mithras Mythology?" coldcasechristianity.com, 5 May 2014.

## theory *9* : The Spiritual-Resurrection Theory

### Assertion of the Theory

When Jesus dies on the cross, his body is laid in a tomb or tossed in a mass grave; it does not really matter. His spirit leaves his body and is carried to the presence of God as might happen to another human being. In that sense, Jesus is still alive in spirit. However in his case, he is further exalted to the right hand of God and is able to participate in the power and being of God.

This puts him in a position in spirit to give his disciples a continuing experience of his life. It is not something happening in their minds as with hallucinations. Jesus in spirit is a reality external to them that they are encountering. He appears to them in visions that are so immediate that they can engender a tactile experience as if the disciples were touching his wounds. The disciples also experience his presence in nonvisual ways; they sense his aura in their midst. They also tap into the power he wielded on earth—power to heal physically, power to transform the inner life of believers, and power to create community. This continuing experience of the life of Jesus likewise is available to contemporary believers just as it was to the original disciples. Jesus lives, is vindicated by God, and is exalted to the status of Lord while the body he inhabited decomposes somewhere in the soils of the earth.

### The Spiritual-Resurrection Theory Requires These Beliefs

*   The term *resurrection* can be redefined as having nothing to do with a physical body but applies to a spirit being raised to heaven.
*   The accounts of the tomb being found empty are invented and false.

- The disciples made a big mistake. They had a real sense that Jesus was alive in heaven and present with them in spirit on earth, but they mistook this sense for his being physically raised from the dead. The misguided disciples claim that Jesus is active beside them in the body for more than a month—walking with them, speaking with them, eating with them—but they felt only his presence; he was not there physically.

### Evidence Against the Spiritual-Resurrection Theory

*Appearance Accounts.* The appearance accounts do not allow for visionary experiences in spirit only; they insist on Jesus's physical presence in bodily form. They take pains to depict Jesus as striding down the road (Lk 24:15), handling objects like bread and fish (Lk 24:30, 35, 41–43), inviting his followers to touch wounds in his arms and side (Lk 24:39; Jn 20:27), and eating with them on multiple occasions (Lk 24:41–43; Acts 1:4). The body of Jesus has special powers to move through barriers and materialize/dematerialize, but these are added without detracting from the customary human dimensions of the body (Lk 24:31; Jn 20:26; see chapter 2).

*Experiences of Exalted Jesus Are Different.* Paul experiences an exalted Jesus on the road to Damascus, where Jesus speaks and calls Paul to come to him as a sheep gone astray that no longer needs to *"kick against the goads."* This episode, after Jesus has ascended to heaven, is described distinctively and differently than the accounts of the appearances to the disciples that happen after the resurrection but prior to the ascension. Paul sees a blinding light from heaven and hears a voice speaking in Aramaic but does not specifically claim to touch or see Jesus in bodily form in that event (Acts 9:4–6, 26:14–18; later, Paul claims to have seen Jesus, but it is not directly tied to the Damascus road intervention; see 1 Cor. 9:1; 2 Cor. 12:1–7).

Similarly, while being interrogated by the council, Stephen sees Jesus already exalted in heaven. When he tells them what he sees, it incites the mob to drag him away and stone him to death (Acts 7:55-58).

*Jewish Conception.* In this era, the prevailing conception of the resurrection among the Jews who believe in it (the Pharisees and most of the population but not the Sadducees) is definitely physical. It involves a monumental feast of food and wine partaken by people with bodies in a new age, not an out-of-body experience of the soul (Isa. 25:6-9).[95] (See also *Background Guide,* resource 5.)

*Jerusalem Base.* Under this theory, the tomb remains occupied by the corpse of Jesus. This begs the question why the priests, rulers, and Romans do not try to stamp out the new movement in Jerusalem by pointing to the body and ridiculing the preaching (see chapter 8).

*Core Message.* As recorded in Acts 2, Peter grounds his initial preaching at the Feast of Weeks (or Pentecost) on certain psalms of David (Ps. 16, 110). He interprets Psalm 16:10 as David speaking of the Messiah, not himself, because David's body dies and his tomb is just down the street. David prophesies that the body of the Messiah will not undergo decay, exactly what Jesus avoids by being raised from the dead. This theory invalidates Peter's preaching if Jesus rises only in spirit (see chapter 4).

---

[95] The noted author and bishop N. T. Wright argues forcefully for the physical resurrection of Jesus as a logical historical conclusion based on the Jewish cultural context of the era. Like most Jews, the early apostles believed in a physical resurrection of righteous persons at the end of the age. Physical resurrection is what they meant when they said Jesus was raised from the dead. See N. T. Wright, *The Challenge of Jesus* (Downers Grove, IL: InterVarsity Press, 1999), 134-37. Also see Wright's magisterial work, *The Resurrection of the Son of God* (Minneapolis, MN: Fortress Press, 2003).

*theory* 10: **The Legend-Grows Theory**

*Assertion of the Theory*

A tradesman in a remote region of northern Israel named Jesus shows a peculiar aptitude for the Hebrew scriptures. He leaves his hillside village and treks down to the shores of the Sea of Galilee. He builds a following of fishermen and other rustics in the agrarian region. He works impressive healings and teaches about a coming kingdom.

On an annual feast in Jerusalem, he stirs up a crowd by riding into the city on a donkey. Then at the temple, he overturns the tables of the moneychangers. These cheats rip off worshipers. The legions of pilgrims from out of town are required to exchange common money for restricted sacramental currency to buy unblemished animals to sacrifice. The disruptive action of Jesus alarms the ruling high priests and the Roman authorities. They arrange to arrest, judge, and execute him on a Roman cross at the outset of the feast to keep the peace and prevent any uprising. Crushed are the hopes of his disciples for they thought he would be the Messiah to free Israel from oppression and restore the nation to greatness. Some of them drift back to their fishing nets.

Over many years, around wells, campfires and marketplaces, people tell stories about what they heard people say Jesus taught and what they imagine happened to him. A myth develops. He becomes more than a teacher, more than a healer. He walks on water, he feeds thousands from a few fishes and loaves, he raises people from the dead, and he is raised from the dead himself. In his death, God saves the world. In his resurrection, God vindicates him. In his ascension, God exalts him as Lord of the universe. Only, *not really*. Over Jesus's actual words and deeds, layer upon layer of imagined teachings and events form like sedimentary deposits on a riverbank one generation after another until finally, the rustic rabbi, who only wanted people to love and forgive each other, is turned by human projection and hope into the savior of the world.

## This Theory Requires These Beliefs

- The idea of Jesus rising from the dead was a later development invented after the original disciples die.
- Historical, documented accounts of the empty tomb are untrue and concocted by later generations of believers.
- That those who encountered a risen Jesus after his death should have had their heads examined, including resistant, hostile converts like James the brother of Jesus and Paul, the faith's fiercest opponent in the early days, who strangely switches sides.

## Evidence Against the Legend-Grows Theory

*Early Source Material.* All the documents we are investigating for resurrection evidence in the New Testament are written in the last half of the first century, twenty to seventy years after the death of Jesus. By ancient Near Eastern standards, these are early accounts for Jesus—compared to the Roman Emperor Tiberius (d. AD 37), whose main accounts start eighty years after his death, or to Alexander the Great (d. 323 BC), whose extant accounts start three hundred years after his death.[96]

*Extremely Early Source Material.* Scholars have dug deep into 1 Corinthians 15:3–8, a summary statement or creedal code for the resurrection events. In Greek, it bears a form of rhythmic

---

[96] The first reliable source for a biography of Tiberius is Suetonius, *Lives of the Caesars,* about eighty years after the emperor's death. For Alexander the Great, first-century authors writing more than three hundred years later include Diodorus Siculus and Quintus Curtius Rufus, with better bios bridging into the second century from Arrian (considered the best of the bunch) and Plutarch. See "Alexander the Great," wikipedia.org.

stanzas that are easy to remember. Paul says he receives it. If we ask when and where, he likely receives it from Peter or James when he stays with Peter for two weeks in Jerusalem. This visit occurs four to six years after Jesus dies (Gal. 1:18; see chapter 7). The creedal formula is created and in use before Paul receives it. It likely is a Greek translation of an Aramaic original. Even some critical scholars date the origin of the formula to within a year or six months of Jesus's departure.[97] This factor invalidates the legend-grows theory for there is no time for a legend to grow. The preaching of the resurrection occurs from the outset of the movement as the book of Acts asserts (Acts 2; see chapter 7).

*Sources in Gospels.* Scholars look for sources embedded in the writings of the gospel authors. The burial account featuring Joseph of Arimathea in Mark has been traced to a source within ten years of the event.[98]

*Replacement Disciple.* When the disciples sense they need a replacement for the deceased Judas, they determine precise qualifications. The person must have witnessed the work of Jesus from the beginning in Galilee to the ascension and specifically including the resurrection. They want eyewitnesses who can give accurate evidence firsthand, not secondhand (Acts 2:21–22; see introduction).

*Change in Disciples.* A slow-growing legend does not explain the sudden change in the disciples about seven weeks after the

---

[97] Gary Habermas, "The Resurrection Argument." See chapter 7.

[98] Richard Bauckham, similarly to the scholar Rudolf Pesch, dates the burial account source before AD 40. See Richard Bauckham, *Jesus and the Eyewitnesses: The Gospels as Eyewitness Testimony* (Grand Rapids, MI: Wm. B. Eerdmans, 2007), 243. Both scholars are cited in James Bishop, "Jesus Fact #5—Jesus' burial by Joseph of Arimathea," jamesbishopblog.com, n.d., n.p. See also James Bishop, "Jesus in the pre-Markan Passion Narrative" at the same website. Also see William L. Craig, "Independent Sources for Jesus' Burial and Empty Tomb," reasonablefaith.org, n.p., n.d. Other prominent scholars cited by Bishop who affirm the high level of historical probability for the burial account include Raymond Brown, *The Death of the Messiah*, vol. 2 (New Haven, CT: Yale University Press, 2007), 1240–41 and John A. T. Robinson, *The Human Face of God* (London: Westminster Press, 1973), 131.

death of Jesus. They change from despairing defeatists to bold proclaimers of an earthshaking message that transforms their generation and many more thereafter (see chapter 4).

*Conversion of Paul.* Paul converts probably two to three years after Jesus leaves earth. He reviews his faith with the apostles in Jerusalem about three years after he converts. Then about fourteen years later, he reviews it again to ensure he and the original disciples are preaching salvation by grace through faith from the same page (Gal. 1:15–2:2). Paul writes letters within about twenty-five years of Jesus dying after going on missionary journeys where he proclaimed the risen Jesus well before he writes. His conversion and message could not be the result of believing a legend because there is not enough time for it to form (see chapters 6–7).

*Ancient Prophecies.* Prophecies Jesus fulfills precede his life by at least five to seven hundred years (Isaiah), by a thousand (David), and by more than a thousand (Abraham and Moses). The ancient prophets introduce these predictions into the OT scriptures, not the generations after Jesus (see chapter 9).

### Conclusion: Alternative Theories Are Uprooted by the Evidence

Alternative theories of what happened to the body of Jesus find it difficult to explain away the quantity and quality of the historical evidence. Two of the theories, the swoon-coma and the fake-death, ask us to believe that Jesus never died on the cross. They assert that the rough-and-ready Roman soldiers did not know how to successfully crucify a condemned person. This view flies in the face of the many records of Romans using crucifixion to deter crime and revolts, the gospel accounts about the suffering of Jesus, and the specific, extra-biblical, Roman-oriented sources from Josephus and Tacitus, who report the death of Jesus in passing as a matter of historical fact.

Two other theories assert that the body was stolen by the disciples or other parties. In the account of Matthew, the theory of the disciples' heist is traced to the temple priests conspiring with the tomb guards to propagate this cover-up. This early theory asks us to believe that the plain-speaking disciples suddenly step up as ingenious con artists. Despite watching the cruel demise of their leader, somehow, they summon up the courage to steal the body. Then they spend the rest of their lives spreading the lie and eventually willingly die for their hoax.

Theories that other groups stole the body flounder for lack of reasonable motives. The detail of the linen strips left behind in the tomb dually attested makes it unlikely that the body was removed. It would be much easier to transport a body if the burial linen remained wrapped around it rather than unwound.

The wrong-tomb theory borders on sexism in that it contends that the women who first arrive at the open tomb have their directions mixed up. This assertion conflicts with two items of evidence: that two of the women watched the hurried burial and that the tomb was new and therefore would stand out in its unweathered state.

The mass-grave theory assumes a crucified criminal would be repudiated and cursed by fellow Jews, who would not permit burial with honor in a proper cemetery. Recent archaeology undermines the premise. A crucifixion victim's anklebone with a nail through it was found in a first-century bone box beside the remains of other family members in a regular tomb.

The group-hallucination theory requires us to believe that tens then hundreds of people hallucinate the same thing. They do so over forty days along roads, in cities, on mountains, and at dinners. They see the same figure, they hear the same message, and they respond to the same challenge to spread the radical news. Males and females share the hallucination. This level of supposed sustained hallucination seems to have no other counterpart in history.

Further, the theory breaks down with the way the hallucinated figure holds objects like bread, eats fish, and invites witnesses to touch him. Finally, it cannot adequately explain how the figure's hostile brother, an outsider, also receives an appearance and transforms into a dedicated leader. The multiple sources for these appearance reports include four separate authors. There is Paul, brandishing a list he received from Peter and James; Matthew and Luke reporting separately from different sources in a mode where neither relies on Mark (because his gospel in the manuscripts that we possess features no appearances); and then John, writing his entire gospel apparently independently of the others (see appearances chart in chapter 2 and author assessments in *Background Guide,* resource 1).

The borrowed-myth theory holds that because pagan deities are said to rise from the dead, the disciples must have lit upon one or more of these myths to create their story. The pagan myths connect with agricultural cycles and float outside history. The gospel accounts make specific, point-in-time historical claims that the resurrection was not symbolic but real, not annual but once for all.

The spiritual-resurrection theory is anticipated in the gospels. To his disciples at one dinner, Jesus denies that he is a ghost and invites his witnesses to touch him. His soul has not gone into the shadows without his body only to appear as a presence or an aura. Along the road, along the lakeshore, he walks and talks and engages in full-bodied, animated conversations.

When all else fails, critics often turn to the legend-grows theory. The resurrection of Jesus was not reported right away they say; it grew over time and generations as memories faded and imaginations went to work. The historical documentation rules out this theory. It proves that the disciples preached a risen Jesus within about five years of the event. More probably, it was within fifty days as Luke asserts in Acts. Either time frame is much too limited for a legend to form. Whether you believe the disciples got it right or wrong, they preached from the start of their movement that Jesus the Messiah had risen physically from the dead with cosmic ramifications.

# EPILOGUE

## EPILOGUE

# BEYOND BELIEF

O ur investigation into the resurrection evidence took us longer than I originally expected because there turns out to be so much of it. Our sources for the evidence nearly all come from the first century when the events allegedly happen. By the standards of the cultural era, and by the criteria of current historical criticism, the source documents and the resulting resurrection narrative emerge with strong reliability (see addition 3 and the *Background Guide* for much more detail on sources).

### Witness Testimony in Context Is Tough to Refute

We have looked over the shoulders of the eyewitnesses. We have seen how the women from Galilee, Mary Magdalene, Mary the mother of James, Salome, and Joanna (and most likely a few unnamed others) reach the tomb at dawn and find it open and empty. At the news, Peter and John come out of hiding, race each other to the tomb, and find nothing but a facecloth and strips of linen lying there; these clues make it less likely the victim is carried out by grave robbers and more likely that he walks out. We have seen how Jesus appears to many witnesses both named and unnamed over forty days. None of them experience him as a ghostly phantom but as a full-bodied, flesh-and-blood person walking with them, eating fish with them, and inviting them to touch his wounds.

We have seen how difficult it is to explain a series of well-attested historical events that happen in the ensuing months and years if no resurrection occurred. It is difficult to explain the sudden change in the disciples like Peter from troubled and traumatized and fearful to intrepid, relentless, and bold. It is difficult to explain the willingness of people such as Stephen early on and James the brother of Jesus later on to go to their deaths for their belief in Jesus as the Messiah. It is difficult to explain the historical enigma of the obsessive-compulsive and violent enforcer of Jewish law, Saul, suddenly switching sides and becoming the bighearted but even more relentless and fervent evangelist Paul.

We have seen the revolutionary historical discovery of an early creed embedded in a letter from Paul. It proves the resurrection message went out early without the time or the need for legendary embroidery layered up over generations. We have seen how the leading disciples base themselves in Jerusalem for two decades or more unconcerned that hostile local witnesses could contradict their message. We have seen how the emphatic point Jesus kept making to his disciples after he rose—that the scriptures of Moses, the Prophets, and Psalms predicted his suffering and rising—is certainly there in the Old Testament prophecies of the Messiah but is much easier to see in retrospect.

All these lines of evidence derived from eyewitness reports recorded in the documents collected in the New Testament produce this result: they raise the probability that the resurrection actually happened in history.

Finally, we surveyed ten alternative theories that deny the resurrection occurred, but all of them come up short and cannot adequately explain the range of resurrection evidence.

### The Witnesses and Writers Do Not Merely Record History

Bear in mind how obvious are the motivations of the gospel writers. True, they preserved the eyewitness material and formed it into narratives from their individual viewpoints. They want to present history to be sure, but they do not want you, their readers or hearers, to stop at the history. They want you to see through the history—beyond belief that earthshaking events happened— to the spiritual new life offered. That opportunity is in a word *salvation* from life without God, or as the gospel of John recounts Jesus picturing it, salvation from living and dying as a branch disconnected from the sustaining power of the root of the vine and therefore destined to wither away. Instead, to us his readers, John writes how he hopes that by believing, we may have life in his name and salvation from life without God to life with God eternally (Jn 3:16, 15:1–6, 20:30–31).

The resurrection then becomes not merely a reality of history but the gateway or if you will the portal to a new reality of life lived with and through the living God starting now in time on earth and stretching beyond time and the blip of one's death into eternity.

Make no mistake—these writers and the witnesses to the resurrection do not simply ask you to increase your knowledge of history; they call you to enter new spiritual life. They urge you to go beyond the historical events of the crucifixion and resurrection to personal faith and an eternal relationship with God. He is the one who created everything, loves humanity relentlessly, reveals his heart in the documents of the testaments both old and new, and makes a path forward to eternal life and a secure relationship with himself through Jesus.

### It Comes Down to Where You Want to Place Your Faith

Our part is to place our faith or trust not in our human efforts but in the work of Jesus in his cross and resurrection. In his cross, he pays the death penalty for our sins; his resurrection verifies the penalty is fully paid, and it proves we too can be raised to life with him after death.[99] The way to eternal life with God no longer is blocked; it is open to all through Jesus. His work secures forgiveness and salvation for all who choose to receive him as Lord. To make him Lord is to put him in charge of your life; the ultimate authority over you is no longer you but him. As Paul put it, *"If you confess with your lips that Jesus is Lord and believe in your heart that God raised him from the dead, you will be saved"* (Rom. 10:9). There is no age limit. No one is too young or too old to receive him (Mk 10:14; Lk 2:36–38). And there is no sin limit; no one is beyond grace and forgiveness. One of the criminals, probably a murderer, who was crucified next to Jesus, believed. He asked Jesus to remember him when he came into kingly power. Responding to that flicker of faith, Jesus assured the condemned man that he would be saved and would be joining him in his kingdom despite dying that day (Lk 23:39–43).

Believing and going beyond belief to a personal relationship with God can be quite a bit easier if you have examined the lines of evidence. It is reasonably credible from the historical evidence (in the face of much supposedly scientific and rational presumption) that Jesus indeed died on the cross yet rose from the dead. Historically speaking, the belief is rational, based on evidence.

Spiritually, God offers and guarantees us an eternal relationship with him, grounded by the work of Jesus in these events. This offer comes out of God's inclusive, personal love for every individual; this is the transcendently glorious message of the resurrection. This God, who broke into history at a specific time and place in the person of Jesus, wants to be with us, no exceptions.

My hope is that these pages have opened your mind and heart

---

[99] This core truth comes in teachings that trace back to Peter (Acts 2:24, 32–33; 1 Pet. 1:3–5), to John (Jn 3:16, 5:24), to Paul (1 Thess. 1:10; 1 Cor. 6:14, 15:20–23, 42–44; 2 Cor. 4:14; Rom. 4:25, 6:4–5, 8:31–39), and to the author of Hebrews, who returns to this truth repeatedly (Heb. 1:3, 2:9, 14–17, 4:14, 5:9, 9:14–15, 27–28, 10:13–14, 13:20).

to God's historical and intricately timed plan to draw humanity back to himself. If you know him already, I hope this investigation has deepened your confidence in his artful ways of working. If you do not know him, I hope that you will call out to him to meet you at the right time and in the right place and that you will be enthralled by his grace, his unrelenting love, and his undying passion to connect with you in a relationship of joy, peace, and empowerment that begins here on earth and endures for eternity.

# ADDITIONS

Four additions are included in this final section in order to enhance understanding of the lines of evidence in the prior chapters.

Addition 1:    Discussion Questions by Chapter
Addition 2:    List of Resurrection Witnesses
Addition 3:    Measuring the Narrative by Historical Criteria
Addition 4:    On the Drama of the Future Resurrection

Addition 1 provides pinpointed questions for each of the ten chapters, especially useful for group discussions. Addition 2 lists the resurrection witnesses denoted in the biblical documents, all in one place for an easy overview. Using a few witness categories, it gives biblical references for each witness and also shows the chapters where this book mentions them. Addition 3 gives the typical criteria historians use to determine what happened in historical events. These criteria are applied to the resurrection narrative, formed from our multiple source documents. For more detailed information on the sources selected and not selected, and for likely dates of source composition, consult the separately published *Resurrection Shock: Background Guide* (resources 1 and 2), as mentioned earlier in the Note on Structure and Usage. In the *Guide* are other resources giving more context to the lines of evidence for the resurrection, including a full archaeological index. Addition 4 portrays the luminous hope of the future human resurrection as revealed to and described by the apostle Paul. In a way the purpose of this entire book is to help you decide whether you desire this revivified destiny after death. It is now open to all of us through the historical events of the painful sacrifice and powerful resurrection of the craftsman from Nazareth who is identified by the witnesses as the Messiah and Lord (Acts 2:36).

## ADDITION 1

---

# DISCUSSION QUESTIONS BY
# CHAPTER

---

The questions provided in this addition are designed especially for groups that want to sift through the resurrection evidence together. By now you must know that the chapters are packed full of personalities, dramatic episodes, Scripture excerpts, archaeological findings and historical connections. So absorbing one chapter per week is the pace most groups may decide to take.

Group members or leaders also may benefit from the supplemental book, *Resurrection Shock: Background Guide*. It is described in the previous Note on Structure and Usage in this book.

Individual readers wishing to have a place to collect their comments may find these pages of questions valuable as well. Specific answers to these questions are not given here or in the *Background Guide*. That is because the questions are not a test. They are meant to catalyze reflection in thought and feeling. They are intended to spark a person's own responses to the witness reports, to the character of the witnesses as recorded in their words and actions, and to the rest of the surrounding historical evidence for the resurrection of Jesus.

¶

# WOMEN ARE THE FIRST WITNESSES TO THE EMPTY TOMB

## DISCUSSION QUESTIONS

(Prelude) Which factors about Joseph of Arimathea make him an unforeseen character who adds veracity to the resurrection account?

Which qualities do you see in Mary Magdalene?

Similarly, which characteristics do you see in the other women who come to the empty tomb including Mary the mother of James, Salome, and Joanna?

To what extent do you find Mary Magdalene and the others credible witnesses?

How does the prominence of women as witnesses to the resurrection given the culture of the time add stronger probability to the accounts?

# ᒫ

---

# APPEARANCE REPORTS INVOLVE
# MULTIPLE WITNESSES

---

## DISCUSSION QUESTIONS

(Prelude) Why won't Thomas believe his fellow disciples when they tell him they saw Jesus?

Which appearances by Jesus make the strongest impressions on you as you read the accounts?

According to the descriptions in the gospel accounts, what do people observe about the resurrected body of Jesus?

Why does the attempt to explain the appearances as hallucinations on the part of the witnesses not adequately account for the evidence?

What types of purposes does Jesus seem to pursue in certain appearances?

# 3

---

# JESUS PREDICTS HIS DEATH AND RESURRECTION

---

## DISCUSSION QUESTIONS

(Prelude) Why doesn't Jesus join with some of his outraged disciples and reprimand the woman who anoints him with expensive oil?

Where in the OT could Jesus have found predictions of his suffering, especially at the level of detail he gave to his disciples privately?

Which images or allusions does Jesus use when he speaks in public about his destiny?

To what extent did the disciples accept or resist Jesus's warnings about his death?

If Jesus himself predicts that his impending death will not be the end but will be followed by his resurrection, how does that make the event more credible?

Ψ

# THE DISCIPLES CHANGE
# FROM FEARFUL TO BOLD

## DISCUSSION QUESTIONS

(Prelude) Why does the way the servant girl of the high priest calls out Peter in public crack the usually strong fisherman?

In your mind, which factors explain the radical change in Peter and the other disciples from despairing to daring?

Why are the disciples practically happy to be flogged for their faith?

How does Peter's speech to the diversified entourage of the centurion in Caesarea Maritima reveal the changes that went on inside the minds of the disciples?

Historians look for cause and effect. For the great effect of the Christian faith spreading rapidly throughout the Western world despite persecution, there had to be a great causal factor, or catalyst. To what extent could the teachings and example of a good but dead rabbi have caused such a fuss?

# 5

# THE DISCIPLES FACE PERILOUS CULTURAL RISKS

## DISCUSSION QUESTIONS

(Prelude) What is it about Stephen's stubborn faith in Jesus that triggers the activist Pharisee Saul to terrorize believers?

What things did Stephen say to the council that ignited their anger and drove them to stone him for blasphemy?

Why might James the leader in Jerusalem have been such a threat to a rogue high priest that he would commit judicial murder?

Most of the apostles ended up being martyred for their faith eventually. How does that fact affect the theory that they invented the resurrection and made up the divinity of Jesus?

# A FIERCE ENFORCER SWITCHES SIDES

## DISCUSSION QUESTIONS

(Prelude) What enabled Ananias in Damascus to gather his courage to face the feared persecutor Saul (also known as Paul)?

Which qualities do you see in Paul as revealed in his adventures?

How does Paul adjust his arguments for Jesus to his ethnically diverse listeners?

How is Paul's witness to Jesus similar to or different from that of other disciples?

How does Paul's personal conversion story and his succeeding years of missions add credibility to the reality of the resurrection?

370 | Resurrection S H O C K

# 7

---

# PROCLAMATION OF THE RESURRECTION IS CLEARLY EARLY

---

## DISCUSSION QUESTIONS

(Prelude) What does Paul crossing paths with the verified historical figure of Gallio say about the historical content in the NT?

How does the Gallio inscription found in Delphi, Greece reduce the elapsed time for the preaching of the resurrection to within twenty-five years?

How does the embedded creed in Paul's first letter to the Corinthians shrink the elapsed time for the preaching of the resurrection to about five years or less?

What difference does it make for there to be just a short time from the resurrection event to the public preaching that Jesus is risen?

# JERUSALEM REMAINS THE EPICENTER
# OF THE MESSAGE

## DISCUSSION QUESTIONS

(Prelude) Although they are separated by multiple centuries, how are Abraham, David, and Jesus all traditionally connected to Jerusalem and to the act of sacrifice to God?

What are some reasons the apostles stay in Jerusalem?

How does staying in Jerusalem actually help the disciples fulfill the commission they received from Jesus?

How does their staying in Jerusalem for years and for some even decades add credibility to the resurrection message?

What makes Jerusalem so central for Jewish faith in the Messiah?

q

# GOSPEL ACCOUNTS CORRELATE WITH MESSIANIC PROPHECIES

## DISCUSSION QUESTIONS

(Prelude) At the synagogue with his hometown crowd, Jesus is surprisingly overt in his claim to fulfill Isaiah's prophecy. What do you think went through the mind of his mother Mary?

Which OT prophecies of the Messiah stand out to you?

Which actions or allusions of Jesus as reported in the gospels reveal passages in which he sees himself in OT prophecies?

In the preaching of the apostles in Acts, which prophecies in the OT seem uppermost in their minds?

# GOSPEL ACCOUNTS CORRELATE WITH MESSIANIC PROPHECIES

## DISCUSSION QUESTIONS, CONT.

The idea of the Messiah suffering was not prominent among Jewish teachers, but Jesus claimed that the painful ordeal was clear from the written texts. How do you account for this sharp difference?

In which OT prophecies do you see specifically a prediction of a resurrection of the Messiah?

Why do you think the Ethiopian official was so quick to ask Philip to baptize him along the road?

What do you expect or not expect about the set of messianic prophecies not as yet fulfilled?

# 10

## ALTERNATIVE THEORIES DENYING THE RESURRECTION

### DISCUSSION QUESTIONS

Which alternative theories of the resurrection do you see people asserting most often?

To what extent do you think the disciples could concoct a hoax and sustain it for years?

Why is the hallucination theory very difficult to establish?

Some scholars favor the view that Jesus was raised in a spiritual sense. They mean he was taken to heaven like any other human believer in God. The disciples, left behind on earth, felt his presence in their hearts because he was such a force in their lives. Yet his bodily remains also were left behind in a grave or bone box. Which items of evidence contradict this explanation?

Other scholars take a decidedly skeptical approach. They assert that the narrative of Jesus in his death and resurrection, his ascension and exaltation, was just a legend that was built up layer upon layer over time by succeeding generations. How does the legend theory run into trouble with several key lines of evidence for the resurrection?

## ADDITION 2

---

# LIST OF RESURRECTION
# WITNESSES

---

This resource lists the names of the resurrection witnesses. With the names are the appearance numbers (from chapter 2, see chart on page 84), the NT verses where the post-resurrection moment is recorded, plus the chapters in this book where each appearance is mentioned significantly. Here are the witness categories.

*Named Resurrection Eyewitnesses*

These people are named as directly experiencing Jesus in one of his eleven specifically denoted appearances (numbers match those in chapter 2), or they are directly mentioned as having experienced all the events in his ministry career.

*Implied Named Resurrection Eyewitnesses*

These people are named in the NT accounts as circulating with the disciples before and/or after the resurrection making it likely that they also experienced Jesus during the forty days between his resurrection and ascension. However, they are not directly mentioned as having seen him.

## Unnamed Resurrection Eyewitnesses

Groups of people are mentioned in the NT as experiencing Jesus after he rose from the dead along with at least one individual, but they are not named. Nevertheless, they would have been eyewitnesses who likely would have spread the message of Jesus.

## Named Post-Ascension Witnesses

These are named persons who experience Jesus appearing to them in a vision or calling to them in an audio-only moment after he ascended.

## Major Prophetic Resurrection Witnesses

These people offer prophecies to the effect that the Messiah will not die but be raised to life.

## NAMED RESURRECTION EYEWITNESSES

| Witness | References with Appearance Numbers | Chapter |
|---|---|---|
| Mary Magdalene | #1: Mt 28:9-10; Jn 20:13-18 | 1 |
| Mary, mother of James | #1: Mt 28:9-10 | 1 |
| Peter | #2: 1 Cor. 15:5; Lk 24:34; #6: Jn 21:1-19; Group apps | 1-5, 8-9 |
| Cleopas | #3: Lk 24:13-35 | 1, 2 |
| Disciples as a Group (termed "Group apps") | #4: 1 Cor. 15:5; Lk 24:33-49; #5: Jn 20:24-29; #7: Mt 28:16-20; #8: 1 Cor. 15:6; #10: 1 Cor. 15:7; #11: Acts 1:1-14, 10:41; Mk 3:16-18 | 2 |
| James, son of Zebedee | #6: Jn 21:2; Group apps | 5 |
| John, son of Zebedee | #6: Jn 21:2; 1 Jn 1:1-4; Group apps | 4 |
| Andrew | #6: Jn 21:2 (probably), 1:44; Group apps | 2 |
| Philip (the Disciple) | #6: Jn 21:2 (probably), 1:44; Group apps | 5 |
| Bartholomew aka Nathanael | #6: Jn 21:2; Group apps | 2 |
| Matthew aka Levi | Group apps; Mk 2:14; Lk 5:27-29; Mt 2:9-10, 10:3 | – |
| Thomas aka Didymus (or the Twin) | #5: Jn 20:24-29: #6: 21:2; Group apps (minus #4) | 2 |
| James, son of Alphaeus | Group apps | 1 |
| Thaddeus, aka Judas son of James | Group apps; Lk 6:16; Acts 1:13 | – |
| Simon the Zealot | Group apps | – |
| James, brother of Jesus | #9: 1 Cor. 15:7; Acts 1:14; Gal. 1:19; Jam. 1:1, 2:1, 5:7-8 | 2, 5 |
| Matthias | Group apps; Acts 1:3, 21-26 | Intro |
| Joseph aka Barsabbus or Justus | Group apps; Acts 1:3, 21-26 | Intro |

## IMPLIED NAMED RESURRECTION EYEWITNESSES

| Witnesses | References | Chapter |
|---|---|---|
| Salome | Acts 1:3; Mk 15:40, 16:1–7; Mt 20:20–28; Lk 24:10 | 1 |
| Joanna | Acts 1:3; Lk 8:3, 24:10 | 1 |
| Susanna | Acts 1:3; Lk 8:3, 24:10 (probably) | 1 |
| Mary, mother of Jesus | Acts 1:3, 14; Lk 2:11–12, 19, 33, 38 | 1, 9 |
| Joseph, brother of Jesus | Acts 1:3, 14; Mt 13:55 | – |
| Simon, brother of Jesus | Acts 1:3, 14; Mt 13:55 | – |
| Judas, brother of Jesus | Acts 1:3, 14; Mt 13:55 | – |
| Philip (the Evangelist) | Acts 1:3, 6:5, 8:35, 40 | 9 |
| Stephen | Acts 1:3, 6:5, 8, 10 | 5 |

## UNNAMED RESURRECTION EYEWITNESSES

| Witness | References | Chapter |
|---|---|---|
| Second Emmaus traveler | #3: Lk 24:13–35 | 1, 2, 9 |
| 500 Believers | #8: 1 Cor. 15:6 | 2 |
| All the apostles | #10: 1 Cor. 15:7 | 2 |

## NAMED POST-ASCENSION WITNESSES

| Witness | References | Chapter |
|---|---|---|
| Stephen | Acts 6:5, 8, 10, 7:54–56 | 5 |
| Ananias of Damascus | Acts 9:10–16 | 6 |
| Paul aka Saul of Tarsus | 1 Cor. 9:1, 15:8; 2 Cor. 12:2; Acts 9:3–4, 18:9–10, 22:6–10, 26:13–18 | 6, 7 |

## MAJOR PROPHETIC RESURRECTION WITNESSES

| Witness | References | Chapter |
|---|---|---|
| Moses | Gen. 3:15, 22:18; Ex. 12:21–23; Lev. 1–7, Num. 21:4–9; Deut. 18:15 | 3, 9 |
| David, son of Jesse | Ps. 16:10, 22:24, 110:1 | 4, 8, 9 |
| Isaiah | Isa. 8:14, 9:7, 11:1–10, 28:16, 52:13–53:12 | 9 |
| Daniel | Dan. 7:13–14, 9:26–27 | 9 |
| Jonah | Jonah 1:1–10, 17, 2:1–10 | 3, 9 |
| Zechariah | Zech. 9:9, 12:10, 13:7, 14:1–11 | 9 |
| Jesus of Nazareth | Mk 8:31, 9:9, 10:34, 14:58–59; Jn 2:18–22; Mt 12:40; Lk 24:27, 44 | 2, 3, 9 |

# MEASURING THE NARRATIVE BY HISTORICAL CRITERIA

S cholars analyze gospel texts to trace what may or may not be authentic to Jesus. They try to sift out what they take to be edited, shaped, or invented material. Most of the effort is focused on sayings and teachings of Jesus.

Our concern in this resurrection investigation is less with individual sayings or teachings by Jesus and more with the core events at the apex of his life—his death, burial, resurrection, and appearances. Our quest centers on whether there are sufficient reasons to believe in the reality of the resurrection of Jesus as a historical event. Many people who hear the message preached or who read a single gospel are struck by the power of the whole, sense its truth and become believers by what is often called seeing through the eyes of faith. There is certainly nothing wrong with taking shortcuts to truth, life and peace, let alone to eternity. Still, other people require more evidence or reasoning before they honestly can believe. Some need to explore the evidence for the event not at first through the eyes of faith but through what may be termed the microscope of historical-critical analysis.

*Applying Criteria to the Combined Resurrection Narrative*

Historical-critical analysis applies common tools of academic history research to the texts of the NT as if these texts were not sacred or inspired but simply like other documents of Roman times. The framework undergirding our investigation is that the resurrection narratives taken together in the NT accounts meet you either way. They seek to win the heart and bring people to faith, but at the same time, they measure up remarkably well to secular historical criteria for reliable documents. They offer simple, honest witness reports to a recognizably miraculous event. Yet looked at through the lens of historical evidence, they also withstand criticism effectively and emerge as highly reliable accounts when viewed in their historical context.[100]

There are discrepancies between accounts, and some differences are more easily resolved than others. However, when we focus primarily on the resurrection narrative, which is drawn from the four gospel accounts (plus a few passages in letters from Paul and in early episodes of Acts), we find it has a remarkable ability to satisfy the supposed criteria of historicity.

These criteria are used by historians in their effort to establish what was done or said. The criteria render a lower or higher probability that an event or saying actually occurred in history as described. These are qualitative criteria. They do not produce a precise, mathematical level of probability. Nevertheless, historical probability is increased by how many of the criteria are met and in what ways. The criteria can be applied to individual sayings or teachings or anecdotes. In our case, we apply the criteria to the resurrection narrative as a whole—to the death, burial, and appearances of Jesus asserted by the NT accounts. This ability of the NT resurrection narrative to address these common historical criteria is presented superbly by Catherine M. Murphy in her

---

[100] For more detail on document reliability, see Craig Blomberg, *The Historical Reliability of the New Testament* (Downers Grove, IL: InterVarsity Press Academic, 2007).

very smart book *The Historical Jesus for Dummies.*[101] This section draws significantly on her paradigm though the examples and conclusions are mainly my own. Let's look at each criterion to see how the resurrection narrative measures up to these criteria.

### At Least One Early Report

More than one source is always better, but historians look for at least one source as close to the event as possible. This criterion puts a limiting principle on rampant speculation. Later writers can invent material out of their own imaginations at will if they are not in some way tied to an early source. Example: there is no early, documented evidence for a romantic relationship between Jesus and Mary Magdalene.

In contrast, the resurrection narrative meets this criterion of one or more early reports. These reports come via multiple first-century accounts in the four gospels along with Paul's 1 Corinthians letter and its embedded early creed, which counts as the earliest written evidence (1 Cor. 15:3–7, see chapter 7). Luke's history of the apostles' missions also provides an early, first-century report of witnesses to the resurrection (see chapters 4–6).

### Multiple, Independent Sources

When different people record events, the credibility increases. It is far better if they are independent sources. That means they do not borrow from each other. If a second source borrows from a first source, the second is dependent on the first and thus is not as highly valued in historical assessment.

There is some value in having a second source implicitly agreeing with a first source in the sense that borrowing from it shows that the borrower has evaluated the preceding source as reliable. Borrowing is less compelling, however, than having

---

[101] Catherine M. Murphy, *The Historical Jesus for Dummies* (Hoboken, NJ: Wiley, 2007).

at least two independent sources come to the same conclusion without consulting each other. The resurrection narrative meets this criterion by having the independent sources of Mark and John plus the letters of Paul. Matthew and Luke tend to follow Mark closely, with 91 percent of Mark's entire gospel included in Matthew and 53 percent included in Luke.[102]

Yet Matthew and Luke expand their gospels beyond Mark's using additional sources. The fact that Luke is self-conscious about investigating thoroughly does add some weight to his borrowing from Mark as it indicates he conducted a certain vetting of his sources (Lk 1:1–4).

### Contains Eyewitness Material

In court cases, when witnesses relate what they have been told by others, it is considered hearsay evidence. It is evidence but not as highly valued as eyewitness evidence. That is when persons see or hear or experience something themselves.

The resurrection narrative meets this eyewitness criterion in several ways. John gives direct testimony to the events including the claim that he *"wrote them down"* (Jn 19:35, 21:24). Luke contends eyewitnesses *"handed down"* their accounts to him though he was not one himself (Lk 1:2). Tradition and continued consensus identify Peter as the eyewitness behind the gospel of Mark.[103] Matthew would count as an eyewitness himself if he wrote the gospel named after him or if he served as a core source for the writer of that gospel.

---

[102] Barker, ed., *NIV Study Bible*, 1437.
[103] For a compelling argument for Peter as the eyewitness source for the gospel of Mark, see Richard Bauckham, *Jesus and the Eyewitnesses* (Grand Rapids, MI: Wm. B. Eerdmans, 2006), 155–82.

## Contains Embarrassing Material

Not just the gospel authors but many authors in history write with a purpose beyond recording objective facts for posterity. They often have a cause or agenda that motivates them to write to convince people to join them or see things their way. This was certainly the case with the gospel writers. When one has a cause, one usually deletes things that might be embarrassing to that cause. Embarrassing sayings or events may lead people to disbelieve your assertions and drive them away from your cause. When obviously embarrassing aspects are left in the account, historians consider this factor raises the probability that those aspects actually occurred.

The resurrection narratives meet this criterion many times over with regular moments embarrassing to the disciples' cause in that culture. The hero, Jesus, undergoes the shame of both betrayal from an insider and denial by his right-hand man. The hero dies a criminal's death, exposed out in public. His disciples are too scared to give him a proper burial, so a member of the usually hostile Sanhedrin does it instead.

In that patriarchal culture, it is embarrassing that women, not men, are the first to discover Jesus is risen. It is they who announce the news to the male disciples, who are hiding out in fear for their lives. Only later as recorded in Acts do the disciples recover their bearings and prove to be strong and bold. That change happens as the full power of the resurrection dawns on them and the inner power of the Holy Spirit starts to flow in them (see chapter 4).

## Other Material Predicated on the Episode

When an event seems to have other established or reasonable events directly dependent on it, that raises the probability it occurred. This principle kicks in when there is a later historical occurrence that is established with its own set of data. Yet that later event can be shown to depend on or be predicated on an earlier event. The earlier event usually has its own set of historical data, but the way it is linked to a valid later event can add to the credibility of the earlier event. Examples help. We saw the way the severe rebuke Jesus gives Peter is highly probable, but it is predicated on Jesus's having predicted his own death. This factor adds credibility to the claim that Jesus predicted his fate (see Mk 8:29-33 and chapter 3).

In the case of the overall resurrection narrative, a major historical occurrence predicated on it is the highly validated enigma of the former persecutor Paul switching sides. This switch is well documented from evidence outside the gospel accounts, mainly Paul's first-person letters and Luke's biographical episodes of Paul in Acts. Archaeological findings and other early writers also support the radical change and missionary zeal of Paul. This later event of Paul's change is predicated on the earlier events claimed in the resurrection narrative in the gospel accounts: Jesus's death, resurrection, and appearances and especially the ones involving Peter, whom Paul visits as a young convert (Gal. 1:18). In this way, the historical documentation for Paul's radical life change and work linked as it is to the resurrection narrative adds credibility to the gospel accounts.

*Discontinuity with Cultural Assumptions*

This means that the claim is new on the historical horizon in that it departs from established belief or practice in a culture. It is not what one would expect in that era. The resurrection narrative meets this criterion by definition with flying colors. Rising from the dead is a miracle in any culture. In Jewish belief of that day, many though not all believed (the Pharisees believed, the Sadducees did not) in a group resurrection at the end of time when all would be judged and some rewarded by God (Mk 12:18; Acts 23:8). Jesus reflects this majority-held cultural assumption in answering a trick question about marriage in heaven (Lk 20:35-36).

To claim an individual rises in advance of everyone else is

new. To claim God does it as a sign that the sacrifice for all of humanity's sins has been fully paid is utterly beyond the pale in the Jewish mind-set. Nevertheless, reading Isaiah 53 in light of Jesus's sacrificial death shows that the concept was in the Jewish prophetic stream but not in the popular consciousness of what the Messiah would be like (see chapter 9 and *Background Guide*, resources 4 and 5).

However, it must be noted that this criterion cuts two ways and that its utility can be disputed by historians. It tends to give higher probability to what is new and different over the status quo. Something asserted may be new to a culture, but that does not by itself verify that what is claimed actually happened.

## Coherent with Major Established Facts

Historians develop a set of facts or high-probability events in a given era using criteria such as these we are listing. After taking all the trouble to establish an event or situation, they assign higher probability to an event that coheres or fits with prior established facts.

The resurrection narrative meets this criterion in several ways. For instance, it coheres with what is known from secular sources about the power structure of that era. It is dominated by the Roman prefect Pilate, the tetrarch Herod Antipas, and the high priest Caiaphas, who was controlled by his father-in-law Annas. That power structure given in the gospels finds validation not only in secular texts but also in archaeological findings. These include the high priest's house and courtyard where Jesus is taken after his arrest; the pavement where Pilate judges Jesus; rock-cut tombs and likely the one Jesus occupied; another tomb where the remains of a crucified man were found; and another tomb containing the bone box or ossuary of the high priest Caiaphas who tears his clothes at what he deems to be blasphemy committed by Jesus.[104]

The accounts of the gospels cohere with these facts established by other means. In a larger sense, the rise of Christianity to eventually encompass the Mediterranean world and later almost the entire Western world is beyond dispute as a historical phenomenon. What cause can be proposed to have had this effect? The claimed resurrection of Jesus certainly coheres with the astonishing spread of this faith. Even those who remain skeptical about the event itself are likely to agree that the belief of the disciples in the resurrection coheres with this world-altering result. The gospels taken together as witness accounts of the resurrection pass these criteria for historicity remarkably well.

### How Acts Measures Up to Historical Criteria

When we turn to Acts, in effect the sequel to the gospel of Luke, we do not have multiple sources covering the same period. Let's take a brief look at how Luke's historical account measures up on its own with the criteria of historicity we are using.

*1. Early report.* Acts covers the thirty years after the witnesses see the resurrection and ascension of Jesus, approximately AD 30–60. The date of Luke's writing Acts is debated, but it indisputably remains a first-century document (no earlier than the AD 60s and no later than the AD 80s; see *Background Guide*, resource 2).

*2. Single source only.* For the thirty years that Acts recounts, we do not have four writings as we do with the gospels that encompass similar times and events. Acts is the single narrative source, but it finds confirming data along the way from several other angles. The letters of Paul confirm in large part the itinerary Luke describes along with some specific episodes (such as the

---

[104] For short sidebars on these discoveries, see chapters 1, 2, and 4. For more detail and sources on each of the findings, see *Background Guide*, Found in the Ground Index, on tombs (1.1–1.3), on the judgment pavement (3.6), and on the high priest's house and bones (4.1, 4.5).

Jerusalem council, covered in Acts 15:1–6 and in Gal. 2:1–10). An author and contemporary of the gospel writers, the Jewish historian Josephus, writing under the auspices of Roman patrons, confirms several of Luke's accounts (the famine in Acts 11:28 and the death of Agrippa I in Acts 12:19–23). Archaeological findings also have conferred credibility to Luke's writing. Terminology, place names, names of officials, and specific buildings and locations that Luke includes all have found verifying evidence in excavations (see *Background Guide*, Found in the Ground index, 4.5–7.3).

3. *Eyewitness material.* In the sequel to his first book, Luke claims eyewitness status for himself in the narratives for much of the second and most of the third journeys of Paul in addition to Paul's two years at the palace prison in Caesarea and in the later rendezvous in Rome. Luke repeatedly uses the pronoun *"we"* (Acts 16:10–17, 20:5–15, 21:1–18, 27:1–28:16). For earlier events, Paul likely briefed Luke on what he had experienced. For the first part of the book, in which Peter is the main figure, Luke would have had access to Mark as a source if not some contact with Peter himself (Lk 1:2). Mark is mentioned with Luke as part of Paul's later entourage (Philemon 24; 2 Tim. 4:11; Col. 4:10; see *Background Guide*, resource 1).

4. *Embarrassing material.* Luke pulls no punches when he reports on the split between Barnabas and Paul over Mark after Mark bails out of the first missionary journey for unstated reasons when they leave Cyprus and land in southern Turkey (Acts 13:13). Later, Paul and Mark reconcile (Col. 4:10). Luke reports on failures as well as successes in the evangelistic efforts including the rejection, physical suffering, and death threats the apostles endure such as the gauntlet they face traveling through Pisidian Antioch, Iconium, and Lystra (Acts 13:50, 14:5–7, 19–20).

5. *Other material predicated on the episode.* This principle applies when a separately established later event depends on or is predicated on an earlier event in question. A later event historically documented outside Acts is the account of the martyrdom of James, the brother of Jesus, by an unrighteous,

rogue high priest (*Antiquities* 20.9.1). Luke does not cover this event, but the account of the death of James is predicated on events Luke does cover, namely the conversion of James (Acts 1:14) and the leadership of James in the Jerusalem church (Acts 15:13, 19, 21:18). In this way, the historically validated death of James is predicated on his becoming a convert and a leader, which adds credibility to Luke's reports of these life changes in James.

In the larger sense, the spread of Christianity in the Mediterranean world, historically verified through archaeology and through texts by later Christian leaders, is largely predicated on the missions of Paul and Peter as recounted in Acts. (See excerpts from Clement's letter to believers in Corinth in chapter 5.)

6. *Discontinuity with prior cultural assumptions.* The major discontinuity with cultural assumptions contained in Acts is the presence and dynamism of the Holy Spirit. The preaching of the message of Jesus begins with the sending of the Spirit. When a crowd gathers at the hubbub over hearing praises to God in their own native languages, Peter tells the hearers at the Jerusalem jam session that this was predicted by the prophet Joel (Joel 2:28–32, Acts 2:16). Evidently, these Jewish pilgrims in town for the festival were not expecting this change in human anthropology. Later, on Peter's pivotal visit to Caesarea, when the Spirit fills Gentile believers as if they were Jewish and full members of God's kingdom people, the original disciples themselves have their cultural assumptions overturned (Acts 10:44–46, see chapter 4). For the rest of Acts, the Spirit then propels the fulfilling of the commission Jesus gives to his disciples.

The way Paul switches sides from fierce enforcer for the high priests against the Jesus believers to evangelist extraordinaire for the other side also cuts against cultural assumptions. The switch definitely consisted of discontinuous behavior for a Pharisee, born into a family of Pharisees (Acts 23:6, Phil. 3:5). A confirmed law-abiding and law-enforcing Pharisee simply would not be the most likely candidate to claim that the roving, grace-giving Galilean teacher Jesus surpasses the national liberator and lawgiver Moses (see chapter 6).

*7. Coherent with major established facts.* The missionary activities of the apostles in Jerusalem, Samaria, Judea, Syria, what is today Turkey, Greece, and Rome all track with how Christianity is known to have spread historically. In the areas evangelized by Paul, archaeological excavations repeatedly have confirmed Luke's data in the book of Acts: on government officials (Sergius Paulus on the island of Cyprus, 13:6–12, Gallio in Corinth 18:12–17); on roads (Egnatian Way, 16:11–12, Appian Way 28:13–16); on buildings (theater, shops and temple in Ephesus, 19:23–41); and on forums (the outdoor platform or bema in Corinth, 18:12). For a rundown on excavations turning up evidence for Paul's journeys, see chapters 6 and 7 along with *Background Guide*, Found in the Ground index, 6.1–7.3.

### On the Reliability of Frequent Speeches in Acts

In the first-century Mediterranean world, literacy rates were not high, and publishing as well as reading written material tended to be reserved for the educated elites. Mass communication heavily relied on orally delivered, in-person speeches. Nearly all the historical writing of that time features some speeches. So it is natural that the apostles are depicted frequently giving speeches about their faith to diverse audiences including ruling councils and kings.

It is probable that Luke is present with Paul at his later speeches on his third journey and in his two-year plush imprisonment at the coastal palace in Caesarea Maritima. For the earlier speeches, Paul probably summarized them for Luke, for they spent much time traveling together by land and sea. As for Peter's speeches, Luke was a colleague with Mark in Paul's entourage, and Mark likely shared the memoirs or notes he had received from Peter.

The longest recorded speech in Acts comes from Stephen, an early Greek-speaking believer in Jerusalem (see chapter 5). It is harder to tell how Luke received notes on that speech. Paul, in his prior life as a persecutor of believers, was on the scene and might have recalled the content. Philip the Evangelist, a fellow deacon with Stephen, may also have been at the scene when Stephen spoke to the Sanhedrin (see chapters 5 and 9). Luke may have gained more information when he and Paul visit Philip on the coast at Caesarea, a stop along the way during their final trip to Jerusalem (Acts 6:5, 21:8).

It is not true to the time to expect word-for-word transmission of these speeches. Rather, the content and general flow of thought presented in that historical moment is what reasonably would have been preserved.[105]

### Resurrection Narrative Meets Criteria of Historicity

With this brief review, we have determined these NT sources are generally credible according to typical historical criteria. They measure up well especially given the limitations of first-century research and writing.

In the area of the resurrection narratives, there is strong concurrence among the multiple sources of the four gospels. In the area of post-resurrection narratives of the apostles, our single source of Acts gains credibility through archaeological excavations and through confirming data in the letters of Paul and the works of Josephus. These sources serve well in our efforts to search in them for lines of evidence for the resurrection. Analyzed in their historical context, these lines of evidence raise the probability that the disciples got it right when they claimed that Jesus was raised physically from the dead.

---

[105] For a full discussion of the speeches in Acts, see F. F. Bruce, *The Speeches in the Acts of the Apostles* (London: Tyndale Press, 1942), 5–27, which also can be read at biblicalstudies.org.uk. Three decades later, Bruce revisited his essay in a festschrift or publication to honor a fellow scholar. See F. F. Bruce, "The Speeches in Acts—Thirty Years After," Robert Banks, ed., *Reconciliation and Hope. New Testament Essays on Atonement and Eschatology Presented to L.L. Morris on his 60ᵗʰ Birthday*, (Carlisle, UK: Paternoster Press, 1974), 53–68. Also available at biblicalstudies.org.uk.

## ADDITION 4

---

# ON THE DRAMA OF
# THE FUTURE RESURRECTION

---

The former persecutor of believers named Saul becomes the most fervent evangelist for Jesus, the apostle Paul (see chapters 5–7). Lest they be in doubt, Paul eloquently writes to believers in the city of Corinth about the drama and ultimate triumph they will share with Jesus their Lord in the future human resurrection (1 Corinthians 15:35–57, c. AD 55).

*But someone will ask, "How are the dead raised? With what kind of body will they come?" How foolish! What you sow does not come to life unless it dies. When you sow, you do not plant the body that will be, but just a seed, perhaps of wheat or of something else.*

*But God gives it a body as he has determined, and to each kind of seed he gives its own body. Not all flesh is the same: People have one kind of flesh, animals have another, birds another and fish another. There are also heavenly bodies and there are earthly bodies; but the splendor of the heavenly bodies is one kind, and the splendor of the earthly bodies is another. The sun has one*

*kind of splendor, the moon another and the stars another;
and star differs from star in splendor.*

*So will it be with the resurrection of the dead. The body
that is sown is perishable, it is raised imperishable; it
is sown in dishonor, it is raised in glory; it is sown in
weakness, it is raised in power; it is sown a natural body,
it is raised a spiritual body.*

*If there is a natural body, there is also a spiritual body.
So it is written: "The first man Adam became a living
being"; the last Adam, a life-giving spirit. The spiritual
did not come first, but the natural, and after that the
spiritual. The first man was of the dust of the earth; the
second man is of heaven. As was the earthly man, so are
those who are of the earth; and as is the heavenly man,
so also are those who are of heaven. And just as we have
borne the image of the earthly man, so shall we bear the
image of the heavenly man.*

*I declare to you, brothers and sisters, that flesh and
blood cannot inherit the kingdom of God, nor does the
perishable inherit the imperishable. Listen, I tell you
a mystery: We will not all sleep, but we will all be
changed—in a flash, in the twinkling of an eye, at the
last trumpet. For the trumpet will sound, the dead will
be raised imperishable, and we will be changed. For the
perishable must clothe itself with the imperishable, and
the mortal with immortality.*

*When the perishable has been clothed with the imperishable, and the mortal with immortality, then the saying that is written will come true: "Death has been swallowed up in victory." "Where, O death, is your victory? Where, O death, is your sting?" The sting of death is sin, and the power of sin is the law. But thanks be to God! He gives us the victory through our Lord Jesus Christ.*

# SUBJECT INDEX

397

Bruce, F.F. 127, 175, 274, 392

## C

Caesarea Maritima 37, 46, 135, 156, 202, 277, 300, 391
Caesarea Phillipi 97-98, 148
Caiaphas, Joseph (high priest) 129, 143, 148, 157
Caligula (emperor) 154-155
canon (New Testament) 6
Capernaum 38, 42-43, 70, 101-102, 105, 122, 125, 266
Celsus 330-331
chart, appearances 352
Cilicia 143, 151, 153, 178, 181, 188, 198, 226-227, 229
circumcision 173-174, 184-185, 247
Claudius (emperor) 189, 196, 204, 209, 220-222, 250-251
Clement (of Rome) 161-162, 342, 390
Cleopas 50-51, 71, 84, 377
Cleopatra 170
Clopus 50-51
Constantine 6-7, 36, 118, 259
Corinth 8, 66, 70, 161, 173, 189, 209, 211, 218-226, 229-230, 232-233, 269, 390-391, 393
Cornelius 2, 135, 138, 185
Craig, William Lane 317, 349
creed 67, 193, 223, 225, 228, 230-231, 233, 356, 370, 383
Creighton, Linda L. 146
criterion, historical (or criteria) 324
cross 2, 11, 30, 32, 41, 43-44, 49, 51-53, 55, 74, 80, 102, 106, 112, 121, 131, 135, 157, 181, 185, 220, 225, 239, 261, 275-276, 285-287, 294, 305, 310-311, 315, 319-321, 324, 335, 343-344, 347, 350, 357-358

crucifixion 14, 29-30, 34, 53, 90, 126, 128, 157, 160, 163, 231, 239, 248, 270, 276, 285-288, 306, 311, 320-321, 323, 327, 333-334, 336-337, 350-351, 357, 406
Cyprus 180, 182, 227, 389
Cyrene (Libya) 151, 180, 321
Cyrus (king) 258, 304

## D

Damascus 67, 154, 166-168, 178-179, 181, 200-201, 206, 226, 230-232, 269, 345, 369, 378
daughters of Philip (the deacon) 299
David (king) 6, 9, 132, 143, 151, 161, 167, 182-183, 187, 238-239, 243, 251, 253, 255-261, 269-270, 278-279, 283, 286-287, 291-293, 295, 341, 346, 350, 371, 379
deacons 151, 159-160, 299-300, 392
Dead Sea Scrolls (DSS) 303
Delphi 209, 211, 220-222, 370
Dio Cassius 220, 251
Diodorus 216, 348
Drusilla 197

## E

Edict of Milan 118
Egnatian Way 186, 391
Elijah 99, 270
Emmaus 50-51, 71, 73, 81, 84-85, 89, 267, 272, 309, 378
Ephesus 157, 177, 189-192, 224, 226, 232, 252, 391
Erastus 218
esplanade (of temple) 246, 258-259, 272, 281

398

Ethiopian (official) 300–301, 308–
310, 373
Eusebius (of Caesarea) 6, 158, 161,
232, 299
Evans, Craig A. 330

**F**

Fairchild, Mary 271
feasts 4, 47–49, 83, 125–126, 147–
148, 169, 215, 241, 243–244,
249, 252, 254, 283, 291, 326,
346–347
Felix (procurator) 197
Festus (procurator) 158, 197–198,
202–204, 206
first fruits 195
fishing 43, 53, 55, 76, 85, 97–98,
121–123, 347
forgiveness 15, 74, 90, 126, 137–138,
140, 149, 183, 201, 249, 268,
292–293, 307, 358

**G**

Galatia 172, 225–226, 229
Gallio 209–211, 219–223, 226, 229–
230, 232, 370, 391
Gamaliel (rabbi) 132–134, 143, 150,
153–154, 178
Geisler, Norman L. 233
Gethsemane 83, 123, 279
Gibson, Mel 296
Gnostics 3
Green, Michael 139
guards, tomb 337, 351

**H**

Habermas, Gary 224, 233, 349
Hadrian 216
heaven 17, 44, 64–65, 68, 78–79, 81,
83, 87–88, 100, 129, 136–137,

144, 153, 163, 187, 200–201,
206, 214, 238, 273, 283–284,
292, 307, 310, 329, 342–345,
374, 386, 394
Hebron 238, 256–257
Hegesippus 158
Herod Antipas 46–48, 55, 97, 145,
147–148, 154–155, 306, 387
Herodias 147
Herod the Great 46–47, 55, 98, 113,
142, 145, 148, 154, 156, 170,
198, 202–203, 246, 250, 258
Hierapolis 159–160
Hillel (rabbi) 133
house (of high priest) 119, 122, 282,
387–388
house (of Mary, mother of John
Mark) 84, 127, 130
house (of Peter) 124–125, 227–228

**I**

Ilan, Tal 35
Isaac 134, 237–239, 258–259
Isaiah iii, 11, 23, 88, 104, 183, 258,
260, 265, 288–290, 295, 297–
298, 300–304, 308–310, 316,
350, 372, 379, 387

**J**

Jacob 134, 239
James (brother of Jesus) 3, 66–67,
79–80, 91, 111, 157–158,
176, 185, 193, 224, 226–228,
247, 250, 252, 273, 328, 331,
339, 348, 352, 356, 368, 377,
389–390
James (brother of John) 46, 50,
54–55, 76, 80, 99, 105, 121, 147,
154, 156, 159, 198, 272, 377

# N

Nazareth 71, 108, 119, 129, 143, 145,
   199, 241–242, 265–266, 270,
   296, 305, 330, 362, 379, 406
Nazirite vow 176
Nero (emperor) 1–2, 160–161, 205,
   221, 223, 232
new covenant 185, 288, 294,
   308–309

# O

Octavian (see Augustus,
   Caesar) 170
ossuary 30, 34, 87, 131, 175, 334,
   336, 387

# P

Panias 45, 98
Pantera (Panthera) 330–331
parable 281–282, 297, 310
Parthenon 190, 330
Passover 4, 14, 47–49, 83, 126, 143,
   155, 215, 223, 241–242, 244,
   249, 252, 288–289, 291, 294,
   309, 321, 335
Patmos 55
Paul (apostle) iii, 7–8, 10, 15, 24, 44,
   46, 66–67, 70, 73, 79–80, 82,
   84, 87–88, 92, 126–127, 133,
   139, 151, 157, 160–161, 166,
   168–180, 182–206, 210–211,
   217–233, 251–253, 269, 292,
   298, 300, 310, 316, 328, 331,
   339, 345, 348–350, 352, 356,
   358, 362, 369–370, 378, 382–
   384, 386, 388–393
pavement, stone 112
Pentecost 80, 126, 138–139, 148, 151,
   215–216, 249, 259, 283, 291,
   310, 326, 346

Peter (apostle) xiii, 15–16, 31, 38,
   44, 53–55, 66–67, 69–70, 73,
   76–81, 84, 86, 89–90, 97, 99,
   106–107, 119–136, 138–140,
   148–149, 151, 153, 155–157,
   159–161, 183, 185, 193,
   205–206, 215–216, 227–229,
   231–232, 247–250, 252–253,
   259–261, 268, 270, 272, 280,
   283, 291–299, 309–310, 337,
   346, 349, 352, 355–356, 358,
   367, 377, 384, 386, 389–391
Pharisees 47, 97, 107, 109, 132–133,
   145, 150, 153, 166, 171, 174,
   180, 195, 199, 206, 227, 241,
   250, 276, 278–279, 283, 293,
   329–330, 333, 337, 346, 368,
   386, 390
Philip (apostle) 76, 97, 156, 159–160,
   299, 301, 377
Philip (deacon or evangelist) 126,
   159–160, 249, 299–302, 308–
   310, 373, 378, 391–392
Philip (son of Herod the Great) 98,
   148, 155
Pilate (prefect) 2–3, 11, 14, 29, 37,
   39, 47–48, 111–112, 147, 306,
   321, 325, 387
Pitre, Brant 277
Pliny the Elder 7, 197
Pliny the Younger 4, 7–8
Plutarch 216, 348
Pompey 219, 225
Pontius Pilate (see Pilate) 2, 11, 29,
   39, 147, 325
Priscilla (Paul's associate) 8, 189

# Q

Qumran 303

## R

Red Sox, Boston 9
Rice, Tim 47
Rome 1–2, 126, 142, 147, 155,
   157, 159–162, 175, 182, 186,
   188–190, 197–198, 202–205,
   220, 232, 247, 250, 253, 320,
   389, 391

## S

sacrifice 138, 153, 176, 238, 257–259,
   289, 294, 297, 307, 309, 342–
   343, 347, 362, 371, 387
Sadducees 107, 132–133, 149,
   180, 195, 250, 278, 329–330,
   346, 386
Salome (daughter of Herodias)
   51–52, 146–148
Salome (wife of Zebedee) 13, 51–
   55, 57, 156, 355, 364
Samaria 82, 102, 198, 214, 248–249,
   299–300, 391
Samaritans 100, 147, 239, 299
Sanders, E.P. 87
Sanhedrin 4, 110–111, 133–134,
   149–151, 153–154, 163, 169,
   179–180, 196, 249, 283, 296,
   306, 330, 337, 385, 392
Sarah (wife of Abraham) 237–238
Saul of Tarsus (see Paul, apostle)
   133, 169, 378
Sea of Galilee 38, 42, 53, 76, 89,
   97–98, 121–123, 159, 347
Seneca (the Younger) 209–210,
   220–221, 223
Sergius Paulus 182, 391
servant figure (in Isaiah) 289, 316
Shanks, Hershel 32, 336
Shelley, Mary 9
Sherwin-White, A.N. 233

shipwreck 204
Siloam, Pool of 100–101
snake, bronze 275–276
Socrates 4
Solomon (king) 128, 132, 149, 167,
   239, 245–246, 258–260, 278
speeches (in Acts) 127, 175, 274,
   391–392
Stephen 126, 144, 151–153, 156,
   160, 169–170, 179–180, 294,
   299–300, 309, 345, 356, 368,
   378, 391–392
Strobel, Lee 9
Suetonius 198, 216, 251, 348
Susanna 42, 48, 57, 378

## T

Tacitus 1–2, 7, 198, 220, 223, 251,
   325, 350
Talmud 3, 34, 133, 330
Tarsus iii, 133, 143, 169, 178, 181,
   188, 227, 232, 378
Temple (Jerusalem) 1, 32, 46, 81,
   83, 100, 110, 112–115, 119–120,
   122–123, 128, 130–134, 138,
   142–144, 148–154, 157–158,
   169–170, 176–180, 190, 192,
   195–198, 200, 202, 209, 211,
   219, 221, 232, 238–239, 241–
   247, 249, 251, 254, 257–260,
   264, 266, 271–272, 279, 281,
   283, 289, 291, 293, 295–297,
   304, 307–310, 330, 340–341,
   347, 350, 391
Thayer, Joseph Henry 50
Theophilus 65
Theudas 150
Thomas (the apostle) 61–62, 66,
   75–76, 78, 84, 86, 89–90, 156,
   365, 377

JESUS SAID TO HER, "I AM THE RESURRECTION AND THE LIFE. THE ONE WHO BELIEVES IN ME WILL LIVE, EVEN THOUGH THEY DIE; AND WHOEVER LIVES BY BELIEVING IN ME WILL NEVER DIE. DO YOU BELIEVE THIS?"

*— Jesus of Nazareth, circa AD 30–31, a few days before his crucifixion to his friend and host Martha of Bethany, as quoted in John 11:25–26 (NIV)*

Printed in the United States
By Bookmasters